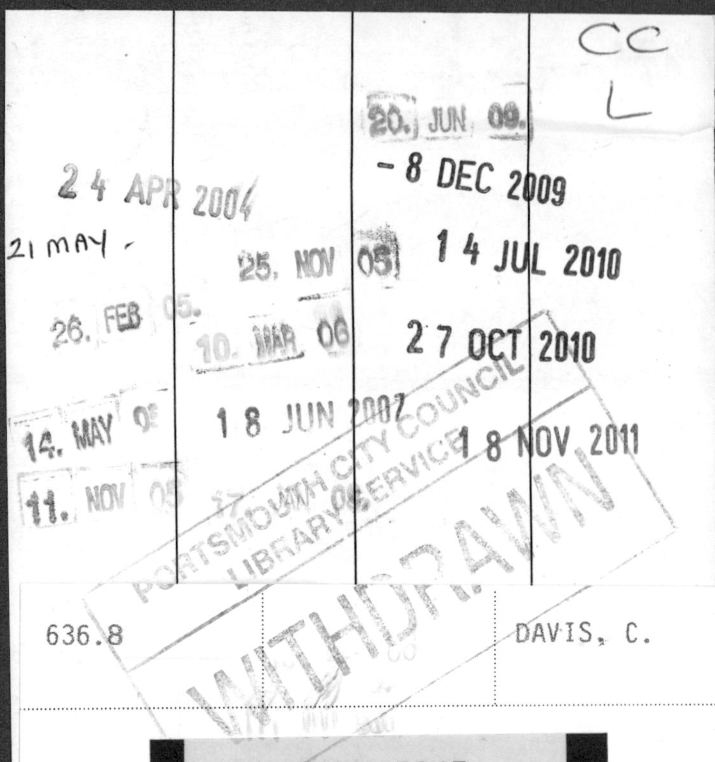
CC
L
20. JUN 09.
24 APR 2004
- 8 DEC 2009
21 MAY -
25. NOV 05
14 JUL 2010
26. FEB 05.
10. MAR 06
27 OCT 2010
14. MAY 05
18 JUN 2007
18 NOV 2011
11. NOV 05
PORTSMOUTH CITY COUNCIL
LIBRARY SERVICE
WITHDRAWN

C800147867

Portsmouth
CITY COUNCIL
LEISURE SERVICE

Essential Cat

Essential Cat

Caroline Davis

hamlyn

First published in Great Britain in 2003 by
Hamlyn, a division of Octopus Publishing Group Ltd
2–4 Heron Quays, London E14 4JP

ISBN 0 600 60836 0

A CIP catalogue record for this book is available from the British Library

Printed in Dubai

10 9 8 7 6 5 4 3 2 1

The advice given here should not be used as a substitute for that of a veterinary surgeon. No cats or kittens were harmed in the making of this book.

CONTENTS

INTRODUCTION

'A home without a cat, and a well-fed, well-petted and properly revered cat, may be a perfect home, perhaps, but how can it prove its title?' questioned the American author Mark Twain (1835–1910) – and he had a point. Somehow, as any cat lover will confirm, a cat does seem to make a home feel more welcoming, more friendly and even safer and more secure. Even those who profess not to like cats tend to change their opinion once they get to know what makes cats tick. For those who adore felines in whatever shape or form they present themselves, life is simply not complete without a cat galloping to greet them, chirruping and sinuously weaving around their legs for attention and then, later, curling up, relaxed and purring, on their laps, for a comforting mutual-admiration session.

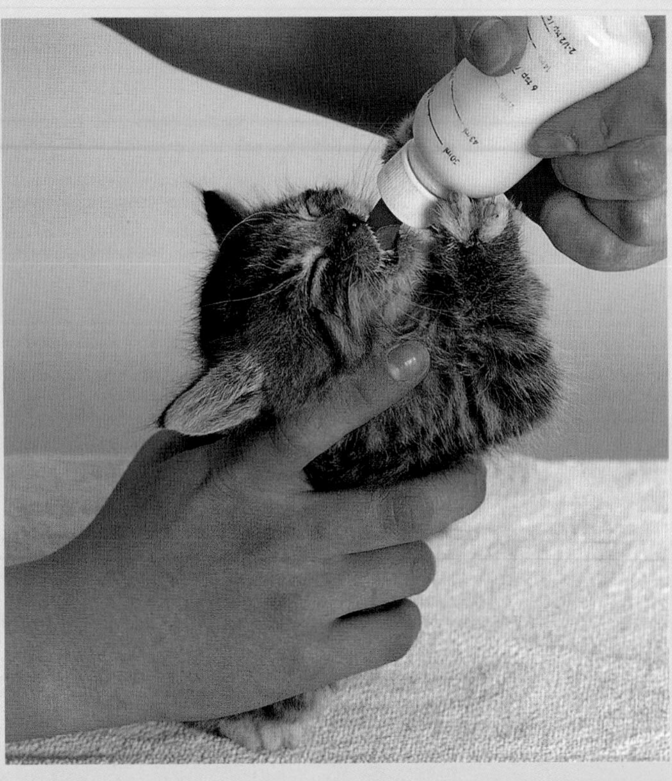

Why do cats make good pets?

In Britain and the USA, cats now outnumber dogs as the most popular pet. Perhaps the main reasons for this are their relative independence and ability to exercise and relieve themselves outside without human assistance, making them less of a tie than dogs, who need companionship and someone to let them out on a regular basis. A cat can also be as affectionate as any dog, and just as much fun to play with. See the checklist for the main advantages a cat has over a dog.

Checklist

- ✓ independent
- ✓ self-exercising
- ✓ quiet
- ✓ clean
- ✓ inexpensive to maintain
- ✓ space-economical
- ✓ strokable

Companionship

A cat not only provides good company, he also imparts a sense of peace and tranquillity in a chaotic, stressed world. Research has shown that having a cat – or another pet – can help us relax and recover from illness, as well as keep us alert and lively as we age.

Cats are naturally self-reliant animals, although we need to protect them in urban areas where they are especially vulnerable to passing traffic. Cats are more independent by nature than dogs, but they can prove to be very loyal and rewarding companions, and will ask for little in return except food, shelter and affection.

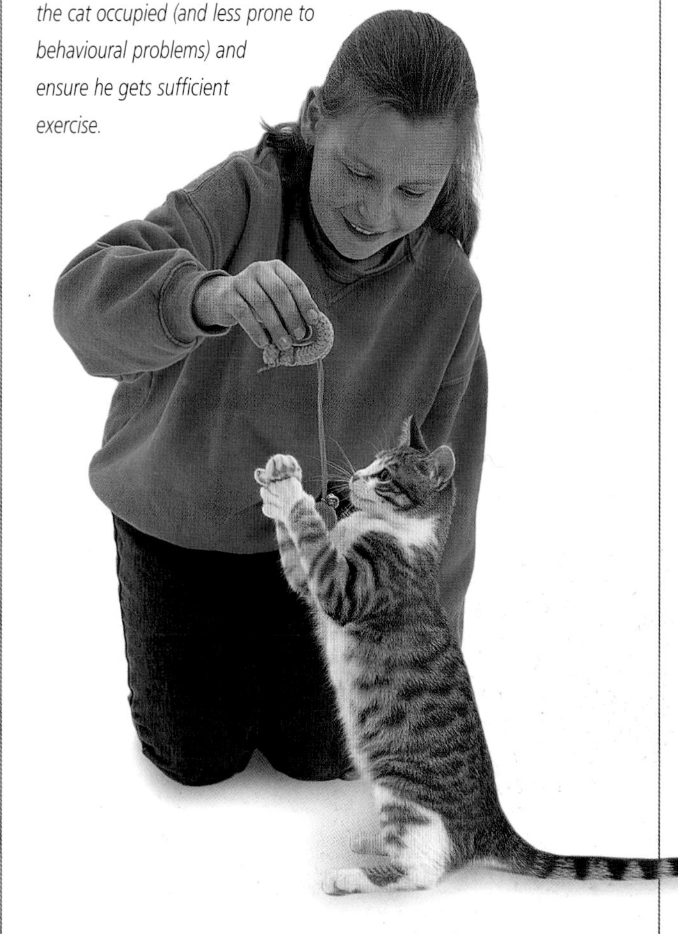

Cats make entertaining playmates for people of all ages. Not only will interactive play with your cat on a daily basis provide great entertainment for you both, it will also strengthen the bond between you, help keep the cat occupied (and less prone to behavioural problems) and ensure he gets sufficient exercise.

Exercise

In general, cats exercise themselves through hunting (if allowed outside) and play. Some owners, whether they live in urban or rural areas, build an enclosed run in their gardens or yards so that their cat can have freedom and fresh air without risking his safety.

Daily care

In comparison with some other household pets, a cat's daily needs are relatively few – longhaired breeds are an exception to this, as they need daily brushing to prevent coat and skin problems. Cats are usually fastidious about grooming and washing themselves, so bathing is not normally necessary, but a daily brushing will help keep shed hairs in the house to a minimum.

With today's high standards in veterinary medicine and feline food, pet cats can live well into their teens – and even longer.

Frequently asked question

Q I am out at work all day and am worried that a cat that is kept indoors all the time will get bored. How can I prevent this happening?

A One of the best ways would be to provide a companion pet. If this is another cat, you should ideally get two kittens to begin with so that they will settle down and remain friendly, whereas an older and a younger individual may not get along too well. See page 21 for the pros and cons of getting one cat or two.

Maintenance costs

Cats are inexpensive to keep. Other than food and cat litter on a weekly basis, the only other regular expenses will be parasite treatments as recommended by a vet, annual vaccinations against the diseases cats are susceptible to, a veterinary health check every 12 months, and toys to play with (you will find small scrunched-up balls of paper and ping-pong balls will do the job admirably). Although an optional expense, pet insurance can be a wise investment – should your pet suffer an accident or illness, any necessary veterinary treatment could cost a large amount.

Feline fact

The Egyptian word for cat is 'mau', which also means 'to see', and it was linked to the concept of the eye of Ra and the eye of Horus – twin symbols of the sun and the moon. Some believe that the word 'miaow' derives from 'mau'.

Advantages

Cats don't bark and howl, so your neighbours won't be upset on that score, especially important if you live in a highly populated, built-up area. As long as he is fed regularly, he has clean, fresh water available to drink, his litter tray is kept clean and he has a safe area in which to exercise and rest, plus some toys to play with, then a cat will be content. If he is sociable and has a warm lap to sit on and a gentle hand to stroke him now and again, he will be a very happy cat, keen to reciprocate his owner's affection.

Type of accommodation

Cats can live quite happily in most homes. Many town and city dwellers keep their cats entirely indoors without any problems. High-rise homes benefit, though, from protective mesh over windows and balconies to prevent cats falling from them accidentally.

LEFT *Ensure that open upstairs windows are secured, so that your cat cannot squeeze through them; better still, fix mesh safety screens to them so there is no risk of your cat falling.*

RIGHT *If you are often away from home for most of the day, getting two cats may be a good idea – they will keep one another company while you aren't there to give them attention.*

CHOOSING A CAT

Cats differ greatly in their needs, personalities and ideal living situations, so it is important to choose a cat who will be happy to live with you, and who you will be proud to own. Do you have time for the daily grooming needed by a long-haired cat? Do you want a sociable, affectionate cat or a more independent companion? Would a more mature cat be a more appropriate addition to your household than a kitten? Be sure to make an informed choice by reading the following pages carefully.

Cross-breed or pedigree?

You may have an idea of your ideal cat in terms of colour, type and temperament – one that looks pretty, is affectionate towards you and behaves perfectly in all respects. However, you must bear in mind that cats are living beings; each is an individual with its own character. You cannot, therefore, buy one 'off the shelf', ready-programmed to be the perfect pet you envisage. You can choose your preferred colour and type but, to a great extent, the way the cat behaves and relates to you will come down to the way you care for, handle and interact with him. Some pedigree cats are known for certain character traits, such as a laid-back attitude and a strong affection towards humans, and this can make the job of choosing a cat easier.

Types of cat

All domestic cats, whatever their colour, coat length or temperament, fall into one of the three main groups.

1 Pedigree (pure-bred)

These cats are bred from pedigree parents of the same breed. The advantage of getting a pedigree is that you know what he will look like when he is fully grown and, providing you have checked out information about the breed, you will have a good idea of his typical temperament and characteristics as an adult.

2 Cross-breed

Such cats are the offspring of pedigree parents, but of different breeds – for example a Persian crossed with a British Shorthair. The resulting kittens could grow up to resemble either parent, or a mixture of both. Some could be longhaired, some shorthaired and others semi-longhaired.

3 Non-pedigree

Cats are described as non-pedigree if one or both parents were cross-bred themselves. Different breeds may have been mixed over generations, which can make the appearance, character and temperament of offspring difficult to predict.

Top tip

Pedigree cats are not necessarily any more loving, clever or naughty than other cats, and their beauty is a matter of taste. Orientals tend to be more demanding of their owners, Persians seem to be more laid-back, and non-pedigrees are generally thought of as being 'hardy'. Whatever the type or breeding, an animal's character is also determined by the way he is reared and his handling by humans. Whether you get a pedigree or non-pedigree, the costs of neutering, vaccinating, feeding and caring for him will be just the same. The only difference will be the initial cost of acquiring him.

TYPE	PROS	CONS
Pedigree 	• Having researched the breed, you can pinpoint your ideal pet, usually knowing what to expect in terms of appearance and character. • Many types and colours exist, appealing to individual tastes. • You can choose the type and colour you want, although you may have to wait a while for your exact requirement. • Pedigree cats are usually raised with the greatest of care, so you should expect a healthy animal.	• Pedigree cats are more expensive than cross-breeds. • Some breeds are prone to hereditary problems, or particular ailments (especially those bred to 'type'). • Some breeds have particular character traits, or care requirements, that may not be appealing you or practical for your lifestyle. • Certain breeds can be difficult to obtain as they are rare, or the demand exceeds availability.
Cross-breed 	• Usually less expensive than pedigrees. • If you know what the parents are like, you have a fair idea of what to expect in terms of appearance and character. • Generally more hardy than pedigrees, but this does depend on the cross and the genetic parentage. • Because the crosses are usually intended, you can normally expect the resulting animals to be well socialized and healthy. Do be aware though that this is not always the case.	• They are not always readily available, especially if you want a very specific cross-breed. • Due to the character and behaviour traits of the breeds involved, certain combinations can be quite explosive, such as Burmese crossed with Siamese. Both breeds are attention-seeking types, highly active and vocal, so the two combined can result in an extremely demanding pet! Some owners may enjoy this, while others could find such an animal exhausting and infuriating.
 **Non-pedigree** 	• Free, or inexpensive. • Wide type and colour choice. • Usually easily available. • Generally uncomplicated in health terms.	• The character traits of the parents are generally unknown, so how the cat will mature in terms of looks, behaviour and character is hard to predict. • You may have to wait a while to find the age, colour and sex of your choice. • You cannot always be sure that the animal has been properly raised and cared for, so look out for signs of ill health and behaviour problems.

Coat considerations

There are two types of coat: shorthair and longhair (the latter is often incorrectly referred to as 'Persian', which is a breed in its own right). Each is exactly as the name suggests, although some coats are thicker than others, depending on the breed of cat. A variation on the shorthair is the 'hairless' (such as the Sphynx), which has only a thin covering of down on the ears, muzzle, tail and – in the males – testicles. Semi-longhaired coats are not as thick, nor as long in some cases, as full longhairs. Some breeds have curly coats (Cornish Rex, Selkirk Rex and the La Perm, which can be either long- or shorthaired).

Coat colours

Cat coats come in many different colours, with the pedigrees boasting the most variations. The basic colours of the cat are simple to interpret – black, white, cream and silver, for instance – but others are more obscure (see the chart below).

Cream

Bi-colour A white coat with dark patches.

Blue Any shade of cold-toned grey.

Blue-cream Dilute version of tortie with a mingled or patched coat of palest grey and cream. There are other colour varieties, including chocolate-cream, lilac-cream, and so on.

Bronze Warm coppery brown which lightens to buff.

Blue

Brown Any shade of dark brown – except in a brown tabby, when it refers to a cat that is genetically black and has black markings on an agouti (grizzled, like a wild rabbit) background.

Cameo White fur with red tips.

Caramel A subtle shade of pale orangey brown.

Champagne Buff-cream with warm honey beige shading to pale gold tan.

Chinchilla White coat with tips of a darker colour.

Red colourpoint

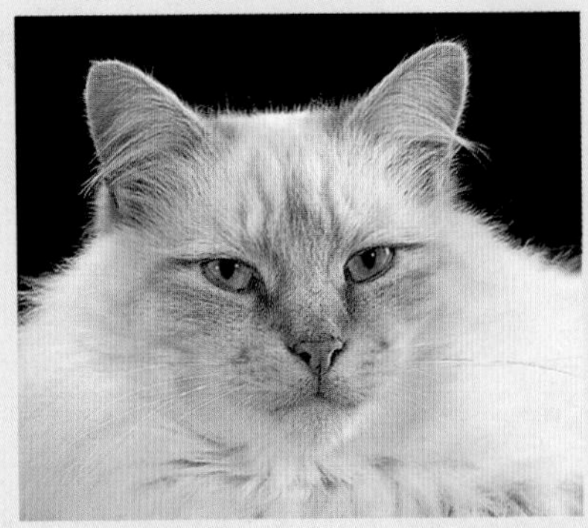

Chocolate A rich, warm brown.

Cinnamon Lighter shades of chocolate.

Colourpoint Self body with the tail, paws, mask (face), and ears of another colour.

Harlequin A bi-colour coat: 50–75 per cent white; 25–50 per cent colour.

Lilac Very pale, warm-toned grey.

Mink A range of colours in the Tonkinese breed.

Self

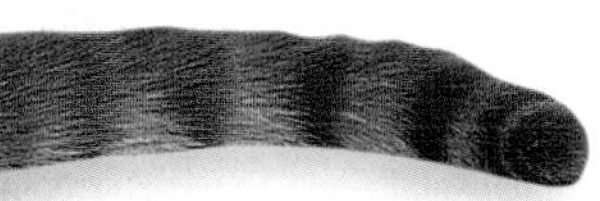

Frequently asked question

Q Which coat type is preferable – shorthaired, longhaired or semi-longhaired?

A You may prefer the look of a semi-longhaired or longhaired cat, but will you have the time and inclination to keep the coat looking good and tangle-free on a daily basis? Can you cope with the amount of hair a long-coated cat may shed around the house? Longhaired cats need grooming every single day to keep their coats and skin in top order, whereas shorthaired cats will take care of most of the necessary daily grooming themselves. Although the latter shed hairs too, it will be a smaller amount than from their long-coated counterparts.

Parti-colour Covers both bi-colours and torties.

Patched Two-tone tabby coat with darker and lighter patches, mingling tortie and tabby. Patched is sometimes also referred to as tortie – which can prove confusing.

Platinum Pale silvery grey with pale fawn undertones.

Red All shades of ginger. Deep coppery tones are the most sought after.

Ruddy A modification of black in the Abyssinian breed to reddish brown and burnt sienna.

Sable A term sometimes used to describe dark brown cats who are genetically black.

Self One colour.

Smoke White undercoat, topcoat hair white at the roots and coloured at the ends.

Sorrel Modification of red in the Abyssinian to brownish orange to light brown.

Tabby There are four basic patterns: *ticked* (each hair has contrasting dark and light colour bands); *mackerel* (vertically striped); *spotted* (as it suggests); and the *classic* (sides are blotched with whorls or 'oyster' marks).

Tipped Hairs are differently coloured only at the ends, which can create a sparkling effect.

Tortie-and-White (Calico) Tri-coloured (black, red and white).

Tortie (Tortoiseshell) A two-coloured (black and red) coat.

Classic silver tabby

Blue, tortie and white

The Sphynx's skin should look like velvet and feel like moss. There are no eyebrows or whiskers. Because he has no protective coat, he must be kept in comfortably warm conditions.

Appearance

Cats come in all shapes and sizes to suit all requirements and tastes. Examples include: the Munchkin with its short legs (said to be suitable as house pets because they are unable to jump onto kitchen counters); the Scottish Fold which has folded ears; the American Curl with curled ears; the Manx which has no tail; the Japanese Bobtail which sports a short curly tail (called a pom); and the lynx-like American Bobtail with their unusual voices.

Your lifestyle

This determines, to a great extent, what sort of pet you should be looking for. In the cat's lifetime you are responsible for his health and mental well-being, and must find others to fulfil this role if you are unable to do so, for instance when you go on holiday or have to be away from home for any reason.

Some breeds are very high-maintenance compared to others, so only consider these types if you are able to provide properly for them for the next 15 years or so. If you acquire a longhaired cat, you must be prepared to learn how to care for his coat properly; if you choose an extrovert, energetic type, then you must have the time to give him all the attention he needs. Such considerations may seem obvious, but animal welfare organizations still have to cope

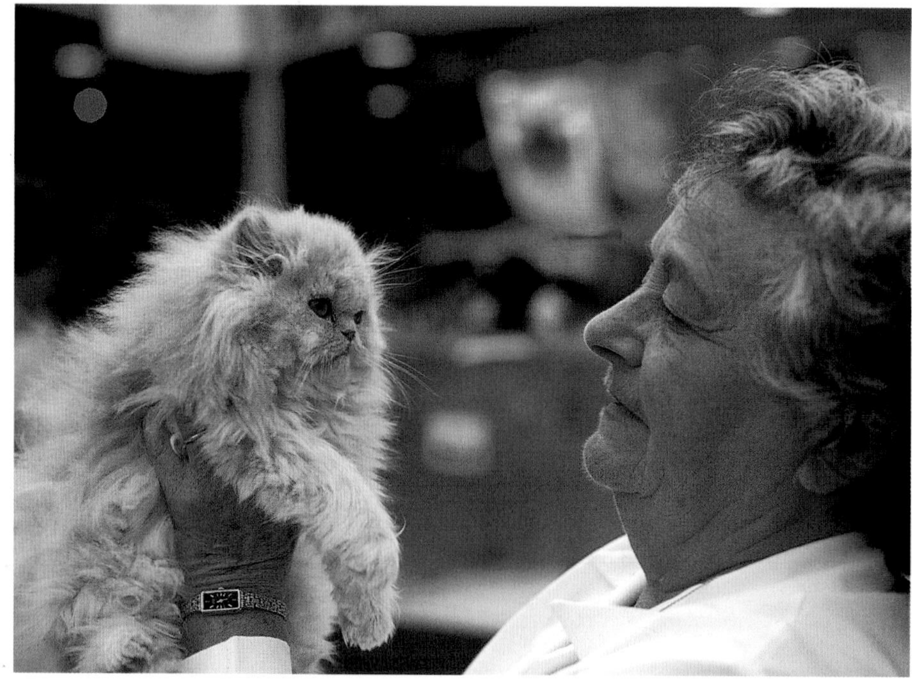

If you want a pedigree cat to show, be sure to choose an excellent example of the breed, but expect to pay a premium price for him.

This 'Peke-faced' Persian may be desirable on the show bench, but 'typey' cats (those with grossly exaggerated features) are often prone to respiratory and other problems due to their physical abnormalities. In addition, some breeds (or breeding lines) display certain characteristic behaviour that may not be desirable to some people, so it pays to research the breed you are interested in thoroughly. If possible, speak to other owners, vets and breeders before making a final decision.

with thousands of pet cats abandoned because their owners felt unable to care for them properly.

Ultimately, picking a pedigree or non-pedigree cat is your decision. You are in the best position to make an informed choice and, therefore, end up with a pet that is the right colour and type. How you will turn your chosen cat into the ideal companion you desire, given your lifestyle and expectations of him, is detailed in the following pages.

Feline fact

The trend for establishing different breeds of cat began early in the twentieth century, and there are now over 50 distinctive pedigree breeds, and hundreds of colour varieties.

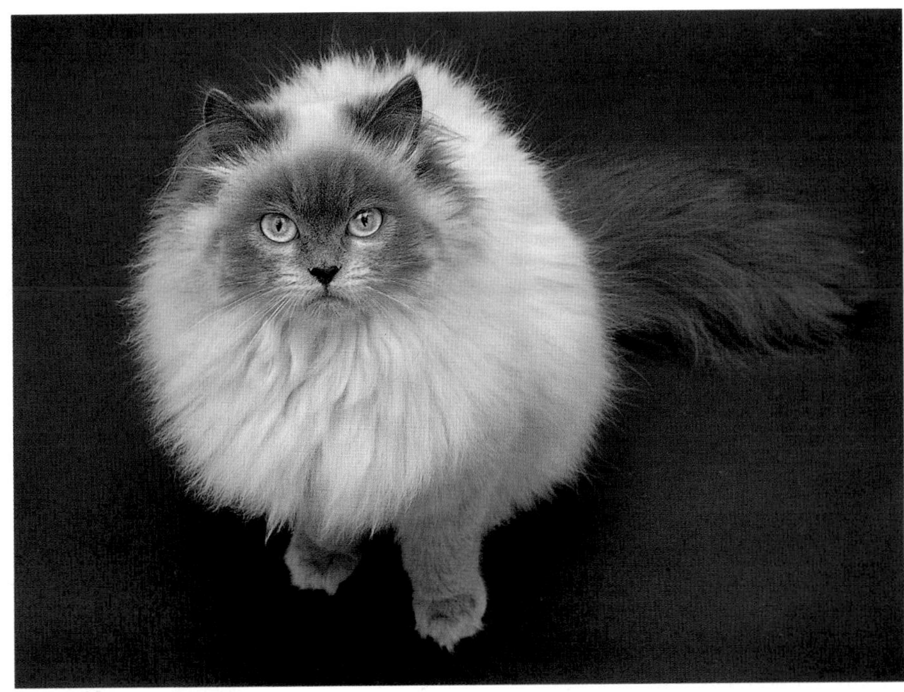

Longhaired cats need regular grooming to keep their coats tangle-free and their skin in good condition. Long coats can hide a multitude of problems, such as ticks and weight loss or gain, so it is essential to check for these regularly.

Kitten or adult?

Many people automatically think of acquiring a kitten, but that may not be the best choice for their circumstances or lifestyle; it is easier to see the character of an older cat, and any difficult or undesirable traits will already be apparent. Consider the points on the checklist before making a decision.

Checklist

- ✓ your lifestyle
- ✓ your circumstances
- ✓ your available time
- ✓ your requirements
- ✓ your other pets (if applicable)
- ✓ the age practicalities (human and animal)

AGE	PROS	CONS
Kitten	• Kittens and young adults tend to be more adaptable than their mature counterparts, but it really does depend on circumstances and their characters. • You can enjoy seeing him grow and develop. • You will, with luck, have many years to enjoy together. • You can train him to behave in the way you want. • If you get two kittens, they will provide company for each other.	• You need to give a young kitten meals at regular intervals through the day, as well as more attention, so he may prove very time-consuming. • Being introduced into a busy family may be frightening for a kitten (unless he has been brought up in such an environment and been well socialized with humans (and possibly other pets) since birth. • If there are young children in the house, a kitten is less able to defend itself or escape from them if need be. • The kitten will not have been neutered.
Adult 	• An adult cat is not as time-consuming as a kitten. • His character is already established. • He is already house-trained. • He is potentially socialized with other humans and animals. • He is potentially neutered.	• He may take longer to bond with you and your family and/or other pets. • He may have a limited lifespan, depending on his age. • He may be more difficult to integrate into your family. • He may be carrying a disease or ailment. • He may have undesirable behaviour traits.

Frequently asked question

Q Which would be better – a male or a female?

A If your cat or kitten is to be neutered, the question of sex becomes much less important. Neutered males may be larger than females, but there will be little difference otherwise. Males, especially those who are neutered, are said to be more loving towards their owners, but much depends on the way the cat is brought up and treated by his owner, as females can be just as affectionate. For more information on neutering, see pages 140–143.

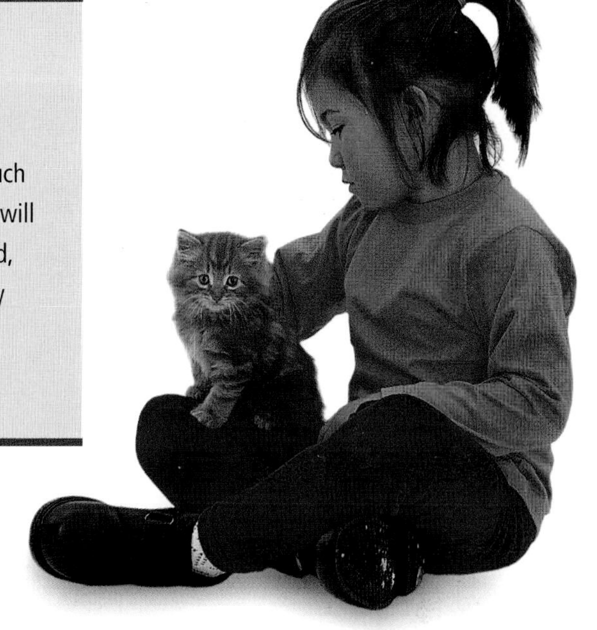

For the safety of both parties, never allow a child to grab at or chase after a cat or kitten.

Cats and children

Children aged three years and under cannot be expected to know how to approach and handle a cat correctly, so close supervision is the best way of preventing them being scratched. Naturally, children of all ages want to explore their new pet and establish a relationship with him, but poking him in the ear or disturbing him while he is asleep are not the best ways to do that. If young people are taught how to handle cats with gentleness and respect, then most children and cats become the best of friends. See pages 94–95 for more information on this subject.

One cat or more?

Cats will be much happier with a companion, whether it is another cat or other pet, especially if you are going to leave them alone for many hours. However, this is usually only the case if they have been brought up together. If you are thinking about having two cats, it would be better to get a couple of similarly aged kittens, or two adults that are used to living with each other, at the outset. See pages 82–83 for detailed information about introducing a second cat.

Sexing cats

Female (near right): *the vulva is the vertical opening immediately below the anus; it looks as though it is almost joined to the anus.*

Male (far right): *the anus – as in the female – is immediately below the tail; the scrotal sac containing the testicles is below this, with the penis concealed in the opening below the scrotal sac.*

When to get a cat

Thinking about getting a cat and actually getting one can be two very different things. Whether you opt for an adult cat or a kitten, you must take into account your personal circumstances at the time. You may want a cat desperately, but would a cat want to be with you right at this moment in your life? See the checklist for things to consider before getting a cat.

Checklist

- ✓ availability of kittens or cats
- ✓ holidays booked
- ✓ work commitments
- ✓ stressful times
- ✓ pregnancy
- ✓ time of year
- ✓ family commitments
- ✓ personal circumstances

Poor timing

The time is not ideal to get a cat if you are:

- moving house
- hectically busy at work and socially
- changing jobs
- being made redundant
- in the throes of an illness
- separating from your partner
- mourning a death in the family
- expecting a new baby
- due to go on holiday
- about to celebrate something that will result in upheaval of the family routine

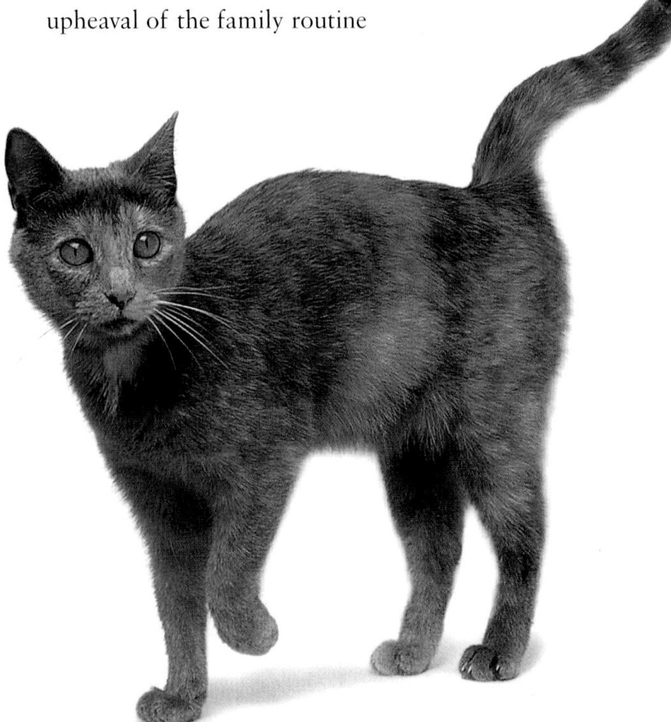

Of course, there are always exceptions to the rules, and many people find comfort in their pets at times of great stress. Such owners may feel that, although they are in turmoil, their pets are not suffering in any way because they remain fed and cared for. However, animals do feel their owners' anxieties (this is called anxiety transference) and feel worried themselves. This may manifest in unusual behaviour such as attention-seeking, or soiling around the home, or the cat may even disappear for a while (some even abandon the family home completely). It is important, therefore, to ensure that you are in a position both materially and emotionally to offer a secure and harmonious home to a cat before you get one.

Frequently asked question

Q I want to get a cat, but I am expecting a baby. Is it best to get a cat before or after the birth?

A It is probably better to wait until you have had the baby before introducing a new pet. This is so that the new cat views the infant as one of the family, rather than an unwelcome intrusion into his life. If you have pets, toxoplasmosis (see page 97) is a concern to new mums, but, providing you worm your pets correctly and adhere to household hygiene rules, this risk should be minimal.

Holidays

Wait until you have been on holiday before getting a cat, because otherwise he will suffer upheaval twice in a very short space of time – initially when you remove him from his former home, and then when you disappear for a while and either leave him in a cattery or with a trusted carer. For him to remain mentally and physically well, a new pet needs a good deal of time to settle in and feel secure in his new home before anything out of the ordinary occurs, such as being displaced from that home, even for a short while.

Did you know ...?

• Insecure cats who feel anxious or threatened in their home, for whatever reason, may spray urine or deposit faeces around the property. Doing this fills their 'territories' with their own individual scents and, therefore, helps them feel safer.

• It takes time to get to know new owners and territory well, which is why cats can be so unsettled for the first six months in a new home.

Cat availability

Sometimes it is not as easy to get a cat as you may imagine. There are several reasons for this:

• If you desire a particular breed, colour or sex of cat or kitten, it may not be available 'on spec'; you may have to reserve your specific requirement with a breeder (or even several breeders) so that when such an animal becomes available you have first choice

• Kittens are dependent on breeding seasons

• Kittens tend to be in high demand at rescue centres, so you may have to wait until one becomes available

• There may not be the exact type of cat you want at rescue centres immediately, so be prepared to wait

Whether young or old, cats are adorable, and it would be very easy to get one on impulse – but it is important to restrain yourself and consider whether the time is right to get a feline friend.

Top tip

Before you get a cat, consider the benefits you can offer him, rather than the benefits you think he can offer you.

Where to get a cat

There are many places to investigate when searching for a feline friend – such as pedigree cat breeders, owners of a non-pedigree cat who has produced kittens, or rescue centres. Which one you choose to explore is your decision, but it helps to be fully informed of the potential advantages and disadvantages of each before you do so.

Checklist

- ✓ breeders
- ✓ local adverts
- ✓ animal rescue centres
- ✓ finding a stray
- ✓ pet stores
- ✓ friends and family

Finding a cat

Your local paper, pet stores, vet surgery notice boards, cat magazines, word-of-mouth through friends and family and rescue centres are all potential sources of finding a cat or kitten. If you want a kitten, bear in mind that he should be at least eight weeks old before he can safely leave his mother. By this time, he should be fully weaned onto kitten food and ideally be socialized with a wide range of people and other animals. Some breeders prefer to wait until their kittens are 12 weeks of age before homing, so that they are fully litter-trained and have had their initial vaccinations.

Top tip

Some cats are naturally quiet and staid in their habits, while others are extrovert clowns. It is possible that you will see both types in the same litter. A noisy, busy household with young children and other pets is not the place for a timid and sensitive cat or kitten, and an outgoing, mischievous feline may prove a little too lively for a quiet and peaceful home.

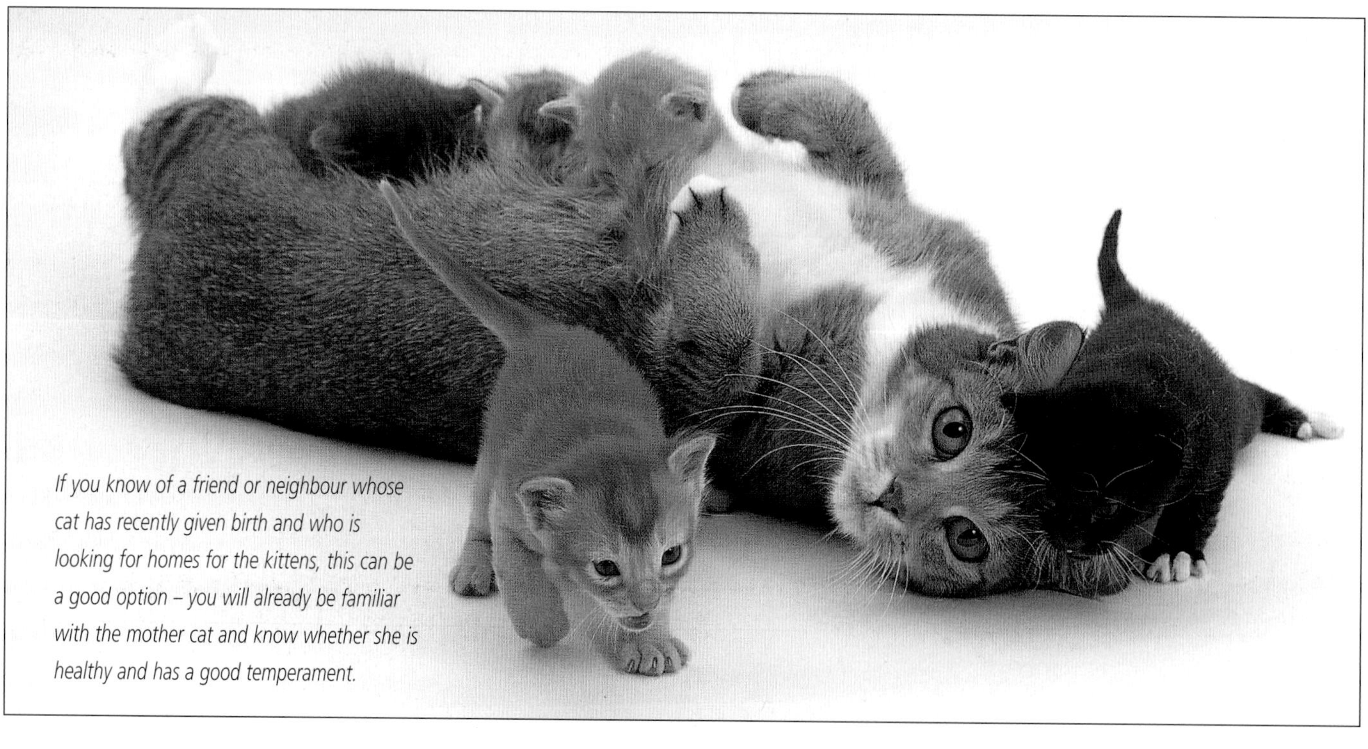

If you know of a friend or neighbour whose cat has recently given birth and who is looking for homes for the kittens, this can be a good option – you will already be familiar with the mother cat and know whether she is healthy and has a good temperament.

Cat shows are held on a regular basis in many countries and can be one- or two-day events. Entry to shows as spectators is not expensive, and breeders who are exhibiting are normally listed in the show catalogue.

Which source is best?

No one source is best, as there are considerations to take into account with all of them.

Breeders

When obtaining a kitten (pedigree or not) from a breeder, try to select him from a whole litter if possible. The appearance of the young cats will influence your choice, but so too should their behaviour and health; it is preferable to pick one that appears healthy (see page 28), outgoing, frisky and friendly and approaches you confidently. Avoid taking on an animal that looks unhealthy (see page 29) since you may be taking on a problem; take your time and look elsewhere for a cat instead.

HOW MUCH WILL A CAT COST?

SOURCE	COSTS
Pedigree breeder	• Depending on the breed and whether or not the cat is of show quality, prices can range enormously.
Rescue centre	• There is generally a charge to cover the cost of neutering and vaccinations.
Stray	• Free.
Pet store	• Prices vary: pedigree cats are more expensive than non-pedigree.
Friends or family	• Non-pedigree kittens or adult cats are generally free 'to good homes'; part-pedigree and pedigrees can vary, depending on the reason for rehoming.

If you find what you think is a stray, make enquiries before taking him in to ensure he is actually homeless and not someone's much-loved pet. Many cats wander away from their own homes as they explore their territory, and sociable ones will happily come into your home for a tasty free meal and some affection even though they are well fed and cared for at home. Old cats tend to look a bit dishevelled and their coats may not always be in good condition, so it is quite possible to mistake such an animal for a homeless stray.

Sometimes it is possible to get an older pedigree pet from a breeder who has no further need for a particular cat, or kittens resulting from accidental matings and not suited to a breeding programme. Breeders sometimes insist that such cats are neutered so they cannot be bred from.

Friends or family

Opting for an older cat can be a good idea if you do not have much time to spend training a kitten, particularly if you are offered a well-behaved animal by a family member or a friend.

Frequently asked question

Q We would like a pedigree, but are unsure about which breed would be best. Without travelling all over the country to see different breeders, how can we learn what the different breeds are and what they look like?

A It is a good idea to visit a championship cat show, where you will see many different ages, breeds and colours all under one roof. You can see how a particular breed of kitten will mature, and you may be able to glean information about the types you are particularly drawn to. You will find shows advertised in cat magazines. If travelling to a show is not possible, then obtain a good book on cat breeds. Having decided which breed you like, the next step is to contact the governing body of pedigree breeds (details of which are also, generally, to be found in cat magazines) in order to get details of breeders of that type of cat.

Did you know ...?

Kittens are not always available all year round; fewer are born in the late winter than during the spring and summer months.

Although your time together may be limited, an old cat has still much to offer in terms of affection and companionship, so don't discount 'oldies' as there are many in rescue centres seeking loving homes in which to see out their days.

Animal rescue centre

If you decide to choose a pet from an animal shelter, find out as much as you can from the staff about his background. Some cats, for example, may not be house-trained if they have spent their lives roaming about on their own, and such animals may not integrate well into a domestic environment. If a cat's age is unknown, there are no reliable indicators for determining how old he is.

Stray cats

Sometimes a cat simply moves into a home where he finds a welcome, or you may come across one you think has been abandoned. However, if you do find a 'stray', be aware that someone somewhere could be grieving over the disappearance of their pet; so make every effort to trace his owners by informing the local authorities and local animal welfare shelters, by putting up 'found' posters in local stores and veterinary clinics, and by having the animal checked for a microchip at the vet's. Once you have satisfied yourself that he is indeed a stray, have him checked over by a vet to ensure he is healthy, and also have him neutered if necessary.

Pet stores

Buying a cat from a pet store can be risky, so be especially critical. Ensure that the animals in the store look well cared for, have adequate space, food and water, and appear healthy. If many cats are kept together in a less-than-ideal environment, and there is a constant turnover of 'stock', there is a high risk of infection being present, which may not manifest until you get your new pet home.

Feline fact

If you pick a cat from an animal rescue centre, then as well as finding yourself a pet you will have the added pleasure of knowing that you have probably saved a life – many unwanted animals have to be destroyed. Elderly cats are more difficult to find a home for than their younger counterparts, so if you require a quiet, laid-back pet do consider a mature cat.

Signs of a healthy cat

Alert, calm demeanour • Supple movement • Normal body weight

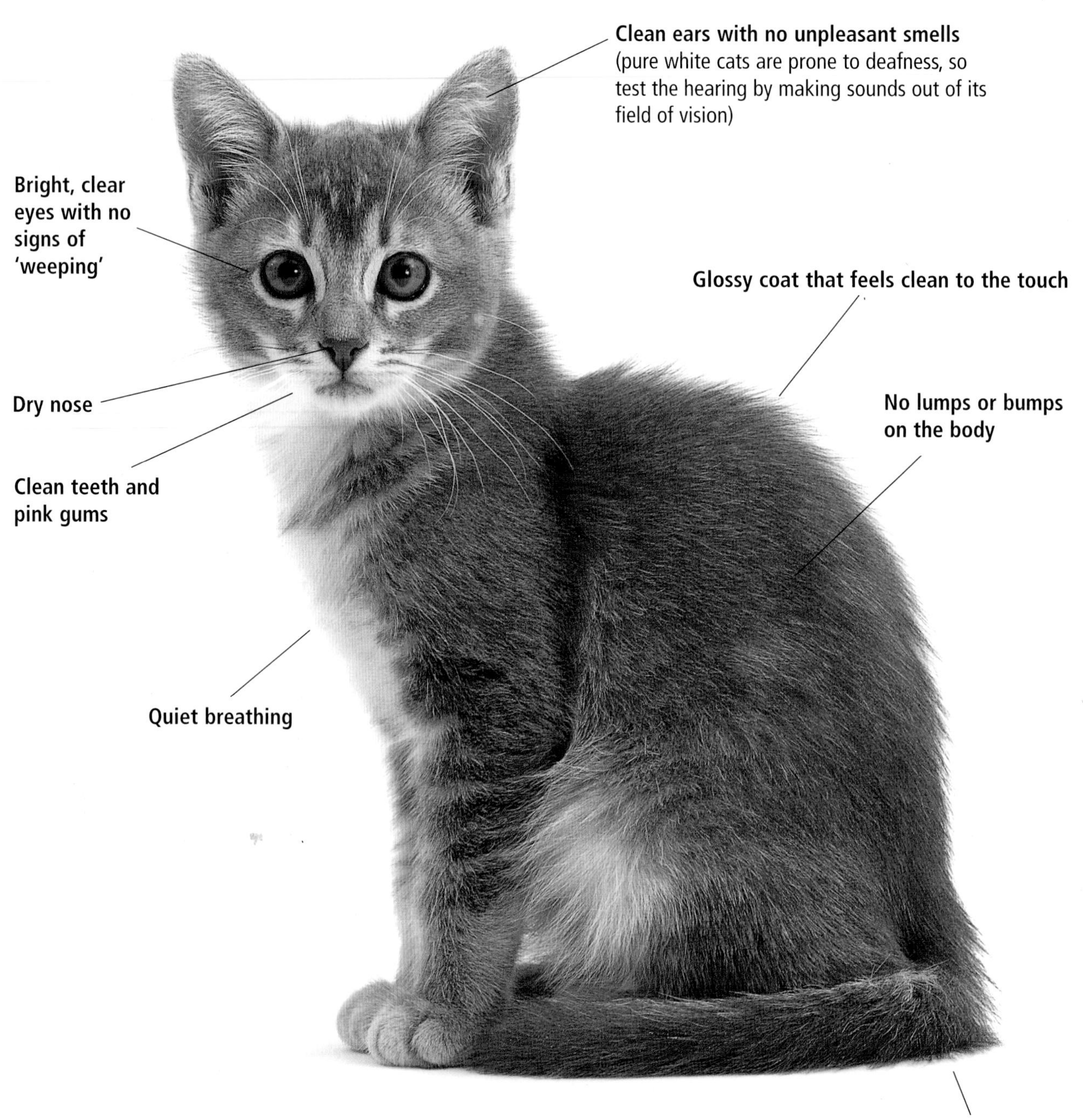

Signs of an unhealthy cat

Depressed demeanour • Constant scratching • Abnormal body weight

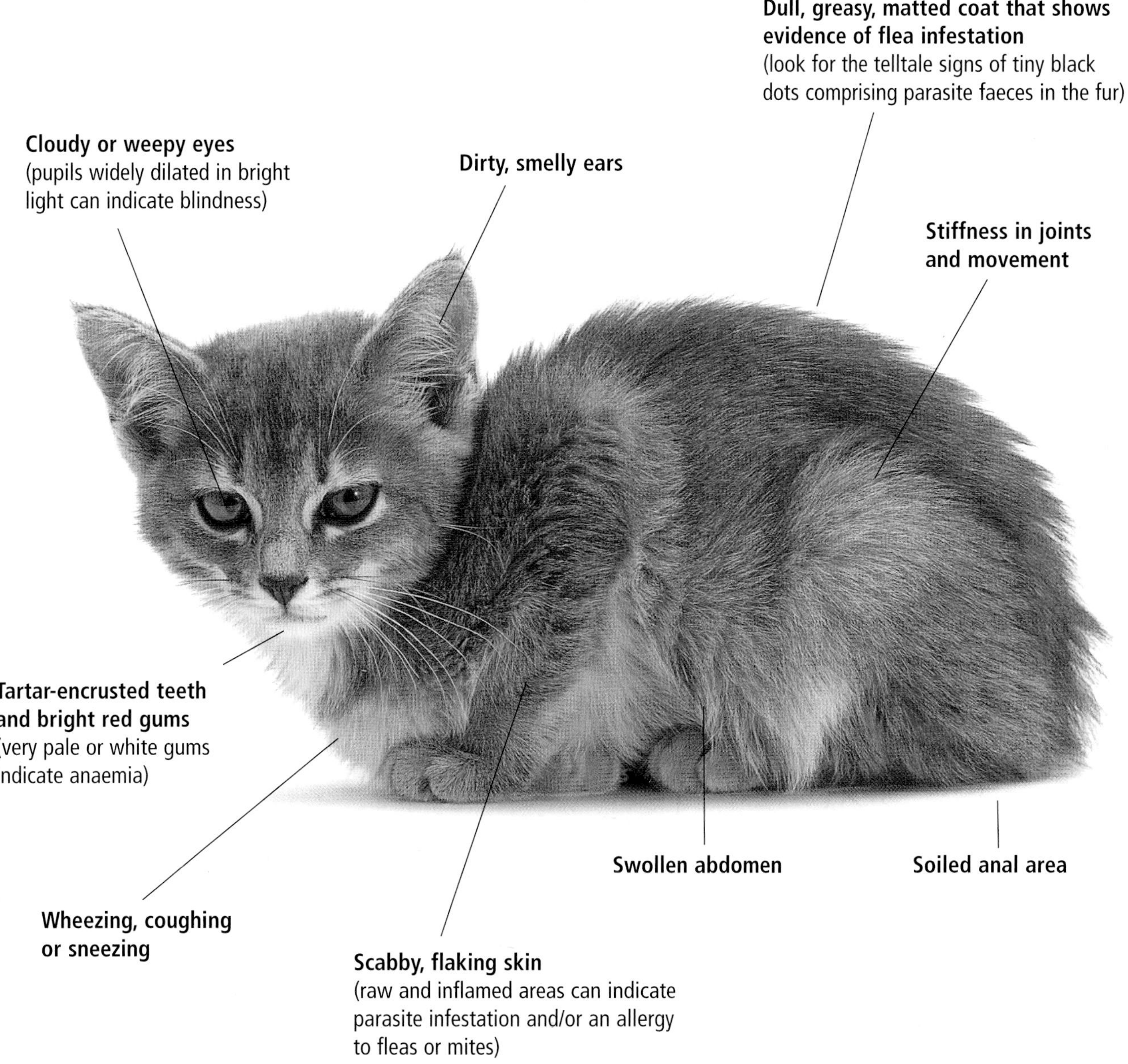

Essential equipment

The vast array of equipment and products available designed for cats – many marketed as being something your pet just cannot live without – can be bewildering for a new or prospective owner. However, many of these items are simply not essential. As long as your cat is warm, has somewhere to rest comfortably, safely and undisturbed, is fed regularly, has a constant supply of fresh, clean water, has somewhere suitable to relieve himself, and has some toys to play with, he will be perfectly happy.

You will not need a great deal of equipment to care for your new cat or kitten, and what you do need tends not to be very expensive. The checklist shows the basic things you will need, although you can add items to this list as you require them.

Checklist

- ✓ food and water bowls
- ✓ litter tray and litter
- ✓ bed and bedding
- ✓ toys
- ✓ first-aid kit (see page 157–58)
- ✓ collar and identity tag
- ✓ cat carrier
- ✓ scratching post

Food and water bowls

Your cat should have his own food and water bowls (see page 42), placed on a wipe-down feeding mat or piece of newspaper to catch any spills. You can buy automatic feeding bowls that dispense dry food at pre-set times. Pedal bowls, if your cat learns how to use them, can also be handy; these are lidded bowls that open when your cat puts a paw on the pedal mechanism, and close when he takes it off.

Litter tray and cat litter

A litter tray is essential even if you allow your cat to go outside. There are two basic types – open and covered (hooded). Covered types prevent the litter being scattered outside the tray, contain smells better and also afford the cat more privacy. However, some cats don't like to be enclosed so will only use an open tray.

Choose a tray big enough for your cat and one that will hold a good depth of litter – cats like to bury their eliminations completely, without wetting or soiling their paws. Lining the tray with newspaper will make cleaning it out much easier. Place the tray on newspaper or a piece of vinyl floor covering, so that any spills will be easy to clean up.

Litter types include (clockwise from top) clay-based litter, fine-grain litter with a grit/sand-like consistency, and wood-based litter comprising sawdust or paper pellets.

LITTER TYPE	PROS	CONS
Newspaper	• Inexpensive • Readily available	• Not very absorbent • Ink can stain a cat's feet and, therefore, floor and furniture coverings • Ink ingested when washing can cause illness • Any newspaper lying around the house may be considered a toilet area
Reusable litter (usually comprising wax-covered corn husks)	• Lasts for a long time, so can be economical • Saves on waste • Non-staining	• Expensive to buy initially • Can be unpleasant to wash and inconvenient to dry before reusing • Non-absorbent • Heavy to carry
Scented litters	• Help to mask smells	• More expensive than non-scented • Can be too strong-smelling, which is off-putting to cat and owner • Can be tempting not to wash the tray as often • The scented chemicals can irritate the respiratory system and foot pads
Paper or wood pellets	• Efficiently absorb moisture and smells • Non-staining • Light to carry	• Expensive
Soil from the garden (if you have one)	• Free • Readily available	• Can harbour insects and other creepy-crawlies • Will stain fur and be tracked across the floor • Heavy to carry
Silica sand crystals	• Soak up urine like a sponge • Virtually eliminate litter-tray smells • Easy to maintain: simply remove solid waste daily and change the whole tray of crystals every few weeks • Non-staining • Light to carry	• Expensive initially • Can be tricky to tidy up if the litter gets onto the floor
Clay or sand-based litters	• Inexpensive • Absorbs moisture efficiently	• Does not absorb smells • The cheaper varieties can leave heavy tracking when wet • Heavy to carry

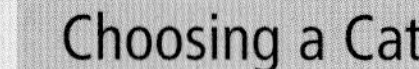

Dispose of used litter, well wrapped up in newspaper or biodegradable bags, with your own household rubbish, not down the toilet, as it could cause a blockage. Consult your vet or local waste-disposal company about disposing of waste from a cat that is receiving radiation treatment.

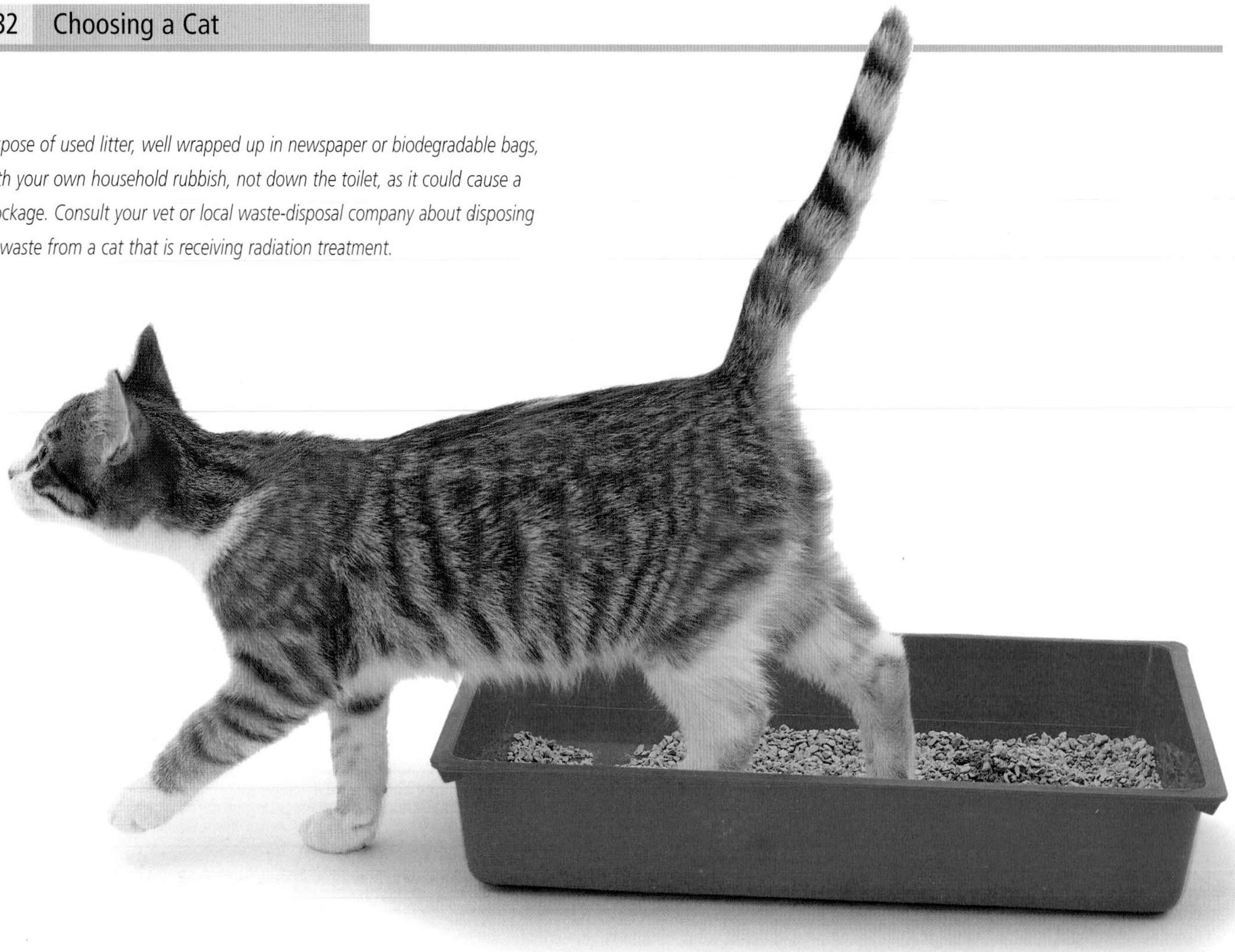

Bed and bedding

There are many types of cat bed (see chart opposite). Blankets, fleece material, a cushion or old pillow, and fleecy veterinary pet bedding all make good, insulating bedding material. Wash materials regularly to remove dirt and help prevent flea infestation.

A warm, cosy bed in which to curl up will be much appreciated by your cat.

BED TYPE	PROS	CONS
Cardboard box	• Cheap • Readily available • High sides keep out draughts	• Needs replacing regularly • Needs extra bedding
Plastic	• Inexpensive • Hygienic • Easy to clean • High-sided types keep out draughts	• Needs extra bedding
Wicker	• Looks attractive	• Expensive • Draughty • Harbours dust and fur; difficult to clean • Cats tend to scratch them to bits • Needs extra bedding
Cushioned or fake-fur bed	• Comfortable • No extra bedding usually needed	• Can harbour fleas if not washed regularly • Can be difficult to wash and dry • Expensive
Covered (hooded) bed	• Most cats feel secure in them • Draught-free • No extra bedding needed with cushioned types	• Can be difficult to wash and dry • Expensive • Some cats do not like being 'enclosed'
Over-the-radiator cradle	• Space-saving • Great for cats who need extra warmth (very young, old, ill, hairless) • Gives sense of security as raised off floor	• Stiff cats may not be able to access them easily • May harbour fleas if not washed regularly
Bean bags	• Comfortable • Warm • Cats love them	• Can be time-consuming to remove the polystyrene beads in order to wash the cover • If the beads escape, it can take a long time to clean them up

Hooded beds can provide a sense of privacy and security, particularly in a busy household.

Toys

Playing with your cat is rewarding for both parties. Cats play most during kittenhood, and if they learn to play with toys during this time they will probably continue to do so during adulthood. Moving toys in ways that mimic prey behaviour will result in more fun for your cat and more interest for you. Darting movements from side to side in front of the cat, rather than up-and-down movements, are more likely to result in play. Toys that move erratically or very fast, then are stationary, are more likely to be 'hunted'. Many stuffed toys contain the herb catnip (also called catmint), which cats find irresistible.

Some cats, Siamese in particular, can be trained to walk on a lead. For this, you will need a harness and a lead designed for cats. Various versions are available, from plain to intricately decorated, and in different colours, but the first consideration is that the harness is comfortable for your cat, and that the lead is long enough for comfort and ease of movement for both parties.

There is a huge variety of toys on the market, specially designed for cats, which mimic the behaviour of prey when rolled, rustled, dangled and dragged along the ground.

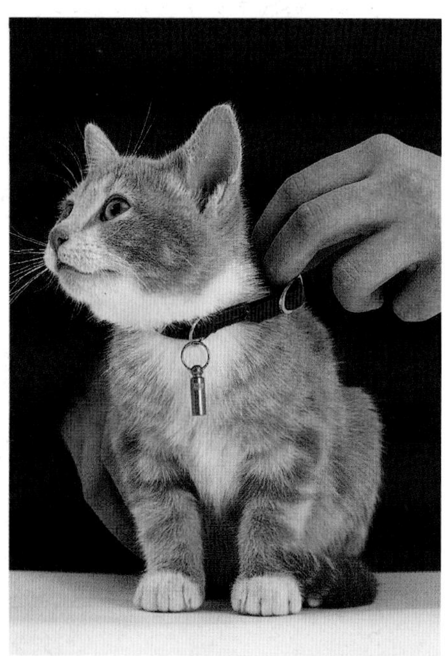

When fitting a collar, make sure you can slide two fingers between it and the cat's neck. Check the collar regularly for signs of chafing, and also to ensure that it still fits comfortably on a growing cat.

Collar and identity tag

Ideally, your cat should wear a reflective or fluorescent collar complete with an identity tag and a bell to warn wildlife and birds of his presence. Collars come in many designs, but you should always use one with either an elastic insert or a quick-release fastening (which opens when under pressure) for safety in case your cat becomes caught up on something.

Cat carrier

For trips to the vet or cattery, you will need a cat carrier. Cardboard ones are cheap and are fine for occasional use, but will not contain a cat that is determined to get out, and are liable to break when wet.

Other types include fibreglass and plastic-coated wire-mesh designs: the former tend to be front-opening and are draught-free, secure, reasonably light and easy to clean, while the latter tend to be top-opening and are ideal for cats that dislike being enclosed too much; they are also easier to get the cat out of.

Wicker carriers look nice, but are hard to clean and not as hardwearing as fibreglass or wire mesh. Choose a carrier you find easy to handle and carry with the weight of your cat in it, and make sure the door closes securely so your cat can't escape.

Plastic-coated wire-mesh carriers are available in several sizes. Large ones are useful if you have two or more cats to transport.

Scratching post

Every cat has a biological need to scratch, to help keep his claws in trim and good working order (this is called 'stropping'). Unless you provide your cat with something he can scratch away at to his heart's content, such as a scratching post, he will inevitably strop his claws on your furniture. Help to train your cat to use the post by rubbing it with catnip (crush a little fresh catnip in your hands and rub them on the post) or by spraying it with catnip essence (available from pet stores).

Make sure the scratching post is stable when in use.

Top tip

If your cat has a preference for a chair or sofa arm on which to strop, then, when you replace the item, keep that arm as a home-made scratching post that your cat will be familiar with. This may stop him transferring the habit to your new furniture.

Indoor crate

Although not absolutely essential, an indoor crate (also called a kittening pen) can prove extremely useful. Those crates designed for dogs afford more space if necessary. The crate provides a secure den during a cat's integration period in a new home, and makes the introduction of it to existing pets more manageable and less traumatic. When you cannot be around to supervise young kittens, popping them in the crate will keep them safely away from wires and other hazards that could harm them.

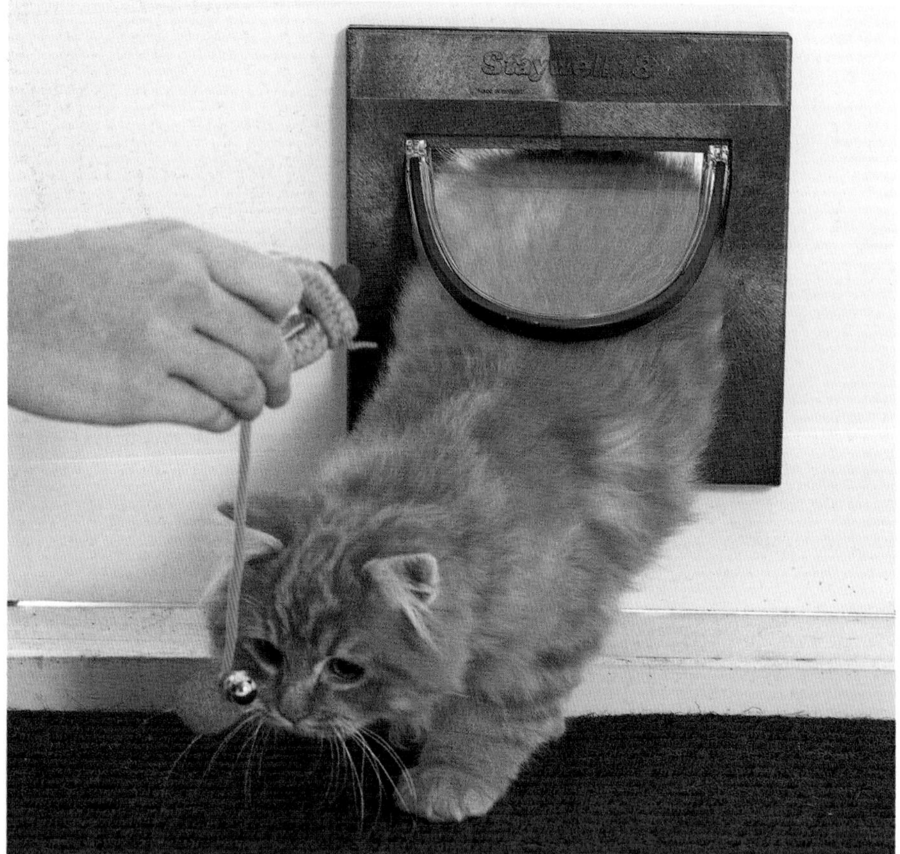

The crate or pen should be large enough for the cat to move around freely within it, and to accommodate his toys, litter tray and food and water bowls. If you only want one for a short period, then it may be possible to rent one from a vet or breeder.

Some types of cat flap can be set into brick walls, which is handy if you don't want to put one in a door or window.

Cat flap

A cat flap fitted in an outside door or window will, when unlocked, allow your pet to enter and leave the house at leisure. Various designs are available, including electromagnetic and electronically operated flaps that will only open to the cat carrying a special device attached to his collar. Fit the cat flap low enough in the door or window for your pet to be able to use it comfortably, and far enough away from the handle or fastening on the door or window to prevent burglars from reaching inside and letting themselves in.

Parasite treatments

You will need to treat your cat for internal and external parasites on a regular basis – the most effective treatments are only available from vets, but are worth spending a little bit more on as they work efficiently, unlike many shop-bought products. See page 138 for more detailed information.

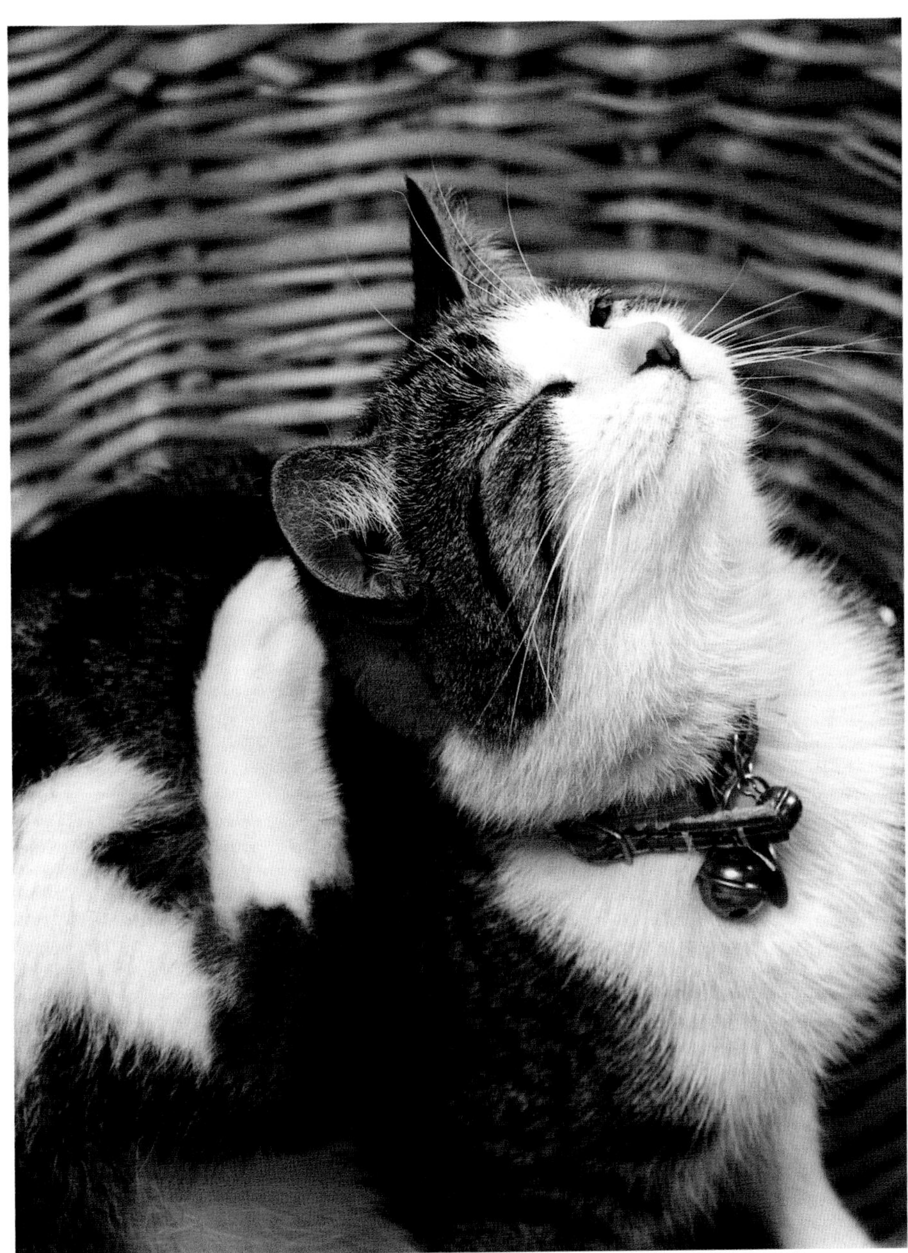

If your cat scratches himself constantly, check his coat for signs of fleas. Fleas cause all sorts of unpleasant ailments, so it is essential to keep your cat and home free of them by means of suitable treatments obtained from your vet.

Top tip

Don't use a flea collar at the same time as other flea treatments, or you may overdose your pet on the chemicals they contain, making him ill.

Feeding your cat

Feeding your cat a well-balanced diet and the right amount of food on a daily basis is essential for his good health. These days the pet-food industry is big business and there is a wide range of feline foods available for cats – many of which are aggressively marketed – so it can be difficult deciding which variety or brand is the best choice for your pet. There are, however, certain dietary nutrients that a cat cannot do without, and these are shown on the checklist. Taking these and your cat's age, health and lifestyle into account when purchasing cat food can help to make the job of deciding which diet is most suitable easier.

Checklist

- ✓ vitamin A
- ✓ vitamin B complex
- ✓ vitamin D
- ✓ vitamin E
- ✓ calcium
- ✓ phosphorus
- ✓ protein
- ✓ iodine
- ✓ amino acids (specifically taurine and niacin)
- ✓ fats
- ✓ fibre
- ✓ water
- ✓ grass

Cats are known as 'obligate carnivores' – they depend on meat and other similar foodstuffs, such as fish, as sources of vital nutrients in order to remain healthy. Unable to exist on a low-protein diet, cats need relatively large amounts of meat-based food per day in relation to their size. In a wild state, the cat hunts, kills, feeds, and then rests. He may gorge himself on a whole rabbit, or several mice and birds, on one day, then go without food completely for the next two or three days. Adult domestic cats are usually fed once a day, but splitting that feed into two meals adds interaction and interest and alleviates boredom. Do not feed your cat on dog food, as this is formulated for canine nutritional needs, not feline ones.

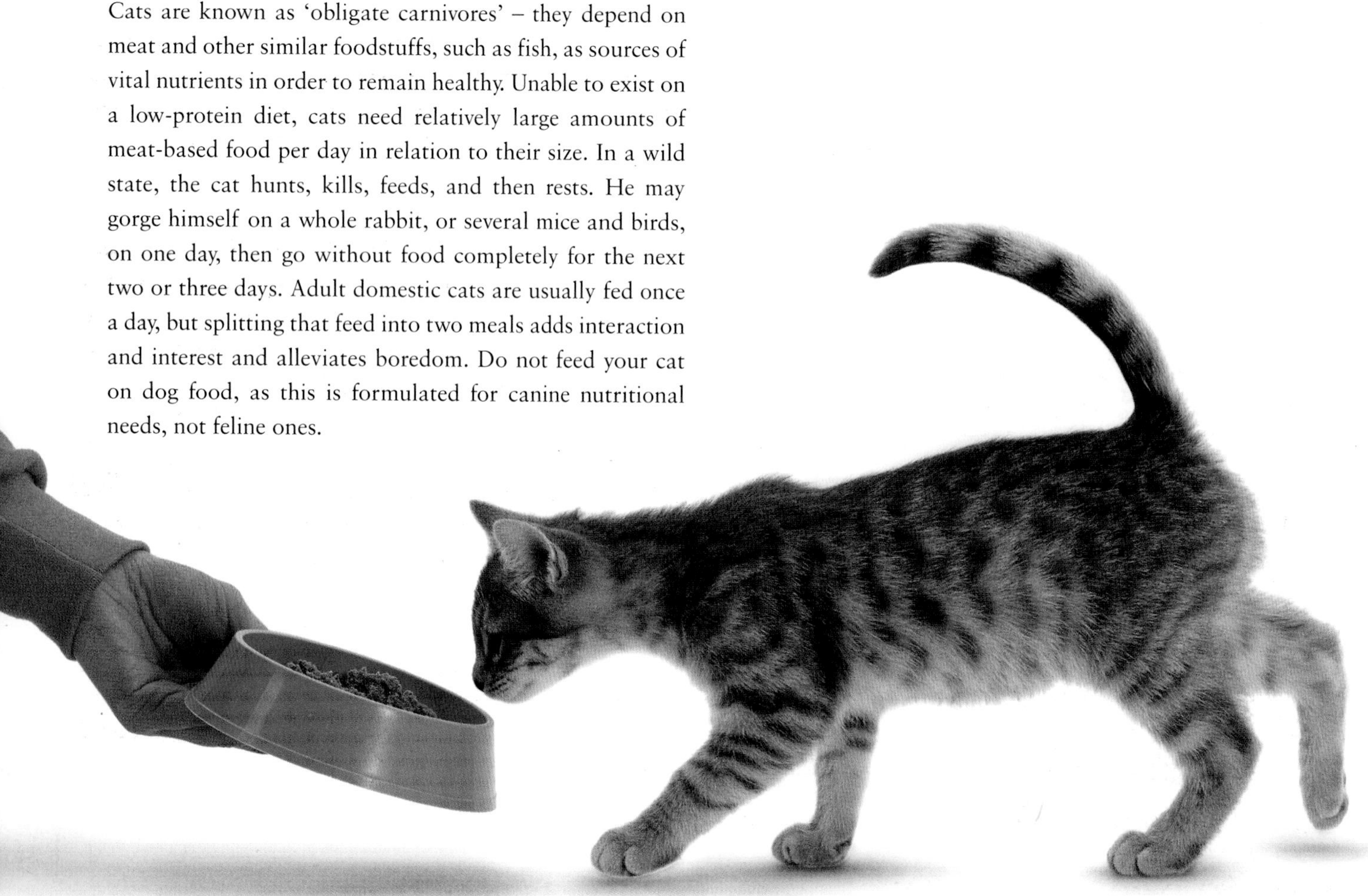

Necessary nutrients

It is important to ensure that the balance of nutrients fed to a cat is correct, as excesses can cause as many health problems as deficiencies. This is why it is better to feed quality commercially prepared foods, rather than a home-made diet through which it is difficult to ensure your cat is receiving all the correct nutrients. For example, a diet of cooked carcass meat alone is low in calcium, vitamin A and iodine, and these deficiencies may lead to osteoporosis (brittle bone disease). A liver-rich diet can cause excess vitamin A, resulting in bony outgrowths around the joints and spine that make movements painful.

Carbohydrates

Although they can digest and metabolize cooked carbohydrates, cats have no nutritional need for them, as their necessarily high-protein diet supplies all the energy they require. However, foods such as breakfast cereals can provide a useful source of energy.

Vitamins

A relatively high level of vitamin A is needed to keep body cells working properly. Vitamins of the B group are important for the maintenance, in particular, of the central nervous system. Vitamin D helps the body produce calcium, essential for healthy bones and teeth, although cats need far less than dogs or humans. Phosphorus is also essential for healthy bones and teeth while vitamin E helps prevent cell damage. As cats can self-produce vitamin C (ascorbic acid; essential for maintaining healthy connective tissue and skin), this does not need to be included in the diet.

Proteins

Proteins present in meat help build body tissue, carry out 'repairs' and make hormones. They also supply essential amino acids that a cat's own body cannot produce, one of which is taurine. A deficiency of taurine will result in visual impairment, infertility and heart disease.

Fats

Dietary fats comprise a concentrated energy source of all nutrients and supply the essential fatty acids (EFAs) that are vital in maintaining total body health.

Fibre

A lack of fibre in the diet can result – especially in elderly, inactive cats – in constipation and other digestive problems caused by sluggish bowels. Fibre providers include cooked vegetables and cereal foods.

Top tips

How much to feed

Follow the manufacturer's instructions on the food packaging; it is generally a good guide to what weight of food to feed per day at each life stage. You can split this weight into as many meals as you wish throughout the day depending on your pet's preference and your daily routine.

Food treats and supplements

On a commercially prepared and therefore carefully formulated and balanced diet, your cat should not need any food supplements (comprising vitamins, minerals and oils), unless your vet advises you to use them. Overdosing on nutrients can prove detrimental to your pet's health.

Eating grass

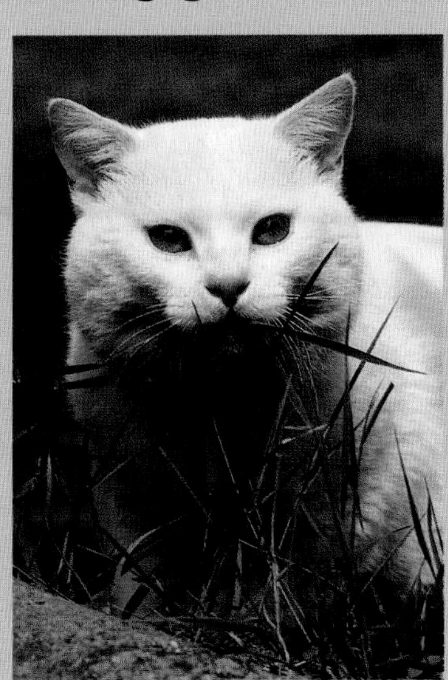

Cats eat grass as a source of folic acid. It also acts an emetic to induce vomiting and so rid the stomach of furballs, worms and other causes of digestive upset.

Commercially produced adult and kitten foods are available in (top to bottom) wet/moist, semi-moist and dry. Try each type to find which one your cat prefers, and appears healthiest on, but avoid giving solely dry food.

Food types

Good-quality proprietary foods are the easiest to feed. They contain all the necessary nutrients in the correct proportions, including vitamins and minerals, which could be lacking from a home-made diet of fresh or cooked meat and table scraps. There are three forms of commercially prepared food.

1 Wet/moist (canned or pouch)

Canned food has a high water content, is available in a wide range of flavours and is usually the preferred choice of cats.

2 Semi-moist (pouch)

Often containing vegetable protein, such as soya, this food type contains less water than canned, and therefore keeps well in a bowl without drying out and losing texture.

3 Dry (packet)

As its name suggests, dry food contains minimal water, so your cat will need plenty of water to drink in conjunction with it. Because of its hard, crunchy texture, dry food helps keep cats' teeth tartar-free and in good condition. However, it is best to use it only as part of the diet, rather than the whole, as some cats become addicted to it, and it can result in urinary problems.

Frequently asked question

I have heard that dry foods can cause crystal formation in the urine, leading to bladder urinary tract problems – is this true?

A Dry foods had a bad press when they first came on to the market as they were linked to a condition called feline urological syndrome (FUS), more commonly known as feline lower urinary tract disease (FLUTD). It was particularly common in inactive cats fed purely on a dry diet and whose water intake was minimal. The condition meant that the cat strained to pass urine, but was unable to because of crystals in the urine partially, or totally, blocking the urethra leading from the bladder. The formula for dry cat foods was changed, and today they are widely used, although it is preferable to choose high-quality brands to ensure the formula balance is correct, and to interchange the dry for moist foods on a regular basis. Fresh drinking water should always be available.

If you feed your cat outside, always do so in a secure place where no other animal can share or steal his dinner.

Life-stage feeding

Different feeding regimes are appropriate for the various stages in a cat's life (see chart below).

Kittens	Kittens usually stop drinking their mother's milk and go on to solid food when they are 8 weeks old; gradual weaning starts at 4–5 weeks. After that, they should be fed kitten food, as this contains all the essential nutrients they need in a form that is easy for them to digest and utilize. Fed correctly at this age, they are on course to grow into healthy and well-developed adults.
From weaning to 12 weeks	Five small meals a day, each of around 25g (1oz).
From 12 to 20 weeks	Four meals a day.
From 20 to 30 weeks	Three meals a day.
From 30 weeks to 12 months (juvenile/adolescent)	Gradually reduce to two meals a day.
From 12 months to 8 years (adult)	One or two meals a day.
From 8 years onwards (elderly)	One or two meals a day, but you may have to increase to two or more depending on your pet's condition and health.

QUICK-REFERENCE FEEDING GUIDE

Age of cat	Body weight	Daily food requirements	Feeds per day
Newborn	0.12kg (4oz)	28g (1oz)	10
5 weeks	0.45kg (1lb)	85g (3oz)	6
10 weeks	0.9kg (2lb)	140g (5oz)	5
20 weeks	2kg (4lb 4oz)	170g (6oz)	4
30 weeks	3kg (6lb 10oz)	200g (7oz)	3
Neutered adult	4kg (9lb)	185g (6½oz)	1
Unneutered adult male	4.5kg (10lb)	240g (8½oz)	1
Pregnant female	3.4kg (7lb 8oz)	240g (8½oz)	2–3
Lactating female	2.5kg (5lb 8oz)	400g (14oz)	4

When to feed

Most owners feed either morning or evening – sometimes both, depending on their cat's age needs or individual preference; some cats do better on meals fed little and often, while others are happy to eat their daily allowance in one helping. Try to encourage your pet to eat his food at a single sitting rather than leaving uneaten food out all day. Wet food, in particular, goes off rapidly, resulting in waste if your cat does not eat all of his portion. You will soon get to know how much your pet will eat at one sitting, which will then enable you to ascertain the right amounts to split his daily allowance into.

Feline obesity is a common problem these days, so it is essential to restrict your pet's daily ration to the

Choose cat dishes that have flat, non-slip bases, and which cannot be toppled over easily. They should be shallow enough for the cat to eat and drink from comfortably, yet deep enough to contain food and water, and be easy to keep scrupulously clean. Suitable materials are (left to right) stainless steel, ceramic and plastic. Discard worn or cracked bowls as these can harbour bacteria, as well as injure your cat's mouth.

manufacturer's or your vet's guidelines on feeding. Treats should be included in the daily ration allowance, and not given as extras. Obesity can lead to all sorts of health problems and drastically shorten your pet's life.

Water for life

Some cats dislike hard water (that which contains a high concentrate of mineral salts – indicated by limescale deposits in cooking utensils and kettles) and will not drink as much as they should for good health. In this case, try offering your pet filtered water, or even try to source soft water. Avoid using bottled mineral water, as this also tends to be high in mineral deposits.

Home-made food

Many cats appreciate 'home-made' foods, but basing an entirely balanced diet around these will be very difficult; a vitamin and mineral supplement will almost certainly be required as well – consult your vet for advice. For ease of feeding (particularly for busy owners), it is simpler to stick to proprietary cat food and only give an occasional home-made meal for a treat, or to tempt a cat that is ill and has lost his appetite. Always allow cooked foods to cool before serving. Items such as cooked porridge, rabbit, poultry and fish, as well as scrambled eggs, are often appreciated – but remove all bones before feeding.

Top tip

Although many cats appear to enjoy eating it, chocolate can make them very ill – and even prove fatal – so do not give it to them as a treat. Give them milk-drop treats instead, or the chocolate drops specially formulated for dogs.

Varying the diet

It is possible to combine a home-made diet with a commercially prepared one, so that your cat has the best of both worlds. A varied diet helps keep your cat interested, and therefore content with life, as well as helping to

ABOVE *Home-made food can be a treat for your cat, but remember that it may not contain the right balance of nutrients for his needs.*

LEFT *Water is essential for life, and your cat should always have access to a fresh supply. Refill the water bowl each day and scrub it out regularly with clean water (do not use detergents which would taint the bowl), otherwise it could get slimy with saliva.*

Did you know ...?

Cow's milk is very high in lactose (milk sugar) which some cats find difficult to digest, resulting in diarrhoea. Some cats are also allergic to the protein contained in cow's milk. Instead, give special 'cat milk' (available from pet-food outlets) which is lactose-reduced yet is still rich in the essential calcium that cats need for strong, healthy bones and teeth.

negate a tendency to be fussy about the food that he is presented with.

A suitable varied diet for an average cat (a fit and healthy adult) with an average weekly energy requirement of 1,400–1,800 kcal (5,880–7.560 kJ) can be made up in many ways. The chart below represents an example of using a variety of different foods over 5 weeks (plus a constant supply of drinking water). At the end of the 5 weeks, you can start again at Week 1.

VARYING YOUR CAT'S DIET OVER 5 WEEKS

Week	Total consumption (to be split into daily feeds)
1	7 small cans/pouches of wet/semi-moist cat food plus 600ml (1 pint) cat milk
2	450g (1lb) dry food plus 300ml (½ pint) cat milk
3	900g (2lb) cooked rabbit meat; 225g (8oz) cooked liver; and 450ml (¾ pint) cat milk
4	450g (1lb) beef; 450g (1lb) melts (spleen); 225g (8oz) oily fish; 300ml (½ pint) cat milk
5	4 cans/pouches of wet/semi-moist cat food; 112g (4oz) dry food; 225g (8oz) white fish; 450ml (¾ pint) cat milk

FEEDING GUIDELINES

- Feed your cat in the same place and at the same time every day.
- Place a feeding mat, or newspaper, under feeding bowls, as many cats like to drag their food from the dish and eat it on the floor.
- Don't disturb the cat when he is eating.
- Leave wet or semi-moist food out for at least an hour before disposing of leftovers, as most cats eat slowly.
- Introduce any changes to diet gradually to avoid digestive upsets.
- Never give spiced food or anything to which alcohol has been added.
- To prevent choking, remove bones from fresh meats and fish.
- Always provide fresh, clean drinking water.
- Do not give cow's milk – provide special cat milk or goat's milk instead.
- Ensure food and water bowls are always clean.
- Never allow your cat to eat chocolate intended for human consumption.
- Consult your vet if your cat shows any reluctance to eat or drink.

FOOD HYGIENE GUIDELINES

- Cats prefer their food at room temperature, so always allow refrigerated foods to reach this before serving.
- Canned foods deteriorate quickly once opened, so refrigerate and use within 24 hours. Decant leftover tinned foods into ceramic, stainless steel or plastic food containers to avoid 'tin contamination' – just as recommended for human foods.
- Place your cat's food and water bowls well away from his litter tray.
- Household disinfectants and detergents can taint food and water bowls and put your pet off using them, so use salt solution (one teaspoon to half a litre/one pint of water) or proprietary pet-bowl cleaners, and then rinse thoroughly in clean water to clean and disinfect them. Clean bowls daily, as cats are very fussy regarding food hygiene – and rightly so as good health depends on it.
- Wash pet-feeding utensils items separately from your own.
- When feeding semi-moist food, reseal the packet to make it airtight in order to retain freshness and prevent moisture loss until the next meal.

Counting the calories

Energy is measured in units called calories. In a healthy cat, the number of calories he requires balances the number of calories that his body uses each day. If this balance is well maintained, the cat stays fit and healthy and his weight remains constant. An underfed cat gradually loses weight and condition as his body draws on the reserves of fat and protein to make up the deficiencies in his diet. Depending on her pattern of activity, a normal female cat needs 200–250 calories per day, while a male needs 250–300. Kittens need more calories in relation to their body weight because they are growing rapidly, they are more subject to heat loss owing to their small size, and their energy requirements are higher.

The right environment

To be mentally and physically healthy, your cat must feel safe and secure in his environment. For you to not worry and be able to enjoy your pet to the full, you need to be positive that you are doing all you can to keep him happy and protected from harm. Fulfilling your cat's natural needs will help keep you both contented – see the checklist for a cat's natural needs.

Checklist

- ✓ safe territory
- ✓ safe, comfortable resting places
- ✓ sense of security
- ✓ personal space
- ✓ toys to satisfy the hunting instinct
- ✓ ample food and water
- ✓ acceptable social interaction

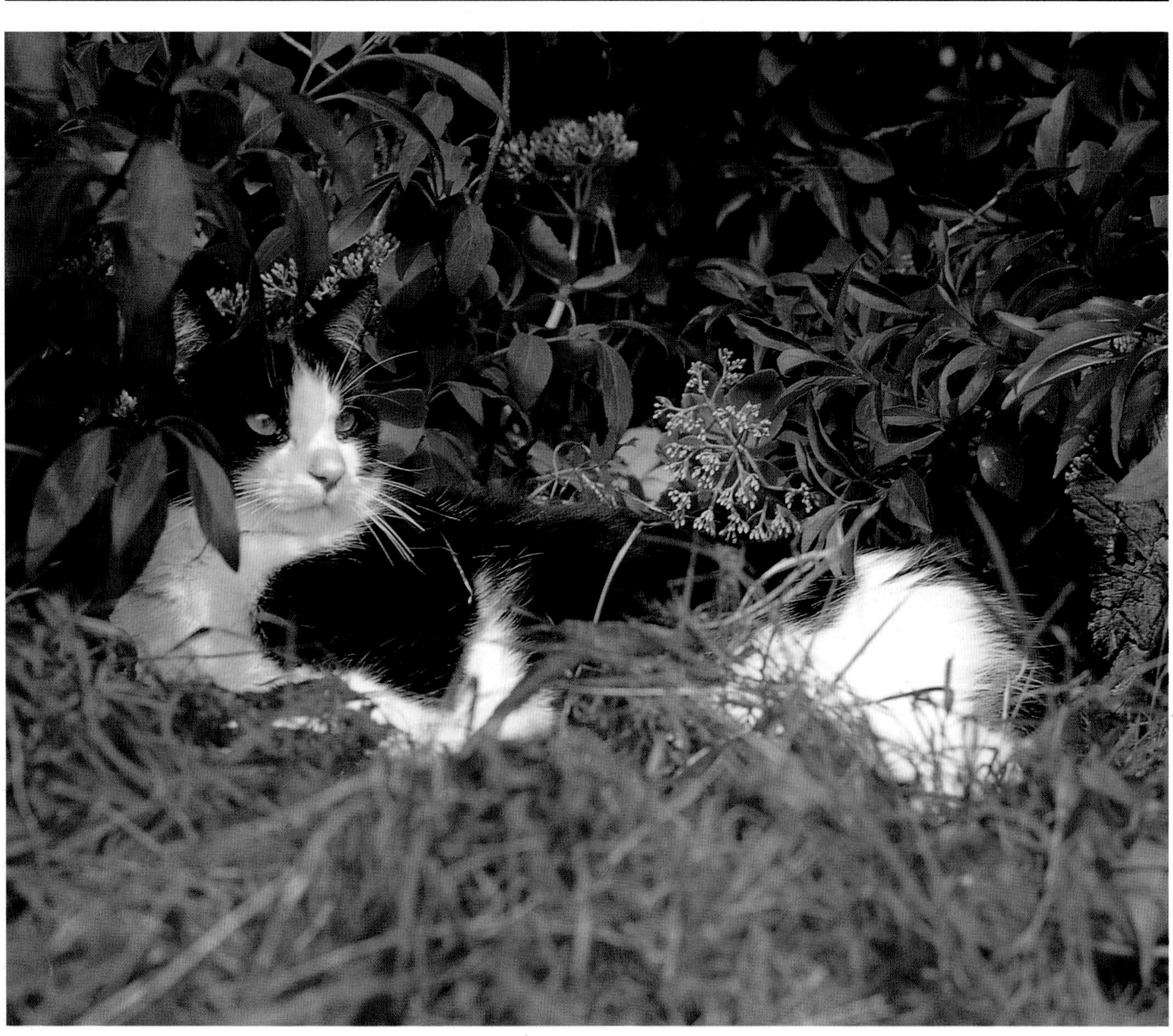

The 'natural' cat, allowed unlimited access outdoors in a safe, rural environment, has perhaps the best life of all, having the freedom to explore, hunt, play and find somewhere comfortable and warm to rest at will. However, only a small percentage of domestic cats enjoy this feline idyll – the rest have no option but to fit into their owners' lifestyles. By considering your pet's instincts and his requirements, you can make his life as natural as possible – and, therefore, more pleasant for you – by implementing a few simple, yet highly effective, alterations to the way you care for him, and to your home.

Home comforts

Most people who keep cats as pets want their animals to be close to them, for the affection and company they provide. To make your home as appealing as possible to your pet, so that he will want to stay in it as much as possible, you must provide him with the facilities most important to him.

To a cat, the most important thing is to mark his home with his own unique smell, and he does this by rubbing his cheeks (where his scent glands are situated) on items and furniture to deposit his scent. Glands between the toes also leave a scent message as the cat strops his claws. Humans cannot smell this scent, but other cats can and know that the territory has a feline occupant.

Surrounded by his own scent, a cat feels more secure, but over-zealous house cleaning by the owner, using lots of strong-smelling disinfectants, polishes, carpet and soft-furnishing fresheners and room fragrances, can keep overriding this feline scent. This may make the cat anxious, as he cannot scent-recognize his territory. In turn, this can lead to more rigorous marking behaviour that may involve the cat spraying urine around the house – and humans can certainly smell this.

High and mighty

You can help increase his feeling of security by providing high-up places where he can rest without being bothered by anyone or by another animal, or simply watch the world go by from a safe vantage point – the chances of him being attacked from above are slim, but high at ground level. This is why many cats like to sit on tables, the top of kitchen work surfaces or cupboards, and the back of armchairs. It is sensible to put any breakable items out of harm's way.

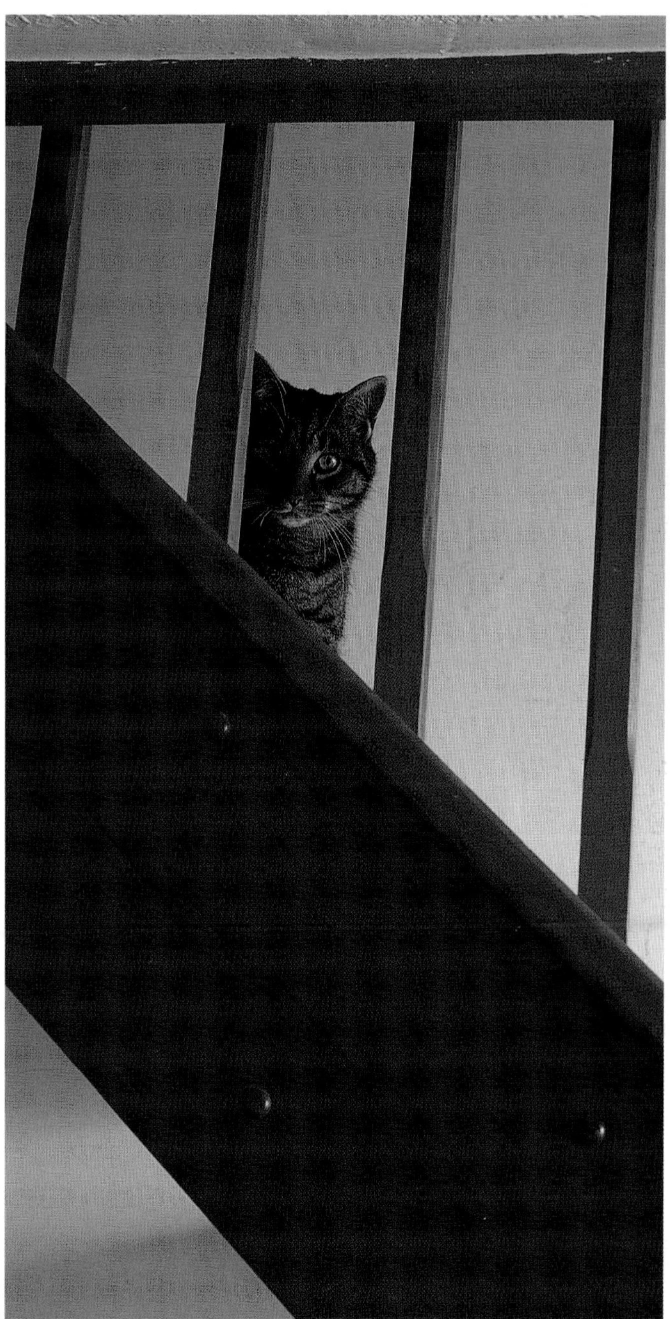

Stairs provide cats with a good opportunity to get up high if they are worried. There they can assess the situation and either run up higher to seek sanctuary upstairs, or make their way back down if happy with what they perceived as a threat.

Personal space

Just as we like to have time by ourselves for a while – to relax, to be alone with our thoughts, or to sleep undisturbed to recharge our batteries – so do cats; and, just as we are likely to become irritable if our personal space and time is invaded, so are cats. So the rule is to let sleeping cats lie. Because an indoor cat will soon view the home as his territory, introducing another one into the house at a later stage may cause many problems. If you are thinking of getting two cats, it is better to get them both at the same time so they can be introduced on 'neutral' ground, and can then establish their own territories within it.

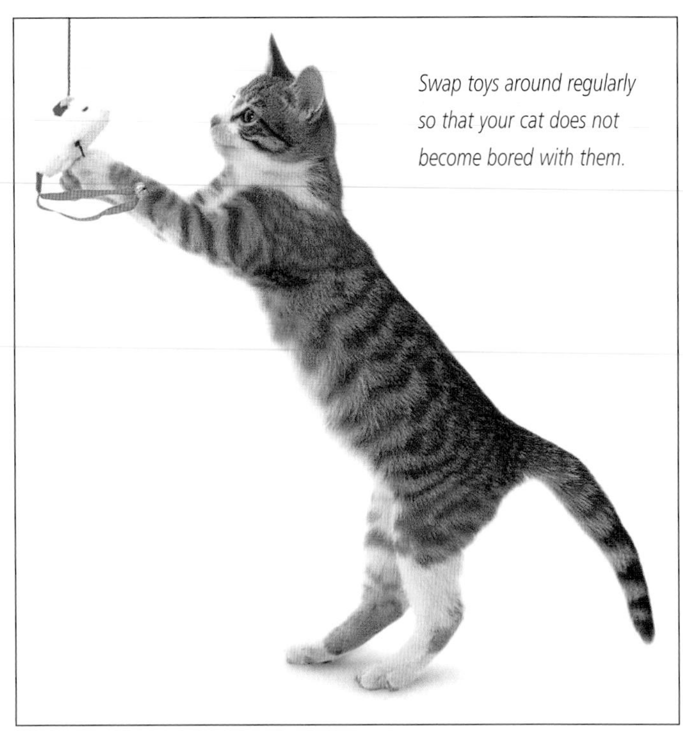

Swap toys around regularly so that your cat does not become bored with them.

Play time

Cats tend to be at their most lively at dawn and dusk, as these half-light times are when prey is particularly vulnerable. While dusk is not usually a problem for owners, dawn can be the time when puss wants you to get up and

Enclosing a property so a cat cannot escape its confines is almost impossible, unless you build a high, solid fence with an inverted top to stop the cat climbing over it – and even then it may not prove cat-proof, as they are so agile.

Feline fact

Night-time is not the best time to let your cat out of the house, especially in built-up areas, as car headlights can 'blind' cats and make them more susceptible to being knocked down.

play with him or feed him, while you want to catch a couple more hours' sleep before going to work. Establishing certain times when you can devote attention to your cat will soon become a regular routine he looks forward to, and make your pet's attention-seeking a thing of the past. To make this quality time interesting and more fulfilling for both of you, invest in a selection of toys that your pet finds entertaining. A length of string pulled along the ground for him to chase, and a ping-pong ball for him to bat about, pounce on and catch, will do fine for starters. Home-made toys can also include cardboard boxes, paper bags and newspaper 'tents'. Should you wish to purchase a selection, there is a vast range of toys specially designed for cats available in pet stores to suit all budgets.

Interaction

Different cats require different degrees of social contact with their owners. Some will be more independent and aloof than their owners wish. Cats that have a low need for social contact may learn to tolerate their owners' attention, but never seem to really enjoy it, so their desire to be left alone must be appreciated and accepted. For a person that requires an openly affectionate feline companion, this can be, understandably, disappointing.

Other cats will actively seek out human company and show signs of distress if they cannot get enough. Certain Oriental breeds, such as Siamese and Burmese, are particularly popular with people who want an 'in your arms' cat, because selective breeding has resulted in a high need for contact with their owners.

Harmony outside

If your cat has access to a safe outdoor environment, then he will have the best of both worlds – freedom to roam as nature intended and a warm bed and sustenance to come home to. There are several things to consider, however, if you allow your cat outdoors:

- maintaining good relations with neighbours
- your cat's safety in the garden and beyond
- preserving wildlife and birds

Keeping everyone happy

Neighbours who object to cats going into their gardens to relieve themselves and/or hunt can make life pretty unpleasant for both you and your pet, so if you have such neighbours it is prudent to take steps to prevent this problem happening. It may be worth considering building a large enclosed pen with shelter to house your pet when you allow him outside. Your pet will then be safe and able to enjoy being outdoors, your neighbours will be happy, and you can relax knowing that all is well and no feud is

Climbing trees

Many people are concerned when cats climb trees, but contrary to popular belief it is rare that those accustomed to being outdoors become 'stuck'; they will usually find a way down safely themselves. When cats do become stuck, it is due to the fact that they are unused to climbing trees, either because they are inexperienced kittens or they have not had much opportunity to do so.

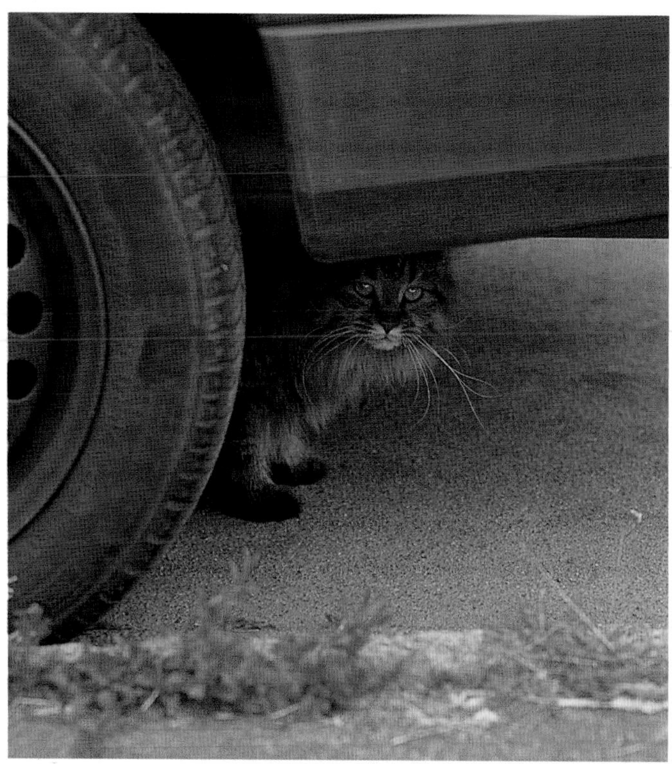

Always check under your car before driving off in it. Cats have a tendency to sit underneath stationary cars, and also, if they can climb in, to curl up under the bonnet of a parked car for warmth.

looming on the horizon. Keeping your cat in an outdoor run has another benefit in that he will be safe from traffic and other outdoor hazards, and from harassment by other humans and animals, and less at risk of contracting diseases from other cats.

Outdoor safety

Outdoor hazards include vehicular traffic, harassment from other animals and humans, poisoning from harmful substances, drowning in water-storage tanks, and contracting diseases from other cats.

• **Poisons** Keep garden chemicals safely locked away where your cat cannot gain access to them. Ensure that if you service the car, any spilt antifreeze and oil is cleaned up; cats find the former appetizing and will lick it, while oil on fur or paws can result in poisoning if ingested when the cat grooms himself. Most cats will instinctively avoid poisonous plants, but kittens – being interested in anything and everything – can occasionally fall victim to them. If you are worried about this danger then, if possible, remove any plants that may prove fatal if eaten – your vet can advise on the worst offenders. Cats can also suffer poisoning from eating contaminated prey animals and birds.

Harness- and lead-training

Some people like to train their indoor cat to go out for exercise on a lead. Siamese cats, in particular, don't seem to mind this, and can be trained to co-operate readily, while other cats resist fiercely. It depends on the individual as to how successful lead training will be. Bear in mind that taking a cat for a walk is not the same as walking a dog; the cat chooses where he wants to go, and when – not you. You will need a cat harness and a light lead long enough for you to remain in contact with your pet without pulling at it. Begin training in the house where your pet will feel safe and secure. Accustom your pet to wearing a harness first, and once he is used to this you can attach the lead. Don't pull on or jerk the lead, but simply allow the cat to wander at will with you following on behind. Be prepared for lead-training to take weeks, or even months.

Start early if you want to lead-train your cat; kittens take to it more readily than adult cats. Never take your cat out on the lead to places where it could be chased by dogs – restraining a frightened feline under these circumstances is difficult and it may end in tragedy.

• **Toad poisoning** Cats do tend to catch frogs, and the occasional toad, before they know any better. Toads emit a vile-tasting, sometimes toxic, substance when under threat. Cats react to this by shaking their head frantically, salivating and pawing at their mouth in an effort to rid themselves of the nasty, irritating substance. If you suspect toxic toad poisoning, consult your vet immediately.

• **Snake bites** Consult your vet immediately if you suspect your cat has been bitten by a poisonous snake.

• **Drowning** Rainwater storage tanks (water butts) can prove lethal to curious cats – once they fall in, they often cannot get out again. Ensure the lids on such tanks are properly secured and weighted down in place so that they cannot possibly be dislodged.

Preserving wildlife and birds

See 'Frequently asked question' on page 89 for information on this subject.

Indoor living

Living in urban environments is becoming increasingly dangerous for cats, mainly because of the continuing growth in road traffic, which leaves many cats at risk of being killed or injured by passing vehicles. For this reason, many owners prefer to keep their cats inside permanently, only allowing them outside to play, benefit from fresh air and gain interest from watching passing wildlife in the safe confines of a pen, either freestanding in the garden or yard, adjoining the house.

If used to having access to outside freedom on a regular basis since kittenhood, some adult cats do not adapt easily – if at all – to living permanently indoors. Boredom can be a major problem with indoor cats, especially active types, and often leads to behavioural problems. If an indoor living routine is established correctly, then it is often very successful, providing you make enough provision to keep your pet stimulated, exercised and entertained.

Suitable ready-made runs are often advertised in cat magazines. A concrete base to put the pen on will enable you to clean and disinfect it easily.

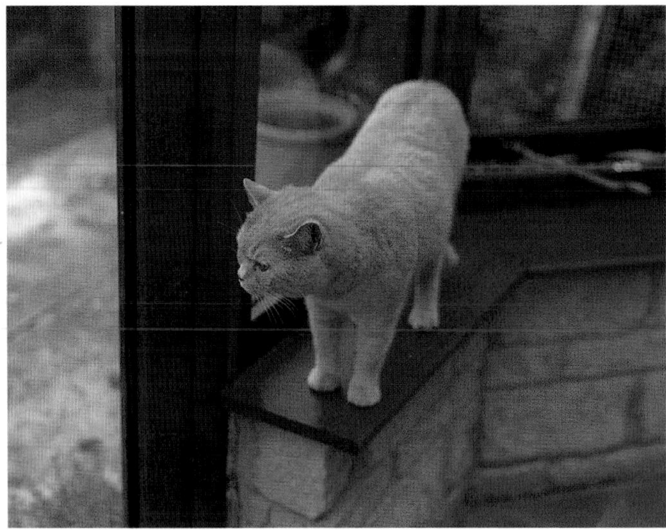

Many indoor cats enjoy being able to watch what is going on outside through a window, and this helps to alleviate boredom.

Hiding dry cat food around the house will encourage your cat to 'hunt' for his food, while providing him with a multitude of play items will help keep him occupied. Some owners even set aside a 'play room' for their cats, equipped with climbing frames, scratching posts and a selection of toys and tunnels – even a shallow running-water feature and indoor garden containing grass and cat-friendly herbs for their pet to explore and drink from or nibble at.

Specific times for play and shows of affection will also provide your pet, and you, with something to look forward to, and help keep feline boredom at bay.

Grass and herb seed kits to create an indoor garden for your cat are available from pet stores and garden centres; indoor water features can be obtained from the latter.

Indoor safety

Although you think your home may be safer for your cat than the great outdoors, there are in fact a number of potential hazards you need to be aware of for your pet's well-being.

- **Cookers or hobs** Cats will insist on jumping onto things, the cooker/hob being no exception, and they can burn their paws as a result. It is safer to keep your cat out of the kitchen while cooking, and to make sure the cooker/hob has cooled down before allowing him back in.
- **Washing machines/tumble dryers** Check these before closing the door and switching on, to ensure your cat has not crawled in there for a nap.
- **Refrigerators/freezers** Check before closing the door that the cat has not nipped in to see what goodies he can sample.
- **Cleaning fluids and detergents** Make sure your cat does not have access to these.
- **Powder carpet fresheners** Cats may suffer paw, skin and respiratory problems from these products, so avoid them.
- **Electric leads** These can prove fatal if chewed, but young, curious cats often view them as irresistible play items. Keep wires to a minimum in areas of the house where cats are allowed to roam.
- **Sewing materials** Keep needles, threads, buttons and elastic bands safely away from your pet.
- **Human medicines** Keep these in a cupboard or drawer, so your cat does not have access to them.
- **Hot water** Keep your cat out of the bathroom while you are running a bath in case he jumps or falls into the hot water; as an extra precaution, run the cold water first and add the hot to suit afterwards.

Feline fact

Fit, healthy cats are good at righting themselves to land on all four feet when falling from a reasonable height, say 3m (10ft) or so, thus saving themselves from serious injury. Sadly, they cannot always do so when falling from great heights, such as from high-rise-dwelling windows and balconies.

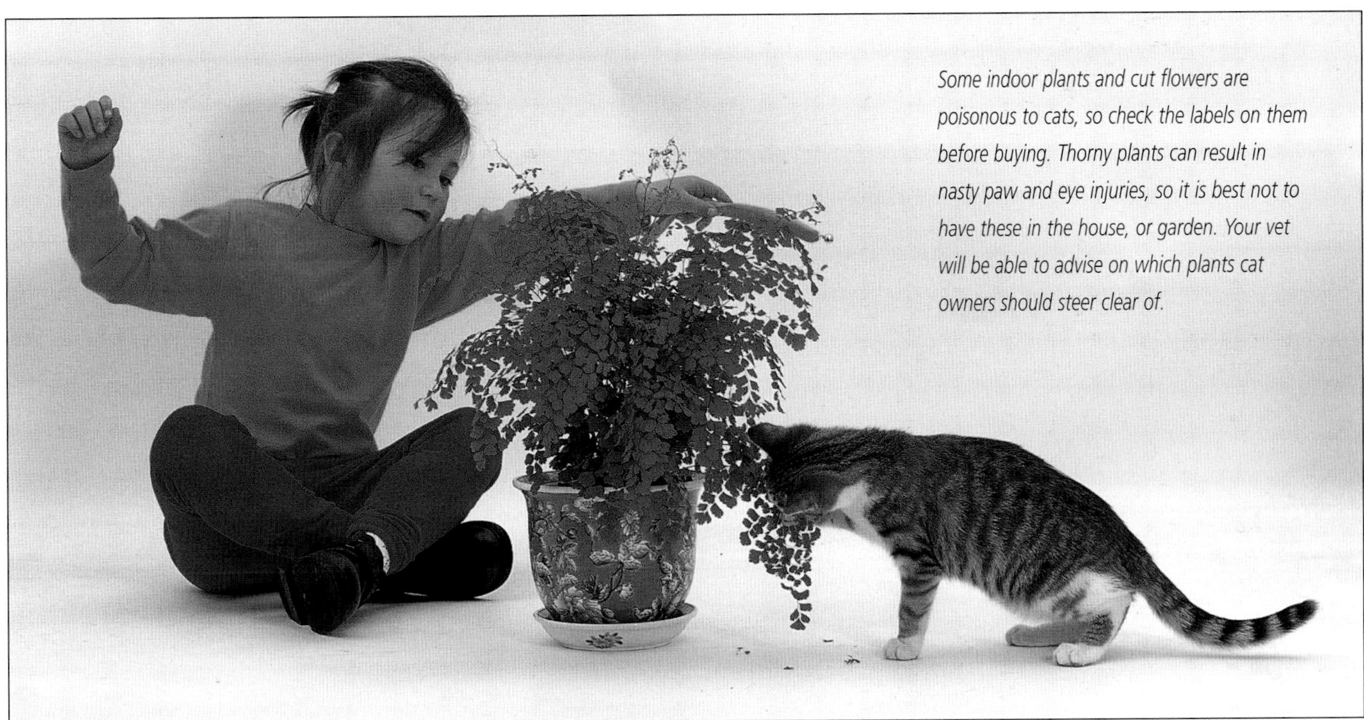

Some indoor plants and cut flowers are poisonous to cats, so check the labels on them before buying. Thorny plants can result in nasty paw and eye injuries, so it is best not to have these in the house, or garden. Your vet will be able to advise on which plants cat owners should steer clear of.

Frequently asked question

Q What should I do if my cat goes missing?

A Cats that are allowed outside are at risk of disappearing for a number of reasons, including being hit by a car, being stolen, being accidentally shut in a neighbour's garage or shed, being mistaken as a stray and taken in by a well-meaning person or by a rescue centre, and climbing into a delivery van and getting out again miles from home. The pain of not knowing what has happened to your pet when he does not come home can be devastating. If your cat goes missing, there are several courses of action to take.

• Contact local authorities to see if there have been any cats reported killed or injured on the roads.

• Contact local vets and rescue centres to see if your cat has been brought in. If your cat is microchipped or is wearing a collar and ID tag, he will be immediately identifiable.

• Ask neighbours if they have seen your cat, and, if not, ask them to check their sheds, garages and other outbuildings.

• Did a neighbour move the day your cat disappeared? Could your cat have 'stowed away' on the removal lorry? You would be surprised how many do.

• Put up 'Have you seen this cat?' posters in the neighbourhood shops, pet stores, schools and post offices (asking their permission to do so first), featuring a photo of your pet and a good description. Offering a reward can sometimes help bring about a speedy result.

• There is a ready black market for pedigree cats, so if yours is a pedigree he may have been stolen; contact the police and have a description of him at the ready.

• Contact a lost-and-found pet service to register your loss – if you have internet access you can find sources there by keying 'lost pet' into a search engine. Failing that, vets and rescue centres often have contact telephone numbers for such services. With luck, it won't be too long before you find your pet, or at least know what happened to him. When this happens, inform the people you told about his disappearance so that they do not continue to look for him.

Bringing your cat home

Before you bring your new pet home, you must prepare for the big event so that it runs comfortably and smoothly and is stress-free for all concerned. Setting a date well in advance for when you will collect your cat will give you time to get ready all the things you will need, shown in the checklist.

Checklist

- ✓ set-aside room or pen in quiet area
- ✓ cat carrier
- ✓ litter tray and litter
- ✓ bed and bedding
- ✓ food, water and bowls
- ✓ toys and scratching post
- ✓ collar and identity tag

When to collect your cat

Wait until you have free time to spare (or take a week's holiday from work) before bringing your cat home, so that you are around to help your new pet settle in. This is especially important if he is a kitten, as he will need more attention than an adult. Naturally, he may be confused or afraid, so your task will be to keep him company, show him where his food, water and litter tray are (and house-train him if necessary), and also introduce him to the rest of the household.

Ideally, you should set aside a spare room in which to keep the cat safe for a day or two while he settles down; prepare this with the essential equipment – food and water bowls, a litter tray, bed and toys. Make sure the rest of the family (especially children) know that the cat should be disturbed as little as possible while in this room to give him the chance to acclimatize to new surroundings in his own good time.

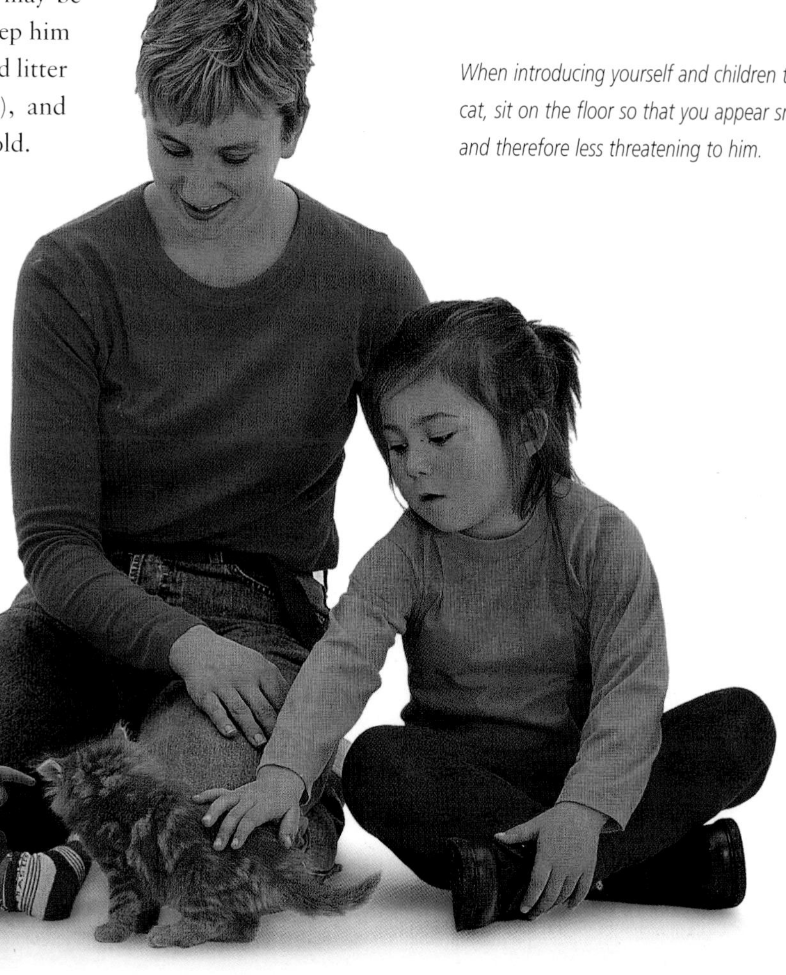

When introducing yourself and children to the cat, sit on the floor so that you appear smaller and therefore less threatening to him.

Many cats run and hide when introduced to a new home; don't try to prevent them from doing this, or haul them out of their hiding places – it is their way of making themselves feel secure. They will come out when they have assessed the situation and feel it is safe to do so. Simply ignore the cat and go about your business, albeit quietly.

If you don't have the luxury of a spare room, put a pen (with the necessary equipment inside) in the quietest area of the house and use this as the 'sanctuary' for the first few days of the cat's arrival.

Pre-arrival preparations

A couple of days before you collect the cat, take the bedding he is to use at home to the breeder, or wherever you are getting him from, so the cat can use it there. The cat's own smell, or that of his mother and litter mates, will transfer to the bedding and make him feel more at home in his new environment (both when travelling home and once there). It is best to take two lots of bedding, in case the cat has an 'accident' on one when bringing him home. Also take a little of his used litter back home with you to transfer into his new litter tray – again for familiarization purposes.

Buy the equipment you will need (see pages 30–37), in particular a sturdy cat carrier (it is not safe to transport a cat unconfined). Find out from the breeder or owner what food and cat litter the cat is used to, so that you can find out where to obtain it, and buy some. Also find out how much the cat is being fed, and how often.

At the collection point, line the carrier with the bedding you left there, put the cat in and shut the door securely. Ensure you have all the necessary paperwork from the former owner (receipt, plus pedigree papers, registration and ownership transfer documents and vaccination certificate, as appropriate) before setting off.

Travelling home

Secure the carrier on a seat with a seat belt, in the back of an estate vehicle, or in the footwell on the floor. The inside of the vehicle should be of a moderate temperature with

Did you know ...?

Cats and kittens often urinate and/or defecate when travelling, so place the carrier on a waterproof liner in the car for the journey. Take spare bedding and some antiseptic wipes (baby wipes are ideal) to mop up any accidents.

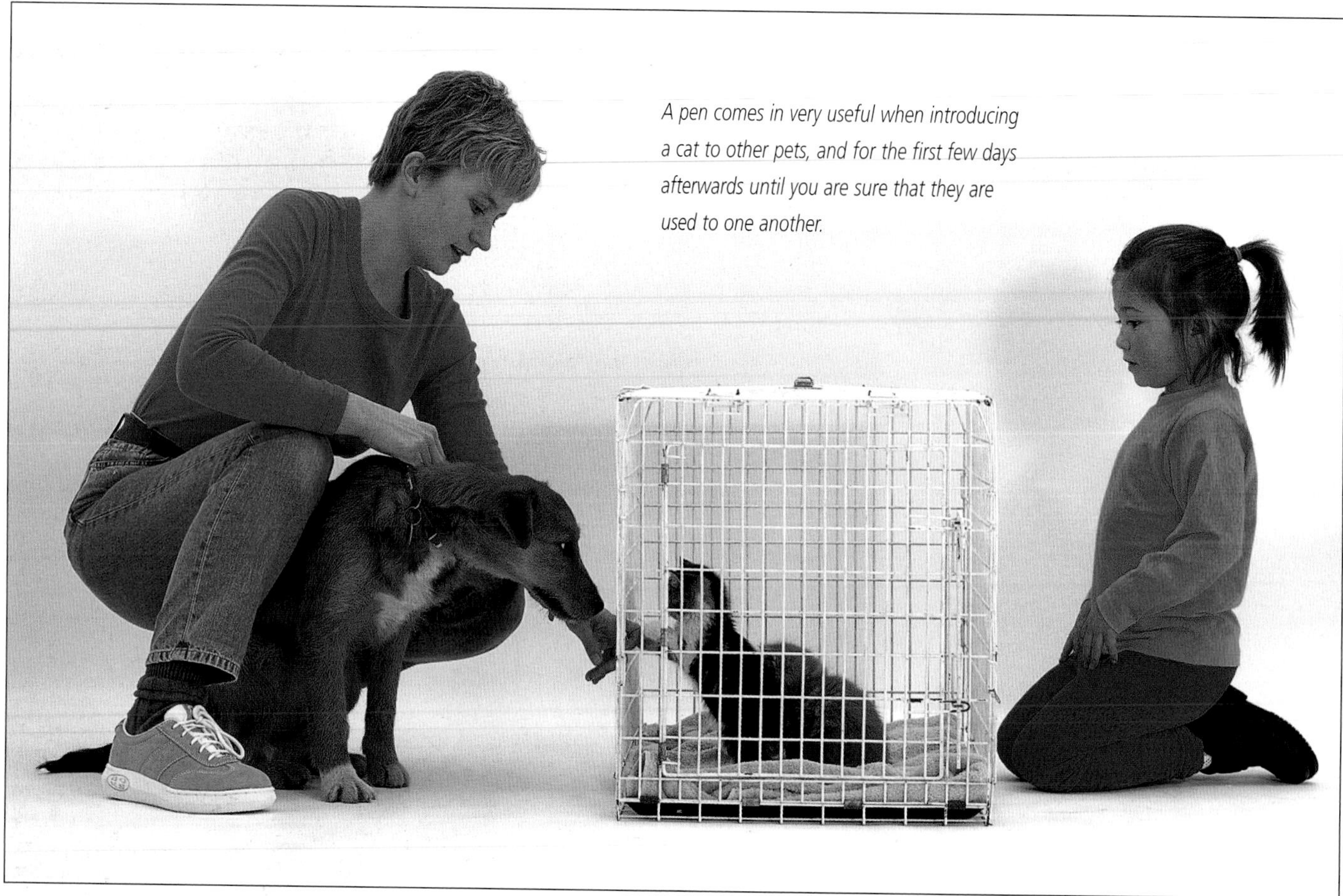

A pen comes in very useful when introducing a cat to other pets, and for the first few days afterwards until you are sure that they are used to one another.

sufficient airflow so that the cat is comfortable in transit; too much heat can be fatal on long journeys. Offer water in a pet drinking bottle at regular intervals if you are travelling any distance. Even if the cat protests at being in the carrier all the way home, do not be tempted to let him out; you or a passenger can talk to and reassure him, which may help him to settle.

Feline fact

It takes time for a cat to get to know his territory well, which is why they are often unsettled for the first 6 months in a new home. Adult cats do not cope well with changes in their territory and find it difficult to adjust to a new one when they move home. It is a common occurrence for felines to return to their old home rather than stay at the new one, particularly if they have not moved far away. Kittens find it easier to adapt.

On arrival home

Transfer the cat from the carrier straight into the set-aside room or pen. Take a few minutes to reassure him before closing the door and leaving him undisturbed for an hour or two to settle down and get over the trauma of travelling. When you do let the cat out into the rest of the house, leave his room or pen door open so he can retreat to his sanctuary if he feels the need to. Make sure children behave quietly and gently around him – do not let them handle him too much (even though they will, naturally, want to) until he has got used to them and does not view them as a threat. Allow the cat to investigate you and his new surroundings at his leisure; feeding him will help you establish a bond.

After this initial introduction, put the cat back in his sanctuary for his first night. He will be undisturbed there; you can also sleep soundly in the knowledge that the cat is safe and not getting up to any mischief. See pages 78–81 for detailed information on socializing your new cat with any other animals you might have.

Top tip

Cats will naturally want to explore their new home fully. To make this safer for all concerned, cover fishtanks, remove impregnated fly strips, temporarily board over open fireplaces, put guards in front of open fires, and keep windows shut.

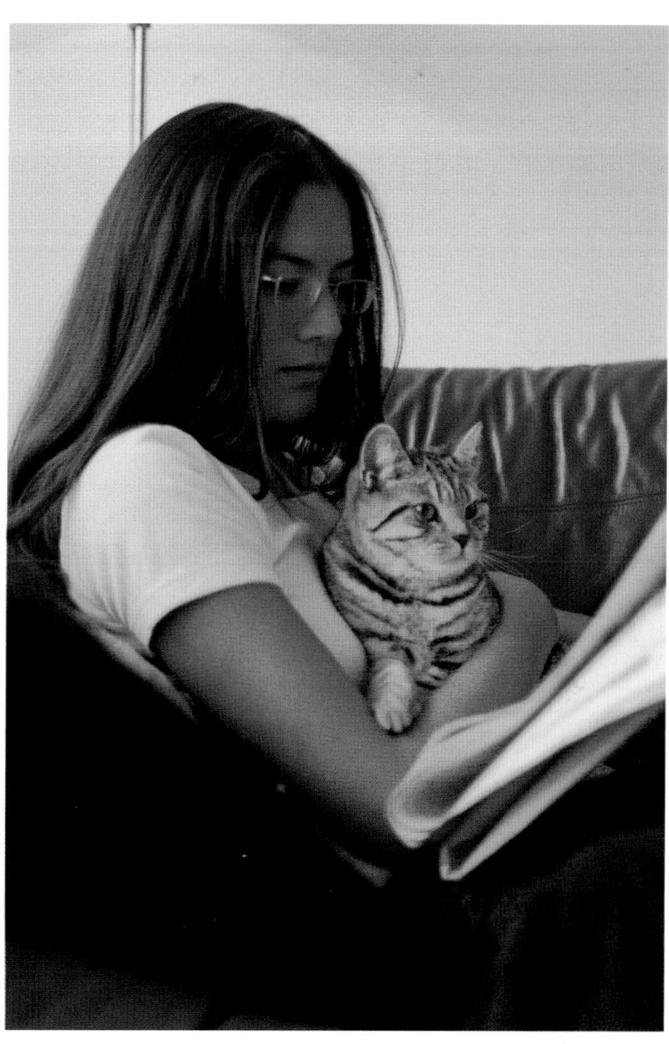

Settling in

Keep the cat in his room or pen for the first week (allowing him out for exercise and gradual acclimatization periods), and then you can allow him free access to the rest of the house. Try to feed and play with him at regular times to establish a routine that he looks forward to and thereby strengthen your relationship.

Do not let him outside for the first 2–3 weeks, depending on the cat's character, otherwise you risk not seeing him again. Friendly, laid-back cats are likely to adjust to their new homes more quickly than timid ones. Once the cat is feeling at home, you can move his bed and litter tray to their permanent positions, showing the cat where they are. You can also gradually introduce him to wearing a collar.

Let a new cat come to you when he is ready to do so – don't try to force him into interaction or you may frighten him, which may get the relationship off to a poor start. Don't try to pick him up if he clearly does not want to be held – restricting him in this way may cause him to panic and lash out in fear. See pages 92–93 for more information on handling and interacting with a new pet.

Frequently asked question

Q How soon after I get a cat should I take him for a health check?

A Give the cat or kitten a couple of days to settle down, then take him to the vet to ensure he is fit and healthy and not suffering from any obvious ailments. Take him sooner if you are worried about anything. If the vet does detect any signs of serous ill health, he or she will help you decide what to do. All good breeders or rescue centres should rehome their animals subject to veterinary approval and refund your money or take him back if there is a problem. If you collect a kitten at 8 weeks, you will need to take him to the vet again at 12 weeks for his first vaccination, plus another developmental check. Choose a vet as close to home as possible, so you can get the cat to the surgery quickly in an emergency. At the check-up, you can ask the vet about microchipping (which may be done there and then) and whether neutering is applicable.

FELINE BEHAVIOUR

Cats have their own unique language. If we observe them carefully, however, we can build up a detailed picture of their body language and actions that helps us guess how they might be feeling, what they want from us and what they need. By making the effort to learn what your cat is saying to you, you will understand him better and therefore be able to give him a better life. Many cats are treated badly or inappropriately because their owners are ignorant of what their cat is telling them. As intelligent humans, it is our responsibility to learn about the language of the animal we keep as a pet.

Body language

Cats communicate with a wide range of facial expressions, vocal sounds and body postures. Many people talk to their cats, and sometimes they seem to understand each other. Cats have a considerable universal vocabulary and some people have tried to translate precisely what they are saying; you too can learn to recognize what your cat is communicating if you observe the points on the checklist.

Checklist

- ✓ watch
- ✓ listen
- ✓ learn
- ✓ understand

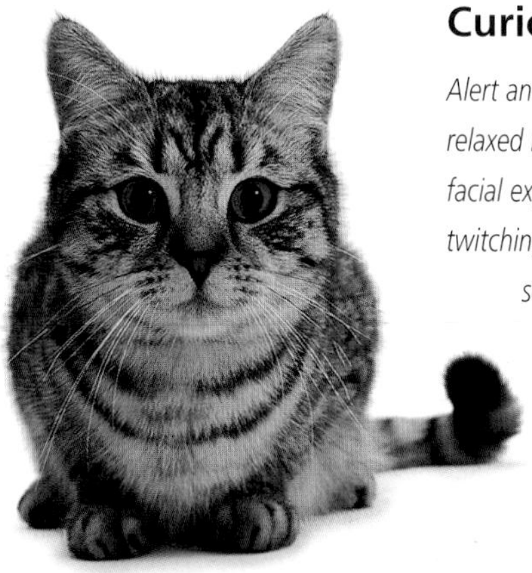

Curious

Alert and interested, this kitten is relaxed but his body posture and facial expression (wide eyes and twitching whiskers) indicates he has seen something that is worth investigating and not considered a threat.

Friendly

Tail up and curled in greeting, and paw raised ready to come forward once sure it is safe to approach and rub against the person or other animal in an effort to make friends quickly.

Playful

This cat is relaxed and playing.

Relaxed

With paws tucked under him, this cat has no fear that they will be needed. Hind legs are outstretched, and he is in a vulnerable position that a tense, wary cat would not adopt. Ears pricked and eyes wide open indicate that something has caught his interest.

Bored

Lethargy, alternated with bouts of almost manic behaviour, is a sign of boredom and stress (it can also be a sign of physical illness).

Sleepy

Dozing and totally relaxed, lying on his side with claws extended as opposed to drawn in for protection, this cat is not ready to run. The face and ears are relaxed and the whiskers are forward. The tail is laid out, not tucked under him. All of these body signs indicate that he is comfortable and relaxed in this otherwise vulnerable position.

Anxious and worried

Tail is tucked under to keep it out of harm's way. Weight is centred over the hind legs in readiness to run or strike with the front claws if necessary. Ears and whiskers are rotated to keep them out of the way in a fight. Eyes are looking upwards, seeking a safer place higher up that the cat might reach. The cat is miaowing loudly to attract a rescuer.

Uneasy or depressed

A combination of tense body posture, uneasy expression, lowered ears, drooping whiskers and tail carried low indicate all is not well with the cat – he may be feeling unwell or out of sorts.

Feline fact

Cats soon learn to miaow for attention from their owners, and do it all the more if we leap into action and deliver what they want. They can train us very well indeed! Female cats also use their voices to great effect when in season to summon a mate; this is known as 'calling', and is used continually until the cat has successfully mated. Males also have their own range of 'love calls'. Cats appear to retain their kitten vocal signals to communicate with their owners, while using an adult repertoire of sounds with other cats.

Wary

Crouched down, back end low, tail tucked under and poised ready for flight, this cat is wary about what he has seen or is approaching. The face is tense and watchful, and the ears pricked to pick up sound information.

Defensive

Faced with a potential threat, this cat flattens his ears, whiskers and tail to keep them safe, and averts his gaze so as not to antagonize the aggressor further. Paw is raised in readiness to strike if necessary. Vocal expression comprises growling or a low-pitched nasal 'yowling' sound.

Frightened

This cat is trying to make himself appear small by lowering his body and angling it away from whatever is troubling him. Tail is tucked underneath and ears are flattened against the head to protect them in event of a fight. Eyes look bigger than normal as the eyelids are pulled back to allow the cat to take in maximum visual information. Fear response dilates the pupils. Vocal expression indicates his fear.

Aggressive

The defending cat has rolled onto his back, so that all four feet can be used in defence, and is striking out at the vulnerable face of his attacker. The aggressor has his ears pulled back out of harm's way and his eyes shut to protect them, and is using his front paws to strike his victim. His back end is positioned and tensed to carry out the assault.

Hostile

Growling, hissing and spitting loudly, ears back and defensively poised to flee or fight depending on his potential foe's actions, this cat is displaying a hostile reception to whatever is approaching him.

Frequently asked question

Q Why do cats purr?

A Purring usually indicates contentment and a sense of well-being; a deep purr can also indicate pain, but if you know your cat well you will be able to tell the difference in his demeanour. Cats start to purr at one week old and can do so continually as they inhale and exhale. Young cats purr in a monotone, while older ones do so in two or three resonant notes. All cats purr at the same frequency – 25 cycles per second – but how exactly they produce the sound is still a mystery, although some scientists believe it originates in the cardiovascular system rather than in the lungs or the throat.

Submissive

This kitten is crouching low to make himself as insignificant as possible and is not retaliating, yet he is poised to make a quick getaway if necessary. Ears are back to keep them out of harm's way.

Did you know ...?

- Nose-to nose greetings between cats are unusual, as it puts both in a vulnerable position. However, cats that know each other well, but have been apart for a while, feel safe enough to do this by way of confirmation of visual recognition, and also to gain information about how the other cat is, where he has been and what he has been doing.
- Cats that know each other well often play-fight. It may look – and sound – violent as they posture and paw at each other as in a real fight, but if you look closely you will see that claws are not out and their bites are inhibited as they leap on one another, roll over and rake with their back feet.

Attention-seeking or hungry

If this Manx cat had a tail, he would raise it in greeting. His ears are pricked, his expression alert and he is standing taller on his paws in an effort to get nearer to a person's face for attention – either for petting or feeding. This posture is usually accompanied by the cat winding himself around legs, rubbing himself against a person and using vocal sounds (from strident miaows to 'chirrups') to gain his owner's ear.

Flehmen response

The Jacobsen's organ in the roof of the cat's mouth allows him to 'taste' smells. To use it, he opens his mouth a little – which looks as if he is grimacing – to draw air in for assessment. It is often used by tomcats to discover the reproductive status of females.

Stalking

Completely motionless, eyes wide for maximum visual information and focusing on the prey, ears pricked for maximum sound information on exact prey location, and back end bunched up ready to spring (wagging from side to side immediately before he executes the pounce).

The wildcat in your home

Despite his independence, the cat has insinuated himself into the hearts and lives of many people, eventually establishing himself firmly as a household pet and also an object of acquisition as specific breeds developed. His chequered history over the centuries – from wild animal to revered pet, hunting partner to object of persecution – has contributed to the character of the cat as we know him today. The cat's main character traits appear on the checklist.

Checklist

- ✓ independence
- ✓ self-sufficiency
- ✓ wariness
- ✓ curiosity
- ✓ watchfulness
- ✓ opportunism
- ✓ instinctiveness
- ✓ caution
- ✓ selective affection

Did you know ...?

- As recently as 1964, a new species of wildcat was discovered on the tiny island of Iriomote, near Taiwan.
- Lynxes are the only wild members of the cat family to live in both the Old World (before the discovery of the Americas in the fifteenth century) and the New World.

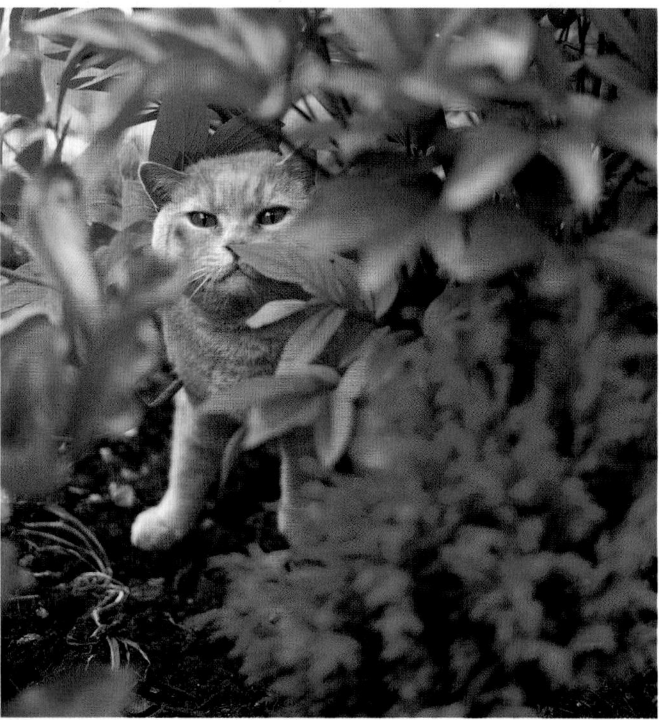

A cat's instincts tell him that finding out who else is in his territory is essential. Knowing who his competitors for food and rivals for mates are is vital for survival in the wild. Even in their cosseted, domesticated world, pet cats have not lost their inborn desire to do this.

Where cats came from

Cat-like animals were in existence long before the earliest human. The precise ancestry of cats is undetermined, but it is believed that Miacids (weasel-like mammals) that existed some 60 million years ago are the ancestors of the family of felines as we know them today, which gradually evolved from those tiny tenacious hunters.

Modern cats

Two and a half million years ago, some 40 species of the cat family emerged from the Ice Age – only the fittest and strongest survived. About 10,000 years ago, early humans developed from their ape-like predecessors and began to grow plants for food and domesticate useful animals. One school of thought is that it was at this point that cats began to form links with humans, attracted by the mice robbing their grain stores.

The domestic cat belongs to the same species as the wildcat of Europe and Asia, bones of which, dating back some 6,000 years, have been discovered in Jericho and Cyprus (a country which had no indigenous cats at that time). It is thought possible that the Cyprus cats were

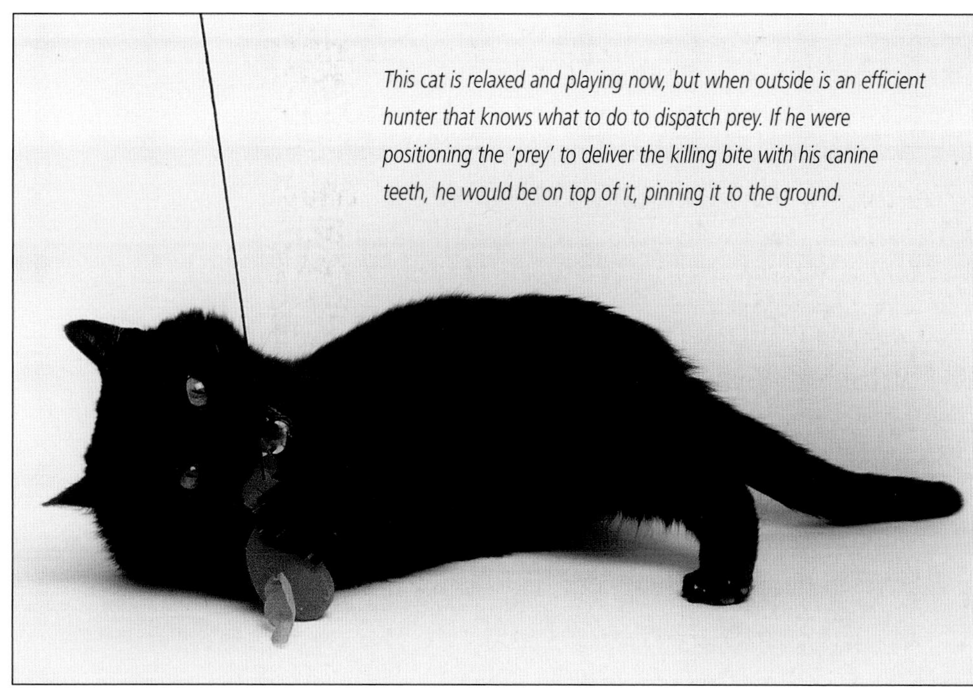

This cat is relaxed and playing now, but when outside is an efficient hunter that knows what to do to dispatch prey. If he were positioning the 'prey' to deliver the killing bite with his canine teeth, he would be on top of it, pinning it to the ground.

Members of the cat family (Felidae)

- Cheetah
- Domestic cat
- Jaguar
- Leopard
- Lion
- Lynx
- Ocelot
- Panther
- Puma
- Serval
- Tiger
- Wildcats of various types

imported by Ancient Egyptians; they were almost certainly kept as pets in Egypt, being revered as sacred animals.

The first pet cats

The Ancient Egyptians (from around 2,000 BC) are best known for domesticating the cat, simply because the cat features so largely in Egyptian artwork dating back to that time. As well as scenes of cats enjoying home comforts, there are also clues that the cat was used to help hunt birds in the Nile delta, by flushing them out of reed cover. Egyptian law not only protected cats, it also forbade anyone to take them out of Egypt; nevertheless, they were exported by traders – Greece and Britain being destinations. The Romans were also responsible for the worldwide spread of cats after conquering Egypt, having found them useful in keeping the rodent population down in army camps.

Living with man

As far as the world outside Egypt was concerned, the cat was probably an animal associated with Roman colonists and wealthy people who kept them as cosseted pets. Eventually the cat became established on farms and homesteads within the Roman Empire, valued for his usefulness in rodent control rather than merely as a pet. The value of the cat was codified in laws enacted in AD 936 by Hywel the Good, prince of southern Wales. The law decreed that a kitten was worth one legal penny until he had opened his eyes; until he was capable of killing mice, he was worth two pence, and when he reached hunting age four pence. The law also covered the stealing and killing of cats, with the punishment for doing so severe in terms of monetary recompense to the owner.

Nowhere was the cat more highly prized than aboard ship, especially after the brown rat joined the black rat in Europe from the sixteenth century. Ships' holds often teemed with rats, and the cat was the only way of keeping them under control. Ships' cats came aboard and went ashore at will, and kittens were often born at sea. In this way, cats of all shapes, sizes and colours were carried around the world.

Feline fact

In the fifth century BCE, a Persian army exploited the Egyptians' regard for the welfare of their cats. When they marched on Peluse, the Persian leader ordered his men to carry live cats in their front line as they attacked the city walls. Rather than risk killing any of the sacred animals, the Egyptians surrendered and the Persians won a bloodless victory.

Normal behaviour

What represents normal behaviour to a cat is instinctive. Some feline actions and behaviours may puzzle, or even annoy or distress, owners, but it is important to understand that they are done for a reason – primarily so that the cat feels safe and sound in his environment. No matter how tame you may think your pet is, you have to remember that he is still very much a wild animal at heart – a little lion in your midst. See the checklist for natural feline behaviour.

Checklist

- ✓ predatory
- ✓ territorial
- ✓ clean
- ✓ alert
- ✓ independent
- ✓ solitary

RIGHT *The body shape and general appearance of today's domestic cat has not changed a great deal from that of his ancestor, the African wildcat.*

ABOVE *The African wildcat is fairly tolerant of humans and can still be found living in and around villages in parts of Africa, scavenging for food as well as hunting.*

Hunting

A cat does not fully know how to pursue and kill prey through instinct alone; his hunting technique develops through learned behaviour as a kitten by watching and imitating the actions of his mother. If a kitten has not been taught these skills, he may later on in life catch a prey animal but not instinctively know how to kill it. To owners, the sight of a cat 'playing' with his catch (repeatedly releasing and recapturing it) can be distressing, and there are several reasons why this occurs.

• The cat is an inexperienced hunter, and therefore a poor killer. He can catch the prey but does not know how to finish it off.

• It is a way of weakening prey that may otherwise bite its attacker in self-defence before the cat puts his face close enough to dispatch the victim.

• He may bring half-dead prey home for his owner – viewed as a litter mate – to play with and to use for practising hunting skills, in much the same way as a mother cat would bring it home for her kittens.

Obviously, pet cats do not need to hunt for food, as their owners provide it for them, but feral cats and wildcats do – hence the need for them to retain the knowledge on how to do so. Undoing millions of years of perfected evolutionary process is impossible and, apart from keeping your cat indoors, or in a pen when outside, you can do little to prevent him from hunting.

Cats often watch birds through the window and perhaps go through some of the motions of catching them, and/or chatter their teeth at them as if frustrated that they cannot get to them.

Displaced hunting

Some cats have a stronger instinct to hunt than others. If they are kept indoors with no opportunity to do so, they may turn their attention to other things that move in the house – adults, children and other pets being the target of their 'attacks'. Sometimes mock chases and bites will comprise social play, and in these cases the bites will be inhibited; in other cases, cats will display real predatory behaviour and, since this is designed to catch and kill prey, considerable damage can be done to the hapless victim.

Giving the cat the opportunity to go hunting outside, or to play with and 'kill' toys, can solve the problem. However, the fact that cats will do this to members of the family with whom they are usually very friendly shows how deep-rooted their hunting instinct is.

Sleeping

Cats spend a large proportion of their lives asleep. As predators, they do not need to spend a lot of time eating as herbivores do, so can afford to rest for much of the day.

Most cats hunt alone, but there have been cases of co-operative hunting by cats from the same family.

This cat is displaying displaced hunting behaviour, pouncing on his owner's legs and feet as if he were a prey animal. However, in this case, the behaviour is more of social play than real predation, as the cat's claws remain sheathed and his bites are inhibited.

To conserve energy and reduce the time they need to go hunting, cats prefer to sleep in warm, comfortable places. They like to nap rather than spend long periods of time asleep, but if relaxed enough to enter a deeper sleep they produce the same brainwave patterns that we do when we dream. During these moments their bodies twitch as if they are running and jumping, so it is easy to conclude that they are dreaming about the day's activities, just as we do. If deprived of deep sleep over a long period of time, cats can become ill.

While asleep, a cat's hearing becomes even more acute than when awake, to provide warning of danger. When they fall asleep on your lap and then wake suddenly as if under attack from hands moving over them, most cats quickly realize that it is only their owner stroking them; but some react defensively and may scratch or bite in self-defence, much to their owner's bemusement.

Did you know ...?

Claws can snag in clothing and cause panic if cats cannot free their paws. Gently detach the claw, holding the cat firmly as you do so to prevent him from pulling away before he is free, and becoming even more stuck and scared.

Stropping

Cats are armed with razor-sharp claws that are hooked at the ends so that they can get a good purchase on prey, and so that they can climb out of danger. Normally kept retracted so that they stay sharp, claws are protracted out of the flap of skin that covers them when used to catch prey or climb.

Claws grow continuously and need to be kept trimmed and, periodically, the old outer casing needs to be removed to reveal the new, sharp claw underneath; this is done by scratching, or stropping, the claws down a suitable surface. Stropping is also done in strategic places in order to leave scent messages. In the garden, trees make good stropping sites, while indoors the furniture tends to be a favourite target – unless the cat is supplied with, and taught to use, a suitable stropping or scratching post.

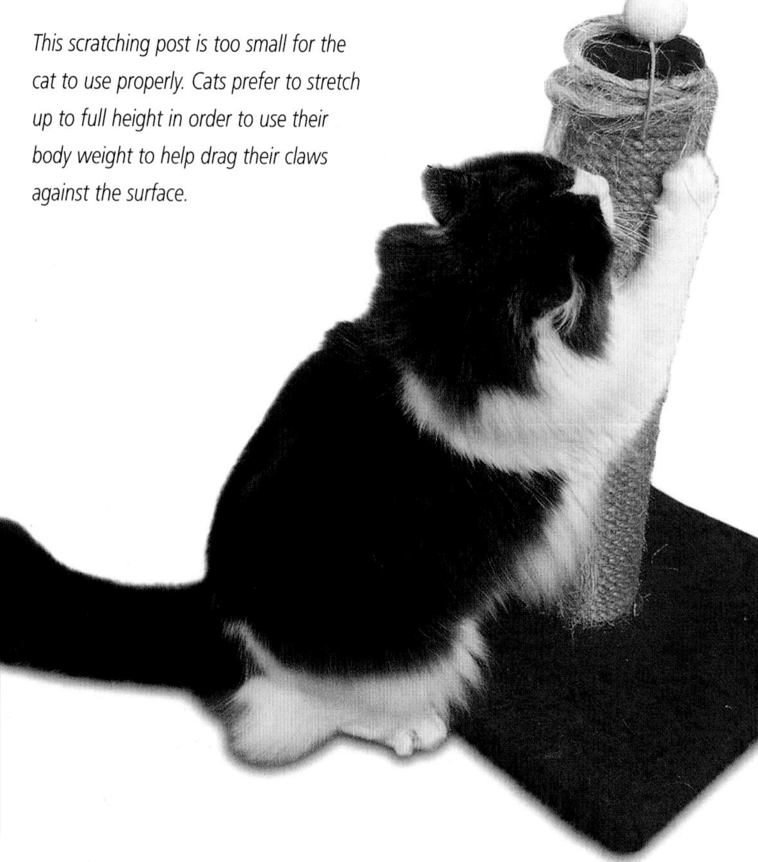

This scratching post is too small for the cat to use properly. Cats prefer to stretch up to full height in order to use their body weight to help drag their claws against the surface.

Top tip

Keeping still is often a favourite strategy for cats faced with hostility from other cats in the household. Such hostility can compromise their welfare if it prevents them from gaining easy access to necessary resources (food, water, litter tray, sleep), so watch out for this happening in multi-cat households.

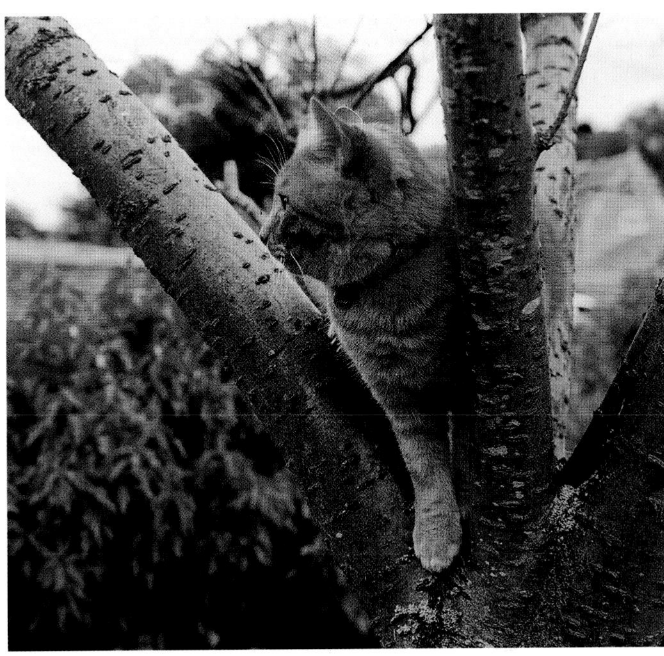

Inexperienced cats or kittens may climb trees or jump up to a high place in panic to escape from danger, and then find themselves stuck because they have not learned how to get down. These cats are genuinely in need of rescue, and may die or fall if none is available. Experienced cats simply wait for the danger to pass before climbing down.

Sitting in high-up places

Most members of the cat family use trees and other elevated places as vantage points for safety, eating and resting, and as hiding places from which to leap down and attack unsuspecting prey below. Cats are equipped with sharp, hooked claws that help them to run up most textured, vertical surfaces. Descent from high-up places is more difficult, as their claws give them little support, so cats will often back down in a hopping motion (rather like bears do) before turning and leaping to the ground.

Playing

Cats play with toys (and each other in some cases) for enjoyment and, more importantly, to develop their hunting and territorial defence skills or to keep them honed. Through play, kittens practise social, hunting and fighting skills to equip them for adult life. They learn to carry small toys, or prey victims their mother has brought them, in their mouth, and defend these from approaching siblings by growling and, if this does not deter them, striking out at them. As cats age, their desire to play and hunt slowly diminishes until, eventually, they are content to sit around and doze for much of the time.

In sibling play-fights, an instinctive restraint prevents them from doing serious damage to each other. Kittens are most actively involved in social play at 9–14 weeks; play with objects reaches its peak at about 16 weeks.

Urinating and defecating

When not leaving scent messages, cats like to bury their waste products so that they are not detectable. Digging a hole in which to deposit their waste, and then covering it up afterwards, ensures the area is kept clean and does not advertise their presence. Cats perform this action from an

Having finished relieving himself in the hole he has dug, the cat will rake soil or litter over his waste products, then sniff at the site to check that the smell is reduced or no longer detectable. Having shaken his paws to dislodge any soil or litter sticking to them, he will usually walk away from the area before settling down and cleaning himself.

early age, as soon as they leave the nest, if an easily rakeable substrate (soil or litter) is available to them. They prefer to use a substrate of clean, dry consistency in which digging is easy, which is why sand or freshly dug earth is a favourite – much to the annoyance of parents whose children have sandpits, and gardeners.

Cats like to hide away when they are relieving themselves, and try to find a secluded place in which to do so where they will not be disturbed or vulnerable. It is important, therefore, to place litter trays in quiet places in the house; if placed in a busy thoroughfare, the cat may prefer to go behind furniture or other inaccessible place instead. Being fastidious creatures, cats do not like using dirty, wet litter trays and will often go elsewhere rather than use them, so it is important to keep trays as clean and dry as possible.

Scent messaging

A cat's sense of smell is very important to him, and is highly developed. Since feline ability to communicate with body language is limited, for safety's sake cats use scent messaging to do so at long distance. Scent messages linger in the environment for some time, informing other cats and animals of the leaver's presence. As well as rubbing their facial and paw scent glands on surfaces, cats also use urine and faeces to mark their territory.

After investigating a scent message, a cat will then add his own to it. If the leaver is familiar without animosity, then a face-rub scent message is sufficient, whereas if a stronger message is required the cat may choose to scratch or spray urine to cover the intruder's scent. In the cases of spraying and defecation scent messaging, cats can discover the messenger's age, sex, state of health and even what he ate recently.

Personal hygiene

Grooming fulfils many important functions in maintaining health. As well as straightening out the coat to make it a better insulator in cold weather, helping remove parasites and keeping the coat and skin in healthy condition, grooming can also cool a cat down in hot weather by spreading saliva on the fur. Cats also lick themselves dry if they get wet, as a wet coat does not provide the necessary insulation. Grooming also plays a part in improving relationships between cats, with the less important cat making an effort to groom the more confident one.

Frequently asked question

Q My cat often deposits faeces outside his litter tray – it is as if he 'misses' the tray. Why does he do this and how can I prevent it happening?

A It sounds as though the tray is not big enough for the size of cat. Use a larger tray with higher sides, and this should solve the problem. Another reason could be that much of the litter is wet or dirty; the cat will shy away from getting his paws dirty or wet, and will position himself on the driest part, which is usually near the edges of the tray, resulting in dropping urine or faeces over the sides. The cure is simple – clean the tray out more often and always ensure the litter surface is dry.

Cats spend about one-third of their waking time grooming.

Feline fact

The back of the head and face are the only places a cat cannot groom itself by licking, so he licks his front paws and then uses them, like a wash cloth, to clean these areas.

Exploring

To maintain physical and mental health, it is important for cats to know their territory well. This is so that they know where to find the best sources of food, where potential enemies lurk and whether any intruders need warning off their patch. Cats like to check their territory regularly to ensure all is well in their world, and will rigorously investigate anything new.

Feline interaction

For cats who do not easily form friendships with others, coping with cats that are not part of their household but share their territory can be difficult. Disputes between cats over territory are common in overcrowded urban areas where gardens are small and cats numerous. One way of coping with this overcrowding is to 'time-share' the facilities, by leaving scent messages advertising the fact that part of the territory is temporarily occupied.

From these messages, and a knowledge of the felines in the area, a cat can tell how long ago the leaver passed by, who he was and whether it is safe to proceed – or whether it might be better to wait for a while, or go in another direction. Face-to-face encounters occasionally occur, but usually result in nothing more than lots of feline swearing and a standoff until the weaker cat backs down, since neither is usually willing to risk debilitating injury.

Hiding

Though armed with claws and teeth, cats are only small, so it makes sense for them to stay out of trouble when they can. Hiding when under threat is a good strategy. Domestic cats will often run and hide and keep still when they cannot get up high or run away from danger in the close confines of a house. Shy cats like igloo-style beds in which they can curl up and hide, therefore feeling secure – this works on the principle that if they cannot see you, you cannot see them.

Exploring their environment vigorously enables cats to build up a detailed map inside their heads; by using this map they are able to find new routes home, even if they have not been that way before.

Territory

The ancestors of our domestic cats did not hunt in packs, but were solitary hunters who patrolled a territory that supplied them with the food they needed to survive. Although our pets are well fed by us and have no need to hunt, they have not lost the desire to stake out an area they can call their own. To them, a territory represents safety and a food supply should their humans fail to provide for them. See the checklist for what comprises an ideal territory.

Checklist

- ✓ safety zones
- ✓ vantage points
- ✓ abundant food
- ✓ water supply
- ✓ potential mates
- ✓ no adversaries
- ✓ resting places

Area

In an urban environment, a tomcat will opt for the largest territory he can lay claim to and defend, which may extend across several gardens; in country districts, it may cover 1.5 square km (1 square mile) or more. House cats usually treat the home as territory shared with their human household, with some core areas that are specific to themselves or others. They will accept that they are not allowed in certain places, at least if that territory owner is around, and may claim a particular chair or cushion as their own, unless forced off it by a more dominant member of the household.

Outdoor cats lay claim to an area that they can defend from other households. This does not necessarily match human house and garden divisions and may include places not on the boundary with their house. A new arrival who finds his own backyard already claimed, and who is unable

A schematic view of feline territories. Toms range over a wider area than females or neutered cats. Various factors influence territory size and, in areas supporting many cats, toms will evolve a network of paths, crossing one another's territory; this helps avoid conflict in most cases.

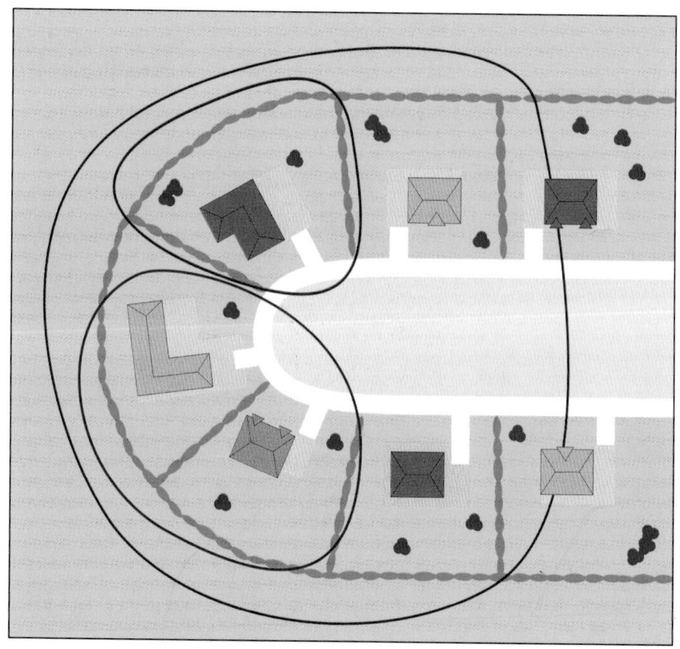

tom's territory
neutered cat's territory
female cat's territory

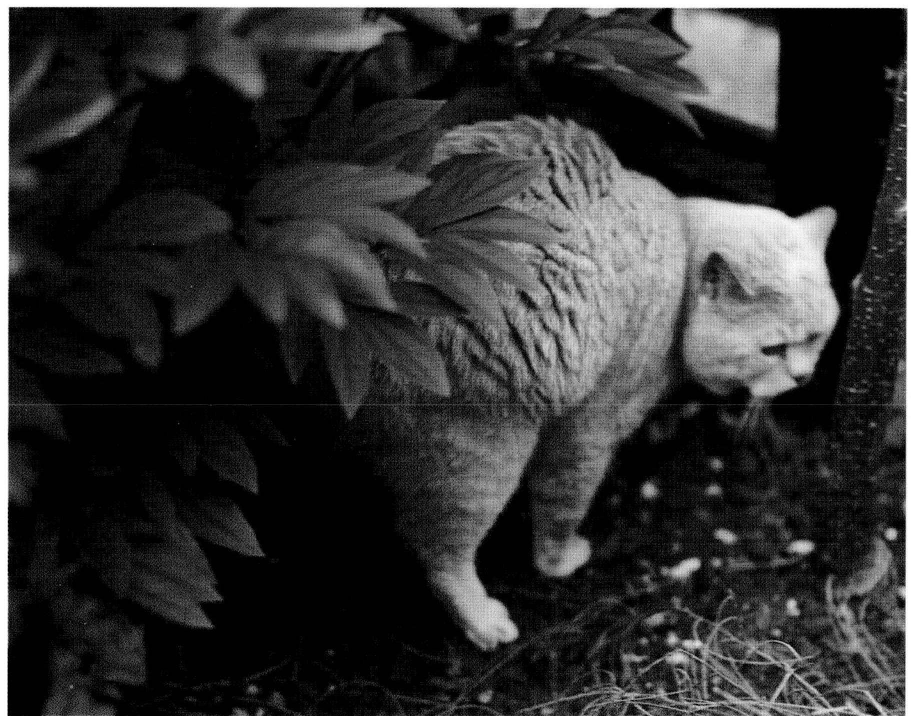

This cat is marking a bush as part of his territory by spraying a small quantity of urine onto it. He is standing as tall as he can, to aim the urine as high as possible, so that the message is at nose height and therefore impossible for other cats to ignore.

Feline fact

Territory is sometimes more important to cats than the family with whom they live.

to drive off the occupant, may occupy somewhere several doors away.

In highly built-up areas where there are no gardens a cat may be reduced to an outdoor territory of little more than a rooftop or window ledge.

Marking

As well as using facial and paw scent messaging (see page 70–71), a cat will often use urine as a stronger form of messaging, and in laying claim to territory. Males generally spray droplets of strong-smelling urine onto every

When a face-to-face encounter happens, the cats usually deal with it by slow-motion posturing, staring and growling until one of them backs down and moves away.

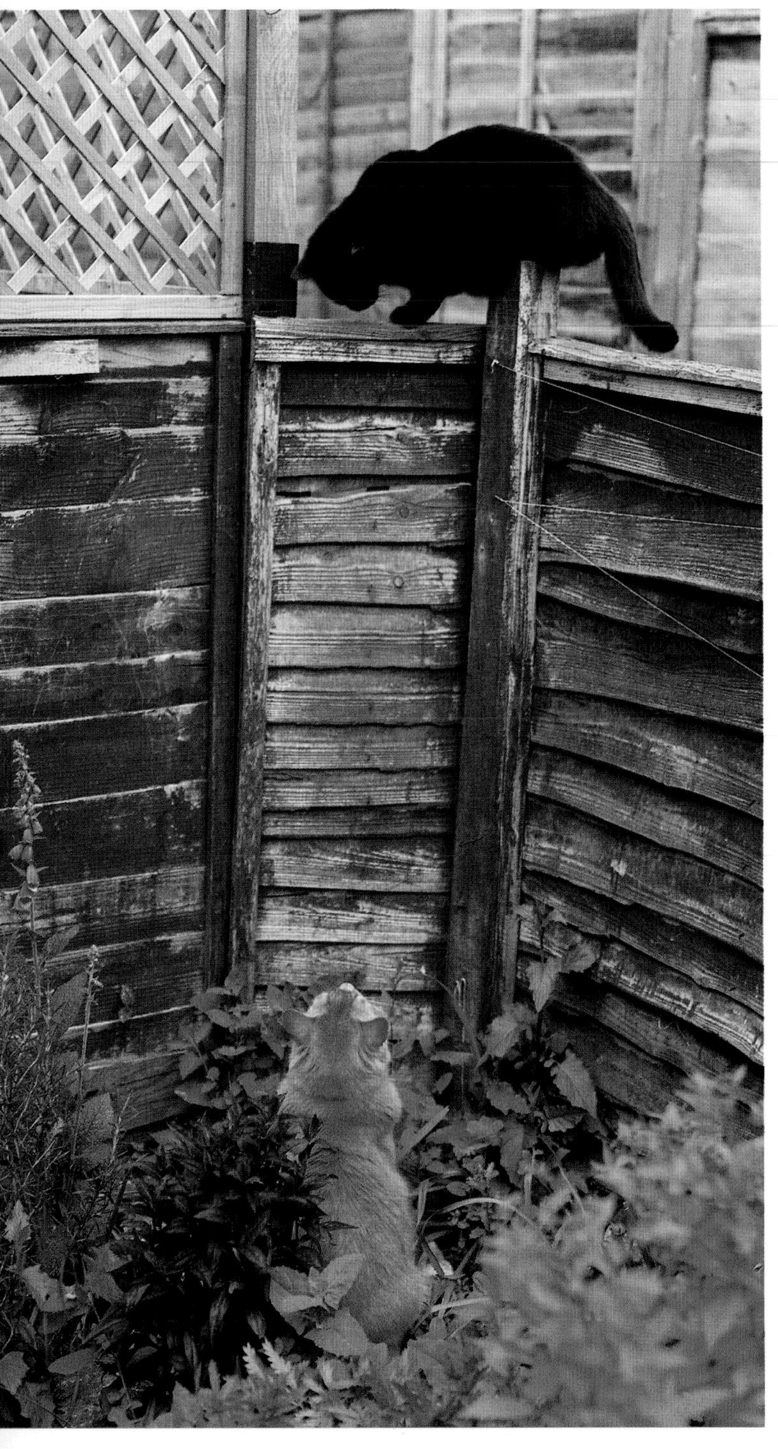

In this territorial dispute, both cats are unwilling to back down. The cat standing on the fence is in a stronger position and may be the owner of the territory, which will give him added strength. Cats can sometimes hold positions like this for hours before one finally decides to withdraw. Once this happens, they do not have a large number of signals to let the other cat know that they have surrendered, so retreat must be very slow to prevent a chase and attack by the victor.

Top tip

Neutered cats' territories are much smaller than those of unneutered cats since they are not seeking potential mates; the males do not spray and the females do not call. Territorial fights may still occur, but will be much less of a problem as neutered cats tend to spend more of their time at home.

convenient object along the perimeters of their ranges. The tom examines a post or bush to see who has been along that way before, turns his back on it, raises his tail, then, with two or three pedalling movements of his hind legs, urinates high and accurately onto the object. Sometimes he will turn back to examine his signature, or back up and rub his tail and hindquarters against the damp patch; occasionally the tom will turn and smell his mark, then strop his claws vigorously.

Female cats also sometimes develop the habit of spraying. Some adopt the typical male position and direct their urine backwards in a fine jet.

Territorial defence

If a cat receives a threat from another cat, or other animal, in its territory, the following happens.

- The cat freezes and looks at the intruder; his tail lifts and starts to flick slowly from side to side. His whiskers and ears point forward and his nose begins to quiver as he tries to identify the threat object.
- As the intruder moves closer, the cat changes his stance.

Did you know ...?

Cats are very curious about anything new appearing in their territory and will investigate it thoroughly to ensure it is not harmful, or to discover whether it could be a good place to rest or hide, or be useful in their continuous quest for food and hunting opportunities.

The point of the lifted tail turns downwards, the chin is drawn in, and the ears flatten as the cat begins to turn slowly to one side. Gradually the back arches and the hairs on the cat's back and tail rise until he has assumed his aggressive posture.

• This menacing display continues if the intruder continues to move forward. The cat faces the enemy but turns sideways to present as large and formidable an area as possible. The hind legs become tensed and ready to spring forward in attack or away in flight. He balances on one front paw, while the other is raised, claws unsheathed, ready to strike. He bares his teeth in a snarl.

• If the unwelcome visitor backs away, the aggressor may move forward slightly, smacking his lips and salivating, while continuing to growl.

• When the threat disappears, the cat sniffs the invaded ground and then marks it with his own scent.

If neither cat will give way and a fight ensues, it is often fast and furious with a great deal of noise; each cat tries to inflict as much damage on his rival as possible using both his teeth and claws.

Fighting is usually a last resort in a territorial dispute, as close proximity to another fully armed and hostile cat is very dangerous. Toms are more likely than females or neuters to fight physically over territory.

Frequently asked question

Q My cat has stopped wanting to go out, and lacks his usual joie de vivre. He has also begun to relieve himself around the house, which is most unlike him. Why is he doing this?

A Rogue cats that bully others can cause local cats to stop venturing out. This can lead to depression and other behavioural problems. Agreeing a time-share system between neighbours for letting cats out can help. Having suffered bullying, a cat may lack confidence to go outside, so accompanying him for the first few excursions can help considerably.

Socializing

Integrating a new cat into a household is simpler if there are no other existing pets. If there are, then successful socialization is possible, providing you go about it the right way and are prepared to be patient. The elements that a new arrival, as well as the household's existing pet(s), need for amicable integration are shown in the checklist.

Checklist

- ✓acclimatization period
- ✓owner respect
- ✓personal space
- ✓privacy
- ✓gradual introductions
- ✓safety zones
- ✓undisturbed resting places
- ✓easy, unthreatened access to food, water and litter tray

Socializing with people

As has been mentioned (see pages 54–57), when you first get a cat, it is important that you let him come to you, rather than force yourself upon him. This is so that the cat does not feel threatened. The best way you can ingratiate yourself into your cat's affections is to feed him well and make sure he has comfortable, safe and warm places in which to rest.

Cats that have been well handled since birth, and brought up in a homely, friendly and laid-back atmosphere, tend to be more sociable and easily adaptable than those that have not. The amount of socialization a kitten has with people while he is two to seven weeks old determines how well he interacts with people later in life. Good experiences in early life produce a friendly and outgoing cat.

Respecting your cat

Some cats enjoy the company of humans very much; others do not. Some cats are friendly for brief periods during the day, but spend the rest on their own doing other things. It is a case of discovering what your cat prefers, and respecting

Getting to know and trust human and animal members of the household will take a while, so be prepared to let the cat approach them in his own time. Once he is satisfied that they present no threat to him, he will begin to interact with them on his own terms. Do not try to force him into physical interaction, otherwise he will become frightened and either keep himself to himself or resort to defensive aggression.

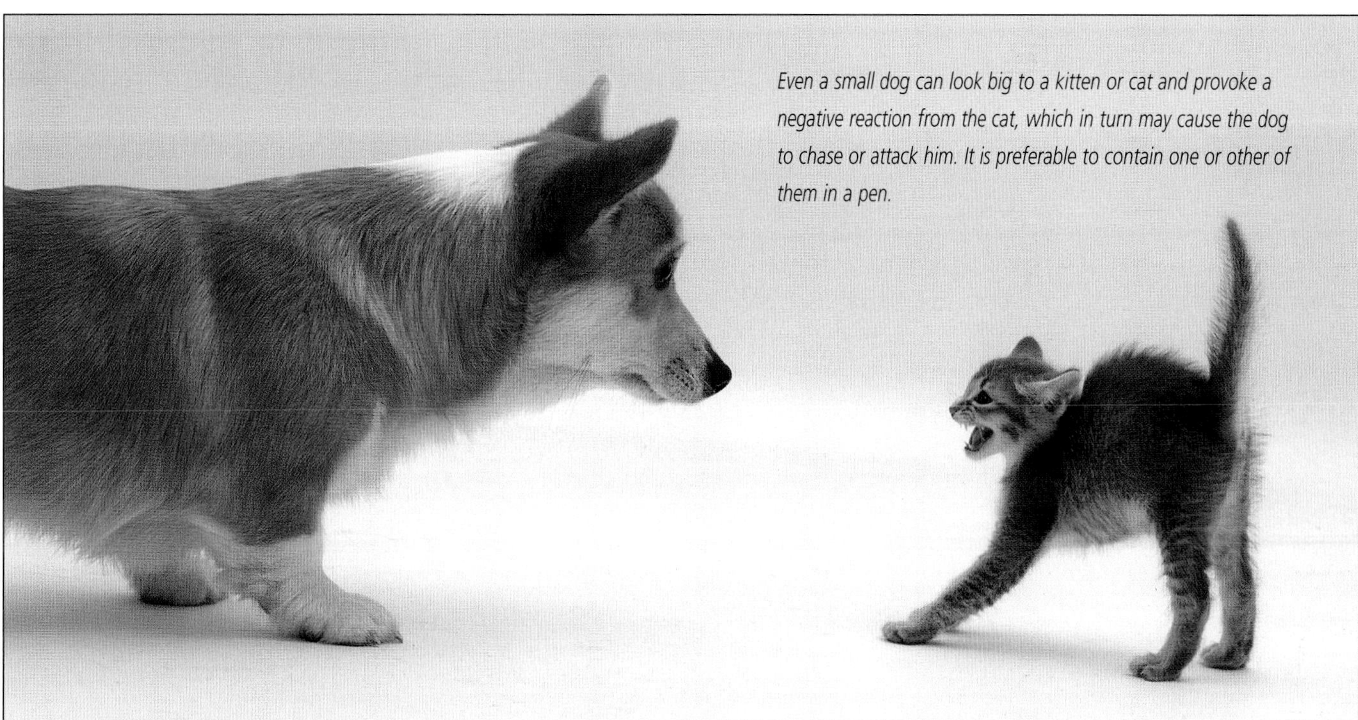

Even a small dog can look big to a kitten or cat and provoke a negative reaction from the cat, which in turn may cause the dog to chase or attack him. It is preferable to contain one or other of them in a pen.

that, in order to build and enjoy a harmonious relationship. If you require a high need for social contact with your cat, choose a breed or type that demonstrates this.

Some cats stay away from humans because of a lack of trust due to poor socialization during kittenhood. These cats are timid and can usually be slowly encouraged to be more friendly and therefore more affectionate through gentle treatment.

Children, often unintentionally, can be a great source of discomfort to cats. They can be too noisy, too rough, too active, sometimes cruel – and altogether too much for a cat to cope with. For this reason, it is important to educate your children to respect pets and treat them as they would wish to be treated themselves.

How you physically handle your cat also has great bearing on how he reacts to you. For detailed handling and interaction information, see pages 92–93.

Integration with other animals

Most cats, especially kittens, will integrate well with other animals in the household (as long as they themselves are well socialized), given a little time. When you bring a new cat home, it may help the introduction and socialization process to go smoothly if you transfer your existing pets' scent onto him. Do this by rubbing the cat with bedding from the pets' beds, or even a little soiled litter from their litter trays, before introducing them all.

Keep other pets away from the new arrival for the first hour or so, and then introduce them with either one or the other safely enclosed in a pen. Don't let dogs behave excitedly or bark around the new cat, or this will frighten him and get them off to a bad start. Usually, if he is well balanced and socialized with other animals, a dog will lose interest in the new cat – especially if you provide him with a toy or treat to take his mind off the new arrival.

Top tips

- Don't leave a new cat alone with other animals in the house until you are sure that they all get along well and are obvious friends. Kittens are most vulnerable, especially when dogs are involved.
- Keep the new cat away from pet birds or small mammals, which may be severely frightened – even if they are not harmed directly – if he attempts to catch them. You will not be able to prevent this instinctive behaviour in your cat, so the answer is to keep the animals apart.

Given time and correct introduction procedures, even the most unlikely animals can become friends.

Did you know ...?

It is very rare for an adult cat to fail to accept a new kitten in the end, no matter how strong his initial reactions are. He does not view a kitten as a significant threat, whereas another adult represents a danger to the existing cat's territorial resources.

Socializing with other cats

Introducing a cat to another cat may need to be a more gradual process, as they are not naturally sociable with unfamiliar members of the same species. Always supervise the initial meetings and never try to force cats of any ages together – they will adjust to each other at their own pace. When they meet, the behaviour displayed from both parties depends on several factors:

- the age of the new arrival
- the sex of the new arrival
- the personality of the new arrival
- the personality of the resident cat

When meeting for the first time, a kitten and a resident cat will probably investigate each other nose to nose (which is why, no matter what age the cats are, it is safer for one to be

A pen is the safest method of introducing two cats; alternate which one is in the pen over several introduction sessions. The body postures of this pair show that they are still unsure of each other and will need more time to adjust.

penned so no harm can come to either). Depending on the kitten's personality, he may become frightened and back away, or show some bravado and even hiss; the older cat may ignore this behaviour and simply sniff at the kitten, or he may become threatening, in which case you may need to intervene. If all goes well, however, the cats will soon grow bored with each other and tolerate their presence without animosity.

In one interesting case, a newly arrived female kitten simply would not take the older existing cat's vocal threats and indifference for an answer – she was a confident youngster who wanted to play and she pestered the older cat until she got what she wanted. The two eventually became firm friends. In fact, when the kitten matured and had kittens of her own, the other cat (a neutered female) took it upon herself to act as midwife and then nanny to her friend's offspring.

If the new arrival is of the opposite sex, or both cats are neutered, then introductions can be easier. However, the personalities of the cats concerned play a large part in integration, and this is something you cannot change – you simply have to work with and around them, taking into account each individual's needs and preferences.

This cat is totally relaxed and comfortable in his environment, so much so that he feels safe to lie in a vulnerable position while the family dog is in close proximity.

Give it time

Ensure that established pets get plenty of attention, so that they do not feel their security and status within the house is threatened by the new arrival. Having their own safe places to retreat to, undisturbed, when they feel the need, makes life easier for all concerned. It may take a week or two for the existing cat to accept the new arrival – longer if this is an adult – but eventually things should settle down amicably. (See pages 82–83 for more information on introducing a second cat into the home.)

Frequently asked question

Q I would like to get a cat, but am worried that my dog won't accept one in the house. What should I do?

A A jealous dog can pose a real threat to a cat. If you lack control over your dog, it may not be a good idea to get a cat as he may be put at a real risk of injury or worse. If the dog is well trained and knows to leave things alone when commanded, you have a good chance of integrating him with a cat. If you give the dog a lot of attention normally, gradually reduce this over a period of time until he no longer expects it constantly and on demand. Once you have done this, the time may be right to get a cat.

When making the introduction, putting the cat, or the dog, in a pen is safest. It is important, however, that you do not unintentionally fuel the dog's jealousy by centring all your attention on the new cat. Giving the dog an activity toy filled with food while introductions are taking place will distract him, and the dog will also associate the cat with something rewarding. Doing this continually throughout the initial acclimatization period should reap dividends.

Promoting health and happiness

Being a good owner means keeping your cat healthy and happy throughout his life. This entails:

• ensuring that your cat has a balanced diet appropriate to his life stage, to enable him to remain healthy
• making certain that your cat is vaccinated against the diseases to which he is vulnerable
• only breeding from your cat if you can be certain that the resulting kittens will be of normal conformation and healthy, and that caring, permanent homes are assured
• having your cat neutered if he or she is not to be kept for breeding purposes
• accommodating your cat's normal behaviour traits
• suitably addressing any abnormal behaviour traits
• having the facilities and time to care for your cat properly
• taking your cat to the vet when he is ill
• keeping your cat throughout his life, unless for any reason you cannot (see the box opposite on rehoming)
• grooming your cat and attending to parasite control as appropriate
• establishing a daily routine that your cat is comfortable with; constantly swapping feeding and letting-out times can soon confuse and distress a cat, which may force him to exhibit what you may consider to be inappropriate behaviour
• always treating your cat gently and with consideration
• never using physical punishment, as your cat will not understand why you are treating him in this way
• not relying on your cat for emotional support, as this can be detrimental to his mental and physical health
• identifying your cat's likes and dislikes

Top tip

Cats feel more at ease within a home where the environment is calm and peaceful, and the unexpected does not arise very often. Animals are quick to feel tension in an atmosphere and become unsettled by it; they may react either by leaving the immediate area or, if they do not have that choice, becoming withdrawn and fearful, and/or suffering ill health.

In relation to humans, cats are relatively small; therefore they feel vulnerable when faced with a creature bigger than themselves, unless they are certain that it is not a threat. For cats that have been mistreated by people, staying out of harm's way is particularly important. A friendly stare from you can often be misinterpreted by the cat who may perceive it as being threatening behaviour on your part. One of the first indications that the cat is ready for interaction is eye contact.

Did you know ...?

Cats blink and narrow their eyes when they accidentally make eye contact. To make friend with an unfamiliar cat, blink and look away when you catch his eye. Even cats that know their owners well don't like being stared at. Although they get used to our eye contact when they live with us, a full-on stare can make them feel uneasy and they will usually turn their faces away to relieve the tension. Another way they make themselves feel better is closing their eyes. If they feel uncomfortable but not threatened enough to run away, closing their eyes lets them think 'if I can't see you, you can't see me'.

Cats soon get to know what time food is served, and anticipate it. Deviating from an established routine, so that feeding times become haphazard, can result in anxiety-related behaviour.

Finding toys that your cat likes to play with by himself will help to alleviate any boredom during the times when you are not available to give him attention.

Rehoming your cat

It is possible that, for various reasons, you may feel that your new pet does not fit into your lifestyle despite all your efforts – the cat is unhappy, which can manifest in many ways, and therefore you are also unhappy. At times like this, you need to take stock of the situation: first of all, is there anything you could do, having read this book from cover to cover, that could improve it? The cat's welfare is foremost, so if there is nothing that you can implement quickly and easily, depending on your commitments, then maybe you and your cat would be better off if you found him a new home where he has a better chance of contentment.

Do not consider this as a failure on your part; view it as positive action to improve your cat's lot. Rescue and rehoming centres may be able to provide you with lots of useful information on how to go about finding the home your cat would be most comfortable with. If you do decide to get another cat after this, before you do so think very carefully about what type would fit well into your home situation.

Should I get a second cat?

Many owners decide to get another cat or kitten to provide their existing pet with a friend and company when they are not there. While the concept may be ideal, the reality is often not – with the resident cat being less than pleased with his new playmate. Being generally solitary creatures, most cats don't require a companion, so is it yourself you really want to indulge?

Once they get to know and are comfortable with each other, play-fights enable cats to maintain their relationship and to learn about each other's abilities and strengths.

Feline facts

- Introducing a new cat to the house can cause fear and/or antisocial behaviour in the resident cat. Some cats react by marking or defecating in the house, losing their appetite, deliberately breaking things such as ornaments, stropping on furniture, sucking clothing, self-mutilation, or obsessively self-grooming.
- Some breeds of cat are more accepting of new cats than others, for example the Persian, the British Shorthair, the Maine Coon and the Birman.

Will I be able to cope?

Before going ahead and getting another cat, ask yourself the following questions. If you can answer 'yes' to them all, then it is safe to go ahead.

- Have you got the time available to help the cats integrate?
- Can you cope with the inevitable routine upheaval of integration?
- Can you afford another cat? (Think of the double food, vet and cattery bills.)
- Do you have the space and facilities for two cats?
- Have you got the time available to care for two cats?
- Could you deal practically and patiently with any behaviour problems that might arise?
- Do you like a challenge?

Introducing a second cat

It is true that cats provide company for each other when you are not around to give them any attention, but only once they are accustomed to each other. Introducing a resident cat to a newcomer is not always as easy as it sounds. Korats and Ocicats, for example, do not tolerate other cats at all well.

Introducing another cat, or any other animal for that matter, once your pet has become established in the household can often cause more problems than it solves, whereas two cats brought up together may well become inseparable friends. This being the case, it is better to get two cats at the start, either kittens of the same age or from the same litter, or two cats that have been used to living with each other. This ideal cannot always be achieved, however, so it is essential to take into account normal feline behaviour, and learn to understand it – then you will be in a more informed position to initiate introducing another cat into the household with minimal stress to all concerned.

Cats do not live by the same code of conduct that humans do, so, instead of smiling and shaking hands on first meeting, they are more likely to swear at each other and then have a punch-up. As this would not start the relationship off well, it is important to follow the dos and don'ts here and not to let this situation occur.

DO:

- Follow the advice given in 'Socializing' on pages 76–79.
- Expect integration to take quite some time.
- Integrate the cats gradually, preferably with one in a pen to prevent either getting injured and to give them both a sense of security.
- Allow them to investigate each other at their own pace.
- When you feel they are eventually ready to intermingle freely, wait until feeding time (when they are both hungry), place them in a room that has 'safety' places which either can retreat to if necessary, close the door and place bowls of extra-tasty food down, well apart, then bring the cats in to eat. Stay with them while they feed to interrupt any antagonistic behaviour (dropping a big bunch of keys is a good distraction). Eating together in this way can help promote successful integration.
- Give the cats separate litter trays.

DON'T:

- Suddenly ignore the resident cat in preference to the new arrival, otherwise the former will feel insecure while the latter may be forced into a jealous confrontation brought on by your attention.
- Put them together and leave them to 'sort themselves out'.
- Leave the cats alone together before the hissing and spitting stage has ended. Only after this is it reasonably safe to allow them to intermingle when you are not around.
- Expect the cats to become buddies overnight. Despite your best intentions, some cats never become great friends and only just tolerate living with each other.

Top tip

Some breeds can be very people-dependent and do not like to be left alone; for this reason it is usually better to get two kittens (not necessarily of the same breed) from the beginning to keep each other company when home alone. Such breeds include the Burmese, the Balinese, the Siamese and other Orientals.

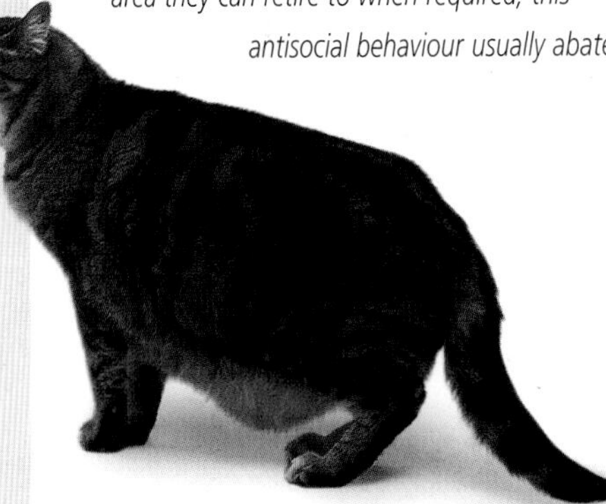

There may be a certain amount of spitting and hissing when the cats are introduced and get used to each other but, providing they each have a safe area they can retire to when required, this antisocial behaviour usually abates.

Behaviour problems

Sometimes, pet cats can display what we consider to be behaviour problems. To the cat, however, such behaviour represents a perfectly normal action in the circumstances. It is up to us to try to understand why these problems occur and then rectify the situation so that the inappropriate behaviour can be cured, or redirected into an acceptable one. See the checklist for the most common triggers for behaviour problems.

Checklist

- ✓ anxiety
- ✓ insecurity
- ✓ feeling threatened
- ✓ feeling fearful
- ✓ courting
- ✓ being in season
- ✓ being driven by instinct
- ✓ feeling unwell

Why cats behave strangely

In view of the constraints and relatively abnormal conditions under which pet cats live, it is surprising how few revolt against domestication or exhibit strange behaviour patterns, but shock and trauma can produce disorders. Rough, unkind handling can result in a totally unbalanced and unpredictable cat, and any form of severe shock may result in reactions that induce collapse of the cranial nerve and death. This can also happen to over-humanized cats on whom care and love have been lavished; here the attack is as a result of the over-stimulation of the nervous system.

Drug and food additives can also cause unusual behaviour in cats, so these are another area to investigate if your pet behaves abnormally; changing a brand of cat food, or being on a course of medication can sometimes induce character changes. Introducing a new pet or human baby to the household can cause fear in some cases and antisocial behaviour in others, so great care must be taken in effecting introductions (see pages 76–79 and 82–83).

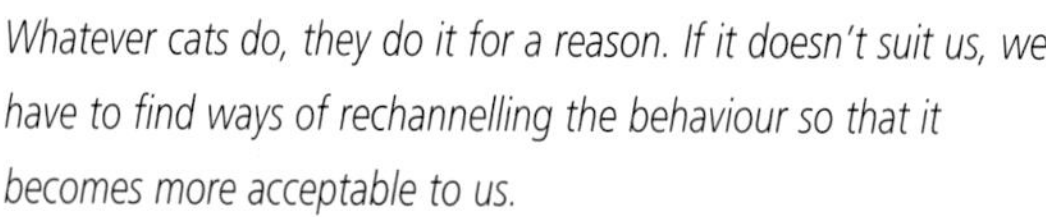

Whatever cats do, they do it for a reason. If it doesn't suit us, we have to find ways of rechannelling the behaviour so that it becomes more acceptable to us.

Feline fact

Cats can derive great pleasure from idiosyncratic behaviour. Some like to play with water, particularly with dripping taps, or to swim. Some are clever enough to use the lavatory. There are cats that like snow and ice, while others won't go out in the rain. Some cats like to roll on cold concrete, or paw at windowpanes. Some also demonstrate covering up food they don't like, as if it were mess in their litter tray. Cats can sulk too – by turning their backs on their owners.

Furniture scratching is a behaviour trait that owners probably view as the most infuriating, yet it can be one of the simplest to prevent (see Scratching furniture below).

Top tip

Place the scratching post is an area often used by the cat, and don't replace it when it looks tatty – this is when cats enjoy it the most, as it is comfortingly familiar and impregnated with their smell.

Scratching furniture

The arms of sofas and chairs make great scratching posts as far as a cat is concerned, while curtains are great fun to run up and hide in; they are not to know that this behaviour is unacceptable to their owners. Provide your pet with alternative scratching areas and hiding places, such as:

- a sturdy scratching post, either home-made or shop-bought (rub catnip on it to encourage your cat to use it) – if your cat likes to climb, choose a multi-purpose play/scratching post or play centre
- cardboard boxes in which to hide
- lots of toys to play with
- if necessary, keep your cat out of the room(s) containing prized furniture and soft furnishings to prevent him damaging them

Urinating or defecating in the house

It is important to identify whether the behaviour comprises 'marking' or is simply inappropriate toilet behaviour. The latter may arise because:

- the cat does not like where his litter tray is positioned – maybe it is too close to his feeding or sleeping area
- the litter that is provided is unacceptable; for example, some cats prefer wood pellets to anything else
- the tray is too small to accommodate the cat comfortably
- the tray is not cleaned out regularly enough

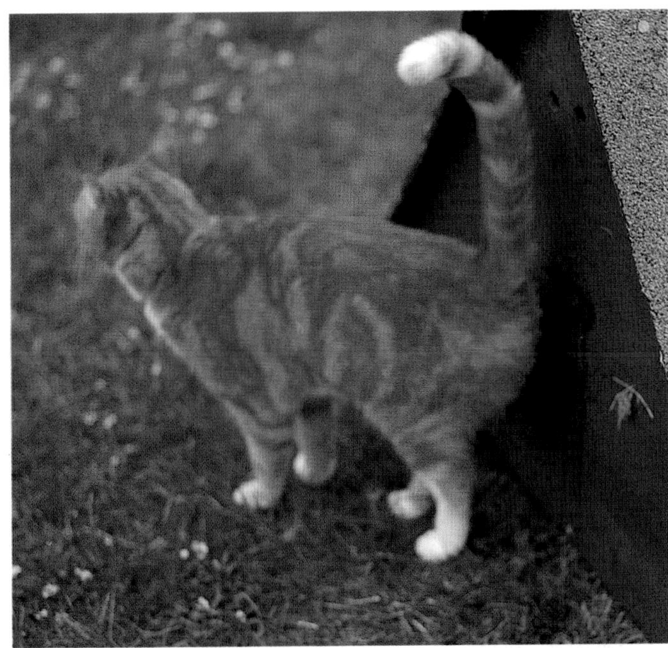

Only a small amount of urine is sprayed when a cat marks, compared with the large volume that is expelled when cats squat to urinate.

Sometimes cats can be encouraged to stray by kindly neighbours who make a fuss of the cat and/or feed him. While they may have the best intentions, it is a good idea to put a stop to this in a diplomatic way by stressing it is for the cat's own safety and continued good health.

Inappropriate toilet behaviour is relatively easy to cure, but marking can be more difficult as the cause of it may not be readily identifiable. When a cat marks or defecates in inappropriate places in the house, it is an indication that he does not feel secure within his territory, and may even feel threatened. Leaving waste deposits in prominent places around the house is a way of marking the territory as his own, thereby warning off perceived intruders – such as other cats, animals or people in the household.

In one interesting case, one married owner could not understand why her previously clean cat started to mark and defecate on the bed. It later transpired that her husband had been having an affair; when he moved out of the marital home, the marking behaviour stopped and the cat reverted to using his litter tray as normal. The wife deduced that the cat was objecting to, or feeling threatened by, the scent of the other woman on her husband!

To help make the cat feel more secure within the home, see pages 22–23, 46–57 and 80–81.

Top tips

- It is a good idea to have two trays for one cat, so that a clean one is readily available if the other is dirty.
- Cats are fastidious and do not like to eat close to their litter tray. Owners often put the food and tray close together, but this can result in a real dilemma for a cat that likes to be clean. Some cats put up with it, but others take to relieving themselves in another part of the house instead.

Straying and fighting

Unneutered cats, on reaching maturity, will make every effort to escape from the house and find a mate. If not allowed to do so, their frustration can lead to all sorts of behavioural problems, including constant attention-seeking, soiling around the home, aggression and incessant vocal expression. Straying can become a real problem for owners who have unneutered male (tom) cats, while those with unneutered females may have toms hanging around the house and garden when their pet is in season. Straying can also lead to health problems – caused by fighting (see pages 74–75) and by contracting diseases and becoming injured – that can prove costly in terms of emotional upset for the owner and any necessary veterinary treatment.

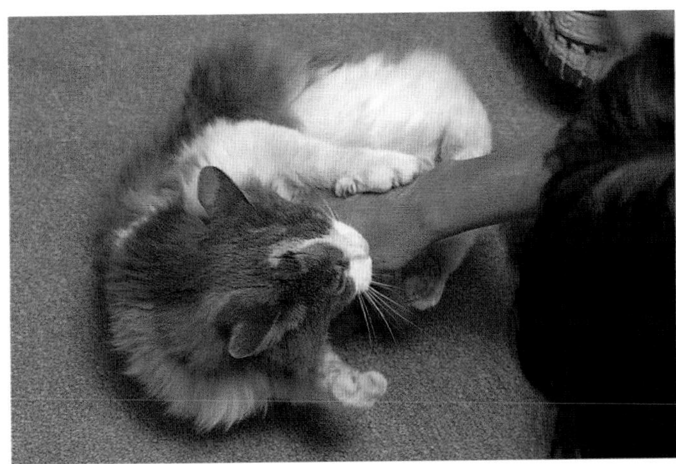

Some cats panic and react defensively when touched on sensitive parts of the body (head, underbelly and legs). 'Attack' on these areas can trigger an aggressive biting and scratching response which is designed to get rid of the hand. Unless you know the cat very well and he trusts you completely, it is best not to touch his vulnerable areas.

Frequently asked question

Q Why does my cat hiss at one of my children and then run away and hide from them?

A This is probably a result of that child tormenting the cat in some way, either physically or by loud verbal abuse, so the cat has learned to regard the child as a threat. To change the cat's perception of the child, you must teach the child how to respect the cat, handle him correctly, and move and speak softly around him. It may take considerable time for the cat to learn to trust that child, so the child should not try to handle him physically until the cat feels unthreatened by such interaction, and will go to the child of his own volition.

Biting and scratching

Pet cats rarely become aggressive unless they are being teased or ill treated. Sometimes a cat reacts violently to being touched because he has been frightened when woken up suddenly, or is reacting to another threat: he may be watching a menacing dog or a noisy vacuum-cleaner when his owner tries to pick him up, and thinks he is being attacked by the cause of his fear. This behaviour is an

When a cat adopts this posture and hisses, it means that he is really worried about whatever he has seen or is approaching him. Fluffing the hairs up on his body and arching his back makes him bigger, in an attempt to scare off the opponent.

This cat's head carriage and body stance show that he is not completely committed to aggression, but hopes his hiss and posture will make the other cat back off and leave him alone.

Did you know ...?

A cat that is feeling unwell or is in pain may display uncharacteristic aggressive tendencies if handled or disturbed while resting; abnormal behaviour like this should be checked out by a vet.

If you ignore the attention-seeking cat, he will usually get bored and go and find something else with which to occupy himself.

understandable response created by the cat's complex defence mechanism.

Sexual disorders sometimes manifest themselves in pet cats when they are not neutered and become frustrated. Neutering usually brings about a marked improvement in behaviour and general health.

Separation anxiety

Some cats – particularly certain breeds, such as the Siamese and Burmese – have a high need for contact with their owners, and can become quite distressed if left alone for any length of time. This anxiety can result in various kinds of inappropriate behaviour being displayed, such as destructiveness or soiling around the house, and even obsessive tendencies such as self-mutilation and cloth- or wool-sucking.

Smells familiar

In many cases of cats with behavioural problems inside the house, it is well worth trying a plug-in cat odour diffuser device (usually obtainable from vets). This works by releasing into the atmosphere synthetically reproduced cat pheromones, which can help settle cats and make them feel more safe and secure in a new or disrupted environment.

Curing these habits can be difficult, since the answer lies in reducing the cat's feelings of anxiety; for example, if you are out at work all day and the cat reacts badly to being left alone, then there are a number of options.

- Impregnate a soft toy with catnip for the cat to play with and cuddle up to for a feeling of security – some cats even respond well to a radio left on at low volume
- Employ a petsitter
- Put the cat in a cattery each day so he has company
- Try to work from home as much as much as possible
- Rehome the cat with someone who is at home all day
- Get another cat to keep him company

All of these options have their drawbacks, and it very much depends on your circumstances and the cat's personality as to which one will work satisfactorily – it may be a process of elimination to find out which option will work best for you and your cat.

Attention-seeking

Cats that seek attention soon learn what patterns of behaviour result in their owners taking notice of them. Some knock objects over or off table tops or shelves, knowing that this will bring their owners rushing to see what is wrong; others miaow, rub around the owners' legs and reach up with their paws. Reading a newspaper can result in the cat playing with it, or lying on it to focus the owner's attention on the cat and not the paper.

The best way to deal with this behaviour, depending on the character of the cat, is to:

- provide him with something else to focus on, such as toys
- move breakables out of his reach

Providing your cat with places to explore will help keep him pleasantly occupied and, therefore, happy.

• make the cat's environment more entertaining and therefore stimulating for him (see pages 46–53)
• get into a routine of giving your cat attention at certain times of the day that are convenient to you, so that he gets his quota of quality time with you, and vice versa; this will keep you both happy

Excessive self-grooming

Cats who are extremely bored or badly reared may indulge in excessive self-grooming. They lick and groom their bodies until some areas are raw, and may even suck at their paws, tail or rear nipples, purring and kneading, regressing mentally into kittenhood.

Eating or sucking cloth

This behaviour (which is similar to that of a young child who will suck on a dummy or snuggle up to a particular blanket for comfort) appears to be related to self-sucking. It sometimes occurs in otherwise well-balanced cats, especially in some strains of Siamese. It is probably easiest to accept this habit and let the cat have his own piece of cloth to suck at. However, if the attraction is for man-made fibres and the cat swallows large amounts of the material, it could become impacted in the stomach and intestines and need removing surgically.

Top tip

Try not to allow a kitten to do things that you may not appreciate later on. For example, always feed him on the floor rather than on a worktop if you do not want him to view work surfaces as a good place to be.

Frequently asked question

Q How can I stop my cat catching mice and birds?

A Most owners dislike their pets catching small rodents and birds, but it is impossible to stop them doing so, unless the cat is kept inside or penned while outside. You can, however, help preserve numbers of wildlife by not allowing your cat outside at dawn (when birds are waking and off-guard in their quest for food) and dusk (when birds are busy finding somewhere to roost). By limiting your cat's access to the outside at peak hunting times, his kill rate will be significantly reduced. Feed birds during the winter season when natural food is scarce, and provide them with water to drink. Position bird-feeding stations so that they are not exposed to feline attack; put them next to trees and bushes so birds have shelter to fly into.

At twilight and dawn, the cat's ability to make the best use of poor light conditions stands him in good stead for catching prey.

CARING FOR A CAT

There are many aspects to cat care and management, and part of the attraction of owning these splendid creatures is the interaction many owners enjoy in keeping their pets healthy and happy. There is something extremely satisfying in knowing that the animal in your care is receiving meticulous attention to all his needs. For many people, the daily routine in looking after a cat, from cleaning out his litter tray to making sure his coat remains tangle-free and glossy, is very fulfilling, and the purring affection received in return is blissfully comforting.

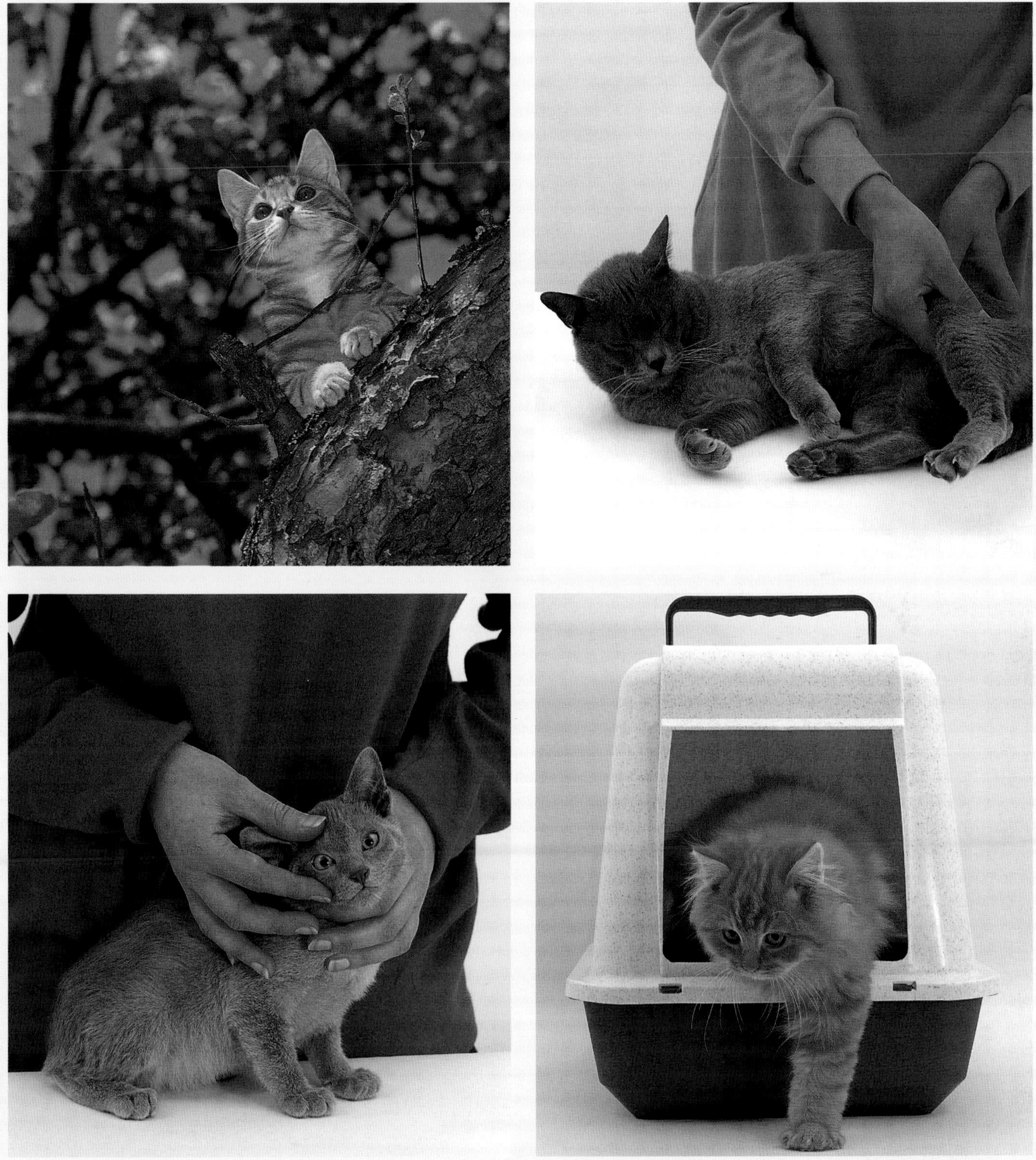

Handling cats

How you handle and interact with your cat will determine his behaviour and reactions towards you. Cats feel threatened and insecure when there is tension in the air, when they hear loud or raised voices, when they are touched roughly, and when they are suddenly grabbed at. Cats respond better to and prefer humans who behave as shown on the checklist.

Checklist

- ✓ touch cats gently
- ✓ be unhurried
- ✓ be at ease
- ✓ speak with a low, soft voice

Stroking

If stroked from an early age, most cats will be used to and enjoy it. However, there are areas on their body where stroking can cause them to worry. If the cat was not well handled as a kitten, or has been badly treated or teased, then it is wise only to stroke 'safe' areas – the back and sides. Avoid stroking the head where all the sense organs are, the sensitive tummy and delicate legs.

Cats often enjoy being stroked at the base of their tails, and will arch their backs in delight when you do this. Scent glands are situated in this area, and the cat appreciates any action that helps spread his own scent onto his companion. However, it is safer not to stroke the base of the tail unless you know the cat very well, as some cats may react defensively if they have had their tail pulled in the past by cruel humans, or if their tail has suffered injury at some time. If your cat scratches and bites you when you attempt to stroke or hug him, see pages 84–89.

Feline fact

From the neck along the back is a 'safe' area in which to stroke an unfamiliar cat. No senses or sensitive areas are being interfered with in this region, and most pet cats will tolerate being touched here. If he likes you and feels comfortable, the cat may then invite you to stroke his head area by trying to rub his face and body against your hand.

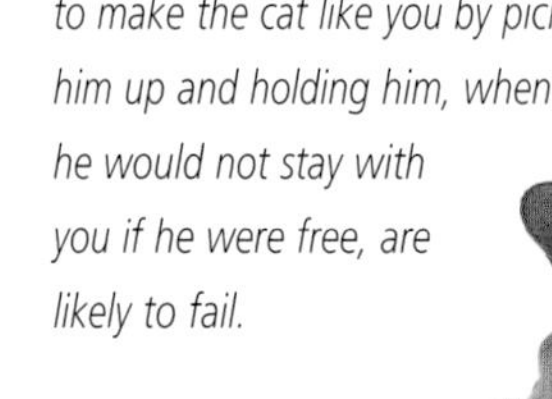

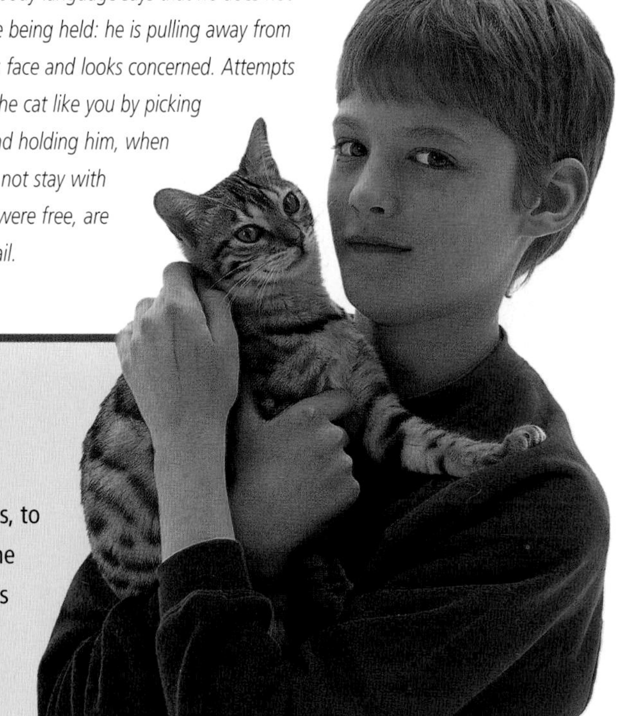

This cat's body language says that he does not appreciate being held: he is pulling away from the child's face and looks concerned. Attempts to make the cat like you by picking him up and holding him, when he would not stay with you if he were free, are likely to fail.

Frequently asked question

Q When should I start handling kittens?

A Handle them frequently between the ages of three and eight weeks, to get them used to people. This is the time for kittens to recognize the difference between safety and danger. Start gentle grooming at this age, especially in longhaired cats, with particular emphasis given to inspecting ears and mouths. Training carried out at this stage is invaluable.

Picking up your cat

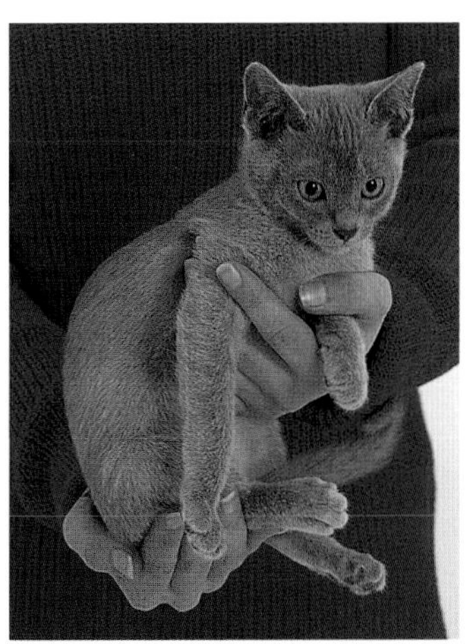

The best way to pick up your kitten or cat is shown here. Gently scoop him up with one hand under its chest, the other hand supporting his bottom, and keeping him close to your body so he feels secure. Don't hold him too tight, or he will claustrophobic and try to escape.

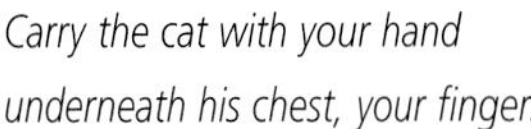

Carry the cat with your hand underneath his chest, your fingers between his fore legs, and keeping him close to your body for support. This leaves one hand free to hold the cat's head, or gently restrain him by the scruff (the loose skin on the back of the neck) if necessary.

Some people find it easier to hold the cat across his midriff, with one hand cradling the cat and the other hand held lightly across the length of his back for security (some cats also prefer this method of holding and carrying).

Looking at your cat's expression can tell you a lot about how he is feeling. Apprehension and worry show in this cat's face. His ears have swivelled back to find out what is going on behind him, and are held slightly back, indicating his concern. Being held, he has little control of what happens to him; he cannot run away, and this makes his fear worse. If you are holding your cat and he displays similar behaviour, set him down gently; keeping hold of him may result in you being scratched or bitten, and your cat avoiding being held in future.

Top tips

- A kitten that has had at least four kind and gentle handlers during his early weeks will be relaxed and friendly with most people.
- To accustom a cat to being picked up and held, start by doing this when you are in a sitting position. Pick up and hold him only for a brief time at first, and then put him down again. Gradually extend the time you hold him until he is content to remain in your arms as long as you are giving him attention; but always allow him to get down if he wants to.
- As they are equipped with sharp teeth and claws, it is sensible not to antagonize a cat during interaction. If you are susceptible to cat-scratch fever – a severe response to infection caused by cat scratches and bites, also called cat-scratch disease (CSD) – take precautions when handling your cat and wear gloves and long-sleeved clothing.

Cats and children

Research has shown that children who grow up with pets in the house, and who are taught to treat them with respect and care, are more likely to develop into well-balanced and responsible adults. What better reason could there be to have a cat if you are a parent? To create harmony between children and a cat, you should observe the rules in the checklist.

Checklist

- ✓ supervise interaction
- ✓ teach children to respect the cat
- ✓ show children correct handling procedures
- ✓ encourage bonding
- ✓ involve children in daily care
- ✓ forbid cruelty

How cats view children

It is surprising just how tolerant some cats and kittens can be with babies and young children, but this is not something you should put to the test. You must teach children not to disturb the cat – especially by grabbing at him – when he is resting in his bed, or they may be rewarded with a scratch. Your cat may sleep for up to two-thirds of the day, which is quite normal.

Feline fact

Cats that have been well socialized with humans during kittenhood, and are treated in a way that makes them content, will successfully fulfil the role of companion and even of child substitute for childless couples.

Interaction

Discourage young children from picking up kittens and cats, because they may squeeze them too hard around the abdomen and put them off being carried for life. Instead, encourage the cat to climb on the child's lap and remain there to be petted. Show children how to stroke the cat, and also how to pick him up and carry him (see page 93). The cat should never be restrained during these encounters; make sure that the child understands that he or she must allow the cat to walk away whenever he wishes.

Prevent all children, especially toddlers, from chasing the cat, as this can put him off young children for life. Similarly, the cat should be able to rest undisturbed without being pestered, as nervousness and fearful or unpredictable behaviour are fuelled by lack of sleep. Provide plenty of areas to which cats can escape from children's attentions – high-up places are preferable, so that your pet can seek sanctuary when it all gets too much for him.

If initial interaction between children and cats is done correctly, most children and cats become great friends. Many cats and kittens bond quickly with children and seem happy to play with them, curl up with them to sleep or watch TV, and 'help' them with their homework.

Frequently asked question

Q How can I prepare my cat for the arrival of my new baby?

A Cats and babies seem to have generated more urban myths than any other combination of animal and human. Some midwives, health visitors and even doctors seem keen to perpetuate tales of woe surrounding pets and a new addition to the family, but common sense is all that is required. If your cat is used to a lot of attention from you, bear in mind that you may not be able to devote so much time to him on a daily basis when your baby arrives. So gradually wean your cat off being too dependent on you; get into the habit of setting aside a time of day that will be convenient to give you and your cat some quality time together for affection and play. Once your cat gets used to this, he should be happy to accept it. Giving your cat other things to focus on, such as new toys, will also help divert his dependency on you for attention and entertainment.

Get the cat used to seeing baby equipment about the house, and seeing you fussing around it. When you have the baby, transfer his or her scent via a clean cloth onto your cat, his bedding and household furniture and surfaces. This will make the baby's arrival in the home less of a surprise to the cat. Be sure to allow the cat to greet the new arrival and 'help' you attend to him or her; having a calm approach to this will ensure the integration process goes smoothly.

Children can sometimes find it hard to express their feelings to parents, or anyone else for that matter. A cat, on the other hand, will not judge them or admonish them and, therefore, can be a source of great solace and friendship.

To cats, children are not the same as adult humans; they move, talk and even smell different. If the two are integrated correctly, they will get along just fine.

Did you know ...?

A common misconception is that a cat may try to sleep in a baby's cot or pram and may smother the child in doing so, but this is highly unlikely to happen. However, to put your mind at rest if you have a baby, it is sensible to use a special net (available from childcare stores) as a precaution, and to keep your cat out of the room in which your baby sleeps.

Hygiene

Young children especially tend to put their hands in their mouths at every opportunity so, while it is rare that a child will pick up any infection (such as ringworm, tapeworm and toxoplasmosis) from felines, it goes without saying that you should take great care to ensure that children wash their hands after handling a cat (and other animals and pets) to minimize any risk. This is especially important if you have a garden that both cats and children like to use; cats will relieve themselves in flowerbeds and, if they get the chance, in sandpits – exactly where children like to play. Keep sandpits covered when not in use to prevent the cat using them as a toilet.

Toxoplasmosis

Contracting toxoplasmosis can be a great concern to expectant mothers, and those with children. Most infections are harmless if the person concerned has got sufficient immunity against them – which is why unborn and young children are at high risk.

Toxoplasma gondii is a microscopic parasitic that can cause abnormalities in the foetus and blindness (it is also to be found in raw meats – primarily pork and chicken – in the human food chain, but is usually destroyed by cooking). Cats become infected by eating raw meat (via prey), and the resulting eggs (contained in cysts) from the parasite are shed in the faeces. These eggs hatch into larvae, and it is these that can cause the damage if ingested by humans.

Some doctors and midwives can be over-zealous in advising expectant mums to get rid of any cats in the household to prevent any risk of contracting the disease, but this really is not necessary providing you follow hygiene rules and wear gloves when handling cats and cleaning out litter trays (or getting someone else to do it), and also when handling soil in the garden. The risks to humans of contracting toxoplasmosis are said to be greatest when handling raw meat and vegetables grown in contaminated soil, or eating undercooked meat, so this puts the chances of contracting it from your cat into context.

If you are concerned about the risks, ask your doctor to carry out a blood test to show whether you are immune to the infection; if you are, this means that there is no risk of you passing it on to the foetus. If you are not immune, then make stringent hygiene practice in your kitchen and around your cat a priority. Ensuring your cat is wormed regularly is also good practice to keep the risk of contracting toxoplasmosis to a minimum.

Cats and children can have great fun together, providing the latter are taught when it is better not to try to engage the pet in play.

Feline fact

Cats don't understand if you punish them for digging their claws in when you stroke them; where children are concerned, it is wise to place a thick blanket over their knees when they are petting a cat to prevent discomfort on both parts. The occasional scratch and bite is part of owning a cat, so it is good practice to ensure that both you and your children are up to date with immunization against tetanus (and rabies, if applicable).

Routine care

Cats look after themselves, don't they? Yes, to a certain extent they do, but for domestic pets to live happy, fulfilled and healthy lives they do need some help from their owners. In order to maintain your cat's mental and physical health, there are certain procedures you must implement on a daily, monthly and yearly basis, shown in the checklist.

Checklist

- ✓ correct nutrition (food and water)
- ✓ grooming
- ✓ appropriate training
- ✓ monitoring behaviour, body eliminations and general appearance
- ✓ stimulating activities
- ✓ checking vital signs (pulse, respiration, temperature)
- ✓ parasite control
- ✓ vaccinations

Body condition

Pet cats can suffer from obesity if they do not get enough exercise in relation to the food they receive on a daily basis. Being overweight can result in serious health problems, and shorten the cat's life. Longhaired cats may look 'fat', but it can be an optical illusion created by all that fur. Depending on the breed or type, the average cat weighs around 4kg (8lb 12oz), and you should be able to feel his ribs but not see them. Any deviation from normal weight may indicate a health problem.

Collars

If your cat wears a collar, check its fit daily to ensure it is not too tight, and is not rubbing or causing allergic skin reactions in the case of flea collars. Kittens grow rapidly, so it is especially important to check the fit of their collars at least once a week.

Check your cat's eliminations on a daily basis to see what state his digestion system is in; loose motions can indicate a problem, as does a constant need to urinate. If either persists for more than a day, seek veterinary advice.

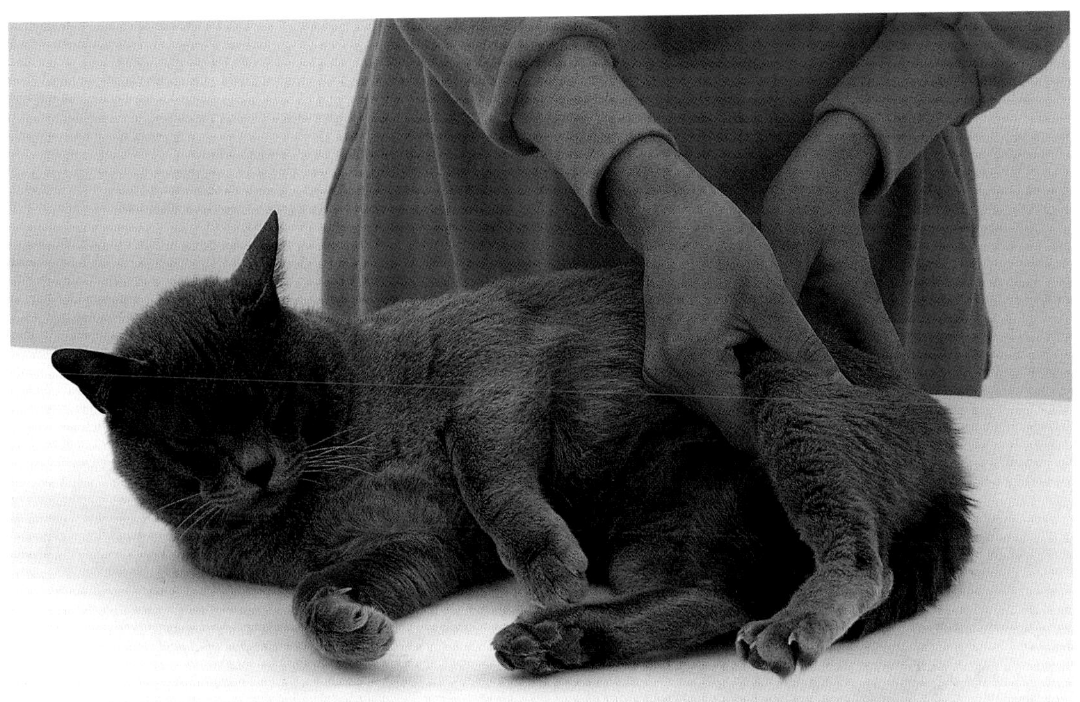

One of the best ways to take a cat's pulse is by placing two fingers on the inside of one of his thighs.

Eliminations

The most important signs of a potential problem are:

- discomfort in urinating and/or defecating
- a constant need to eliminate (shown by the cat frequenting his litter tray, often with no satisfactory result)
- blood in the faeces or urine, or other abnormalities, such as loose or very hard motions
- not as many eliminations as usual
- any deviation from usual elimination – you should closely monitor this, and if it persists for more than a day seek veterinary advice

General demeanour

If you know your cat well, you will soon notice any difference in his behaviour and demeanour. If he is normally bright and active, but suddenly appears depressed, this may indicate he is feeling unwell. If there are other signs of illness, then it is wise to take him to the vet for a check-up. Make a note of symptoms as this may help the vet work out what is wrong. If your cat deviates from his usual eating habits, this also warrants investigation. He may simply not appreciate a change of food brand or, more seriously, he may be suffering from a mouth ailment such as an abscess, or a digestive disorder that is affecting his appetite.

Training

Be sure to maintain rules about what the cat can and cannot do on a daily basis, so that you don't confuse him. If, for example, you don't allow him to scratch furniture, don't dangle toys over the arm of a chair, as this may lead to him digging his claws in the material, which in turn may encourage him to strop. If you don't usually allow the cat on the bed, don't be tempted to let him 'as a special treat' one

Feline fact

A cat's vital signs – temperature, pulse and respiration (TPR) – alter depending on his age and the time of year; in hot weather, for example, the vital signs will be higher than usual. Find out what your cat's vital signs are by taking them over a period of a week (in summer and in winter) to discover his average during warm and cold seasons. As a guide, feline vital signs are:

- **temperature:** 38–39°C (100–102°F)
- **pulse:** 160–240 heartbeats per minute, depending on the age of the cat (the younger he is, the faster the heartbeat)
- **respiration:** 20–30 breaths per minute

Top tip

Being fastidious creatures, cats dislike eating from dirty bowls. After each meal, throw away uneaten wet food and wash out the bowl. If you heap fresh food on top of old food left in the bowl, the cat will probably not eat it.

Cats normally spend a lot of time self-grooming. If your cat fails to stick to his usual hygiene routine, it may be a sign that all is not well, so take him for a veterinary check-up.

day, otherwise the cat will then think he is allowed to do it all the time. Make sure the rest of the family also adhere to these rules.

Special occasions

At times when celebrations occur, cats need extra-special care to ensure they don't become stressed with all the noise and extra people in the house, or ill through eating anything unsuitable for them. Festive decorations and Christmas trees, for example, can prove irresistible to curious cats, so make sure trees are well secured in their stands, lights are plugged into a circuit breaker, and decorations are shatterproof. Some cats can be fascinated by tinsel; if your pet persists in trying to eat it, you will have no option but to remove it from the tree.

Keep the cat separated from any celebrations by settling him in a quiet room with a warm bed, some toys to keep him occupied, his litter tray and food and water; go in to check on him from time to time to reassure him that you are around. Even though you may be tempted to, do not give your pet foods that he does not normally receive, otherwise he may suffer unpleasant and painful digestive upsets.

The use of fireworks seems to be on the increase, and most animals are terrified of them; if they are going off in the neighbourhood, keep your cat safely indoors. Having the TV or radio on can help drown out the noise of the fireworks which animals find distressing. If you do plan to host a fireworks party, ensure the cat is kept inside, preferably in a room in the other side of the house, and choose 'silent' fireworks that you can now buy. It is also courteous to inform your neighbours of a forthcoming fireworks party, so that they can keep their pets safely inside when it occurs.

Did you know ...?

Cats rapidly learn that certain kinds of behaviour result in a reward such as us feeding them or opening doors for them. These behaviours can then become signals that they display regularly when they want something. It is possible to train cats, for example, to sit on command, using plenty of varied, high-value rewards, such as favourite tasty food morsels. Getting cross or saying 'no' never works, and cats become resentful and fearful if such tactics are used.

AT-A-GLANCE MAINTENANCE CHECKS

FREQUENCY	WHAT TO DO
Daily	• Clean food and water bowls • Feed and supply fresh water • Check eating habits • Clean out litter trays and check for abnormalities in eliminations • Give your cat some quality time – attention and play • Check your cat is warm enough, depending on his age and the time of year • Groom longhaired cats • Check collar fit • Check body, legs and paws for signs of injury
Weekly	• Groom shorthaired cats • Check ears • General check for elderly cats – vital signs • Check litter and food stocks for forthcoming week • Wash and disinfect litter trays; totally replace litter • Check for weight loss or gain
Monthly	• Parasite control – worm and deflea cats that have access to outside (see page 138 for more information) • General health check – vital signs (see Feline fact on page 99)
Every two months	• Parasite control for indoor cats (do this monthly if you also have a dog that is allowed access to outside) • Check and clean teeth (see pages 134–35 and 164 for more information on this subject)
Every six months	• If you choose injections to control fleas, they need to be administered every six months • Veterinary check-up for elderly cats • Vaccination booster vaccinations for outdoor cats in highly feline-populated areas (see page 138–39 for vaccination information)
Once a year	• Veterinary check-up (see page 137) • Revise nutrition needs depending on your cat's age (ask your vet for advice if necessary) • Yearly vaccination boosters for indoor cats

If you take the time to learn what represents normal behaviour for your cat, you will soon be able to tell when he is feeling ill, or is displaying signs that something is not right and requires investigation.

Kitten care

You need to put in some work for that cute kitten to grow up into the perfect pet. It is not hard to do this – common sense, inclination and the will to apply certain principles and procedures into training your young cat how to behave and perform as you wish him to will earn rewards. All you need for basic kitten care is shown in the checklist.

- ✓ patience, kindness and gentleness
- ✓ understand feline behaviour
- ✓ appropriate veterinary attention
- ✓ consistent training
- ✓ set rules and adhering to them
- ✓ correct handling
- ✓ quality time together
- ✓ reward appropriate behaviour

Sleeping

Cats sleep for up to 60 per cent of their lives. They spend a larger proportion of their time asleep when they are kittens, and again when they reach old age. It is normal for kittens to sleep a great deal; because of their bursts of frenetic play, during which they use a lot of energy, they need to replenish their energy levels frequently through resting. It is essential that kittens are allowed to rest undisturbed as and when they wish, to make sure they have the necessary energy to develop into healthy, well-adjusted adults.

Feeding

Kittens play hard and grow fast, and so require appropriate nutrition to cope with these demands on their bodies. Luckily for owners, manufacturers make this easy by providing a vast range of food especially formulated for young cats. Choose food for the appropriate life stage to ensure you are fulfilling your pet's nutritional needs. See pages 38–45 for further information on feeding kittens.

Good early experiences of interaction between kittens and children provide an excellent basis for a lifelong affection for each other. Children who love and respect cats are likely to develop into adults who practise good care and welfare to all animals.

Handling your kitten

The way in which you physically interact with your kitten will have great bearing on how he reacts to you and other people when he matures. The better you handle your pet as a kitten, the better he will accept physical contact as an adult. For this reason, aim to give your kitten an all-over check at least once a week, preferably every day.

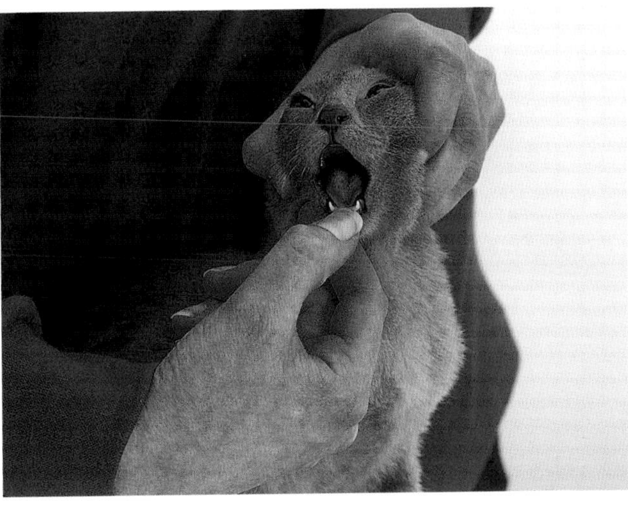

Accustoming your kitten to regular inspections of his mouth will reap dividends when you come to clean his teeth, and also when checking his mouth later on; your vet will also appreciate this training. In addition, it will make it easier for you to administer medicines orally.

Accustoming your kitten to handling and touching all over will make being examined by a vet less stressful for him.

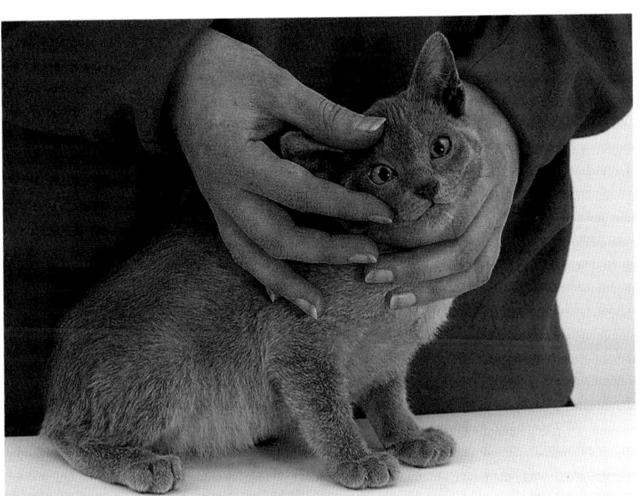

The head is a sensitive area, so the earlier a kitten becomes used to the feeling of a head examination the easier it will be for him to bear one whenever this becomes necessary.

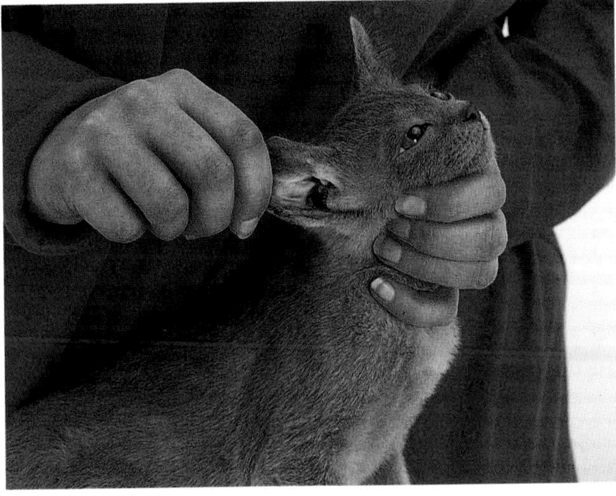

Ears are sensitive, and therefore you should touch and handle them accordingly. Getting your kitten used to ear inspections will make life easier for both of you later on, should he ever need treatment for ear mites or a build-up of wax.

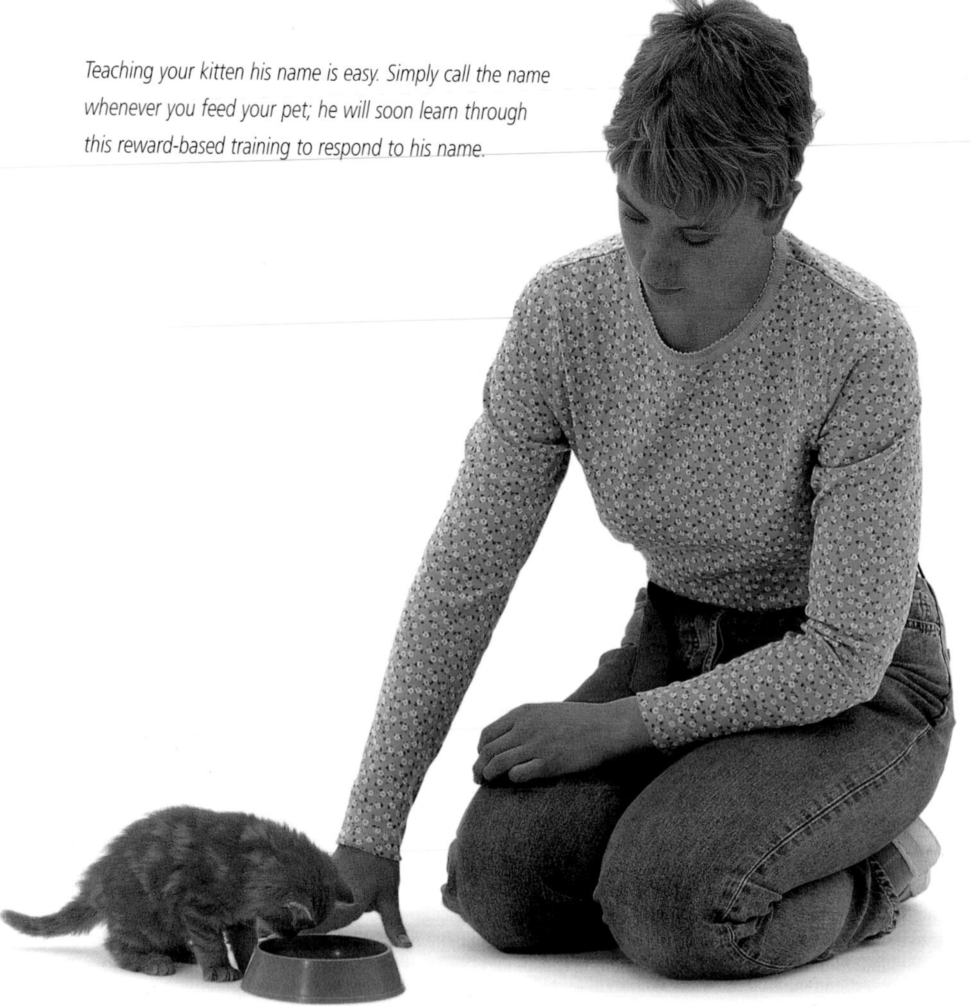

Teaching your kitten his name is easy. Simply call the name whenever you feed your pet; he will soon learn through this reward-based training to respond to his name.

Top tip

Before you bring your kitten home, ask the breeder or owner for a diet sheet so that you can buy in a supply of the same food items. The diet sheet should also include details of mealtimes and how much food to give. This will reduce the risk of you overfeeding your kitten or supplying too rich a menu, either of which could lead to him having a stomach upset.

Juvenile behaviour

After sleeping and eating, playing rates highly in a kitten's priorities. He will amuse himself for hours with a selection of toys. These do not need to be expensive, shop-bought ones for your kitten to have maximum fun: ping-pong balls, cardboard tubes and old soft and cuddly toys will do the job just as well. Make sure, though, that none of the toy items can break or come apart easily, as inquisitive kittens will soon chew off and swallow a teddy's button eyes, or dangling string, which could result in a tummy upset requiring veterinary attention, even surgery.

You can both enjoy hours of amusement simply by dragging a length of string along the ground for your kitten to chase, pounce on, and 'kill'. Never leave balls of wool or lengths of string unattended with a kitten, however, for the reasons given above.

Fishing rod-style toys, again, should only be used when you are there to supervise their use; cats risk strangling themselves by being allowed access to these play items when their owners are not around to supervise.

Praise, reward and punishment

Cats love praise and appreciate rewards, but they do not understand punishment as humans do; therefore they cannot respond to physical or verbal reprimands in the same way that humans might. For this reason, you must praise and reward any desired behaviour. Your kitten will soon learn that certain behaviour produces good things, and will therefore strive to attain these, whereas other types of behaviour produce no satisfactory response on your part, and therefore are unrewarding for him. If your kitten displays any kind of undesired behaviour, try to convert it into something more desirable (see pages 84–89).

Never physically reprimand your kitten, as this will not do any good; it will only serve to frighten him and alienate him from you. Remember that building trust takes a good deal of time, but destroying it can only take a second of inappropriate response on your part.

Behaviour training

Start as you mean to go on. Instilling desired behaviour traits in a kitten will usually result in a sociable and well-behaved cat, bearing in mind the praise, reward and punishment ideals described above. For example, if you let your kitten sleep on your bed, then he will naturally expect to do so as an adult. So think ahead – behaviour you may find acceptable in a kitten may not be quite as desirable in an adult cat, yet the cat will not understand why you have changed your response. If you don't wish your cat to sleep on your bed as an adult, don't let him do so as a kitten and therefore come to expect this as the norm; denying him access to your bed later on may result in behavioural problems.

For many owners, training a kitten to perform a range of basic, acceptable actions by means of kind, gentle and effective methods is a mutually rewarding exercise. It really does help to be open to the feline view of the world to be able to communicate effectively (see pages 58–75).

Litter-training

Usually, a kitten will be litter-trained when ready for rehoming. However, once in his new home you will need to show him where his new toilet facilities are. Try to use the same type of tray and litter as he had in his previous home, so that the change will not be too radical – cats are creatures

Young cats are vulnerable outside, so do not let them out unaccompanied until they are well grown and have familiarized themselves with the garden and surrounding area with you in attendance.

of habit. Bringing some of the kitten's used litter home with you and placing it in his new tray may help acclimatize him to his new facilities.

Did you know ...?

- Friendly feline mothers are likely to produce sociable kittens, because they show their offspring that there is nothing to be afraid of.
- The genes a kitten inherits from his father will determine how friendly he will become. His mother's genes will also play a part, but the effect is not so strong.

Environment and safety

Being naturally bold and curious – the world inside and outside the home is one big exciting playground to them – kittens can get into all sorts of trouble and distress if left to their own devices. See pages 46–53 and 76–79 for information on keeping your kitten or cat safe.

Going outside

After keeping your kitten indoors for a few weeks, he will have become self-confident enough to venture outside. While he is small (and only when his course of vaccinations has been completed), you should only let him out when you are around to supervise him until he gets used to his outdoor environment and is able to find his way around the garden and back into the house. This is the ideal time to introduce him to a cat flap (see the 'Frequently asked question' on page 108).

Kittens are at risk from adult cats in the area, as well as dogs and other hazards, including traffic. Being cute in appearance, kittens are also much more likely to be picked up and taken home by well-meaning people who, seeing him all alone, think he has been abandoned. This is why it is so important that young cats are supervised outside until they become 'streetwise'.

Vaccinations

For a multitude of reasons, some people are in favour of vaccinating cats, while others are against it (the frequency of booster jabs being a particular bone of contention). On balance – particularly from the veterinary point of view and in the absence of scientific evidence to prove otherwise – vaccinations are to be recommended against the nasty, often lethal diseases that cats can fall victim to. Some insurance companies insist that cats are vaccinated before they will issue policies; if vaccinations are not kept up to date, the insurers may not pay out in the event of a claim, so check the policy terms before signing up. See pages 138–139 for further information regarding vaccinations.

Two kittens will provide great companionship and entertainment for each other. Play-fighting may sometimes look – and sound – alarming to the owner, but kittens rarely damage each other. This is all part of the essential defend-and-fight learning process, which teaches them to assess other cats' strengths and weaknesses, for when they may have to defend themselves against feline intruders and other outside aggressors.

Veterinary health checks

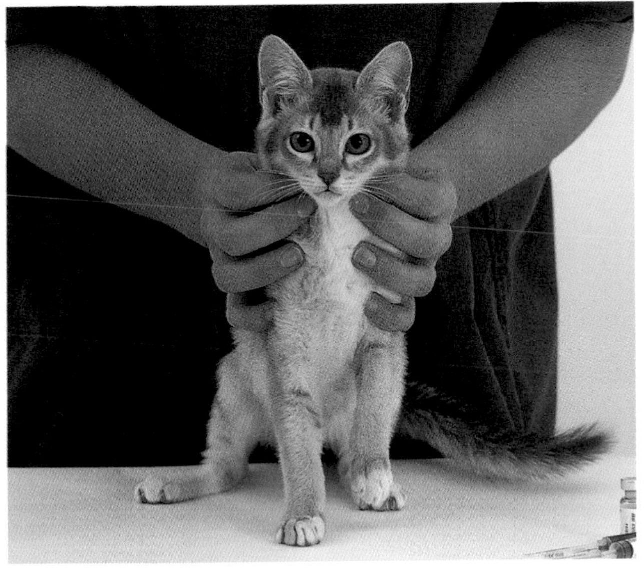

Checking your kitten's body condition will tell your vet how good his physical state is.

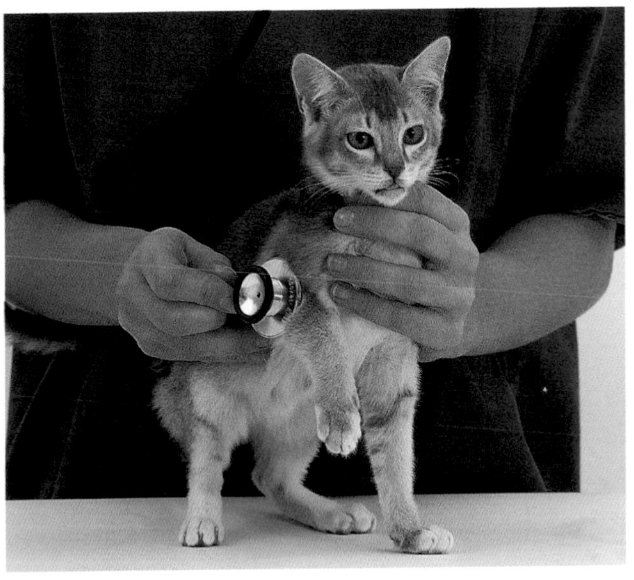

A full veterinary examination will involve a number of basic tests, including a heart function evaluation using a stethoscope to listen to the heartbeat (see Feline fact, page 99 for vital signs readings).

An initial check-up is likely to include a rectal temperature reading. For ease of use and minimum discomfort for both parties, an aural thermometer is available for owners to check their pet's temperature (see Feline fact, page 99 for vital signs readings).

Your kitten will lose his milk teeth at the age of about five months; your vet will be able to tell if teething is occurring without problems, and, if not, will advise on treatment accordingly.

Accustom your kitten to having his teeth cleaned from the start, so that he comes to view it as a normal process. Trying to clean an older cat's teeth if he is not used to it is extremely difficult, and often impossible. (See Brushing teeth on page 115 for more information on this subject.)

Visiting the vet

Take your kitten for regular check-ups, so the vet can monitor his development and catch any potential problems early, and also so that your kitten becomes accustomed to going to the clinic and is therefore not frightened by the experience. Many vets like to see their patients just for a cursory look-over and a cuddle, so that the animal does not view them just as someone who does only unpleasant things to him.

Worming

Internal parasites can cause all sorts of problems, even death, so it pays to consult your vet regarding a worming programme for your kitten. A typical regime is to deworm kittens aged four to sixteen weeks every two weeks with an appropriate roundworm product. When the kitten is six months old, it will require deworming every two to six months, depending on its lifestyle, for roundworms and tapeworms. Consult your vet for advice. (See page 138 for more information.)

Frequently asked question

What is the best way to teach my kitten to use a cat flap?

A Once your kitten knows his name and is used to going outside under your supervision, you can introduce him to a cat flap. Some self-confident kittens quickly learn that desired access to inside or outside is achieved by pushing against the cat flap, but others may need a little more encouragement. In the latter case, kittens tend to be quite food-motivated, so a little bribery can have the desired effect. Simply encouraging the kitten through the flap (which can be taped open at first if necessary) with a tasty morsel of his favourite food will usually do the trick. Take it one stage at a time – slowly but surely – and continue at your kitten's pace. Don't try to hurry your pet, as this will probably have the opposite effect. Never try to push your kitten through the cat flap in an attempt to show him what to do – this may frighten him and perhaps put him off cat flaps for life.

Flea control

If your kitten enjoys an outdoor lifestyle, or comes into contact with other cats or dogs that do, then he will almost certainly require defleaing on a regular basis. Fleas can cause all manner of unpleasant ailments, including anaemia and flea allergic dermatitis, and can be a problem all year round if not kept under control. Your vet is the best person to ask regarding a suitable flea control product for your kitten. (See page 138 for more information on fleas and how to control them.)

Trimming claws

Unlike outdoor cats, who are able to keep their claws worn to a reasonable length naturally, cats that are kept indoors may need a bit of help to ensure their claws remain in good condition and do not get too long. It is easier to get kittens used to having their claws trimmed than it is to start the procedure with older cats. Ideally, claw-clipping, if necessary, should be carried out by an expert. If you do opt to do it yourself, however, ask a vet, an expert breeder or a professional cat groomer to show you how to do it – this is the best way of learning how to trim claws humanely to the correct length.

Trimming the ends of the claws does not hurt the cat, as long as the nail bed or quick (the thin vein that runs down the nail, and which you can usually see) is not nicked; if it is, great pain will ensue – as well as profuse bleeding. If you catch the quick, the cat is unlikely ever to put up with having his claws clipped again.

Providing your kitten with a good-quality wooden scratching post (complete with bark if you can find one – perhaps even a tree branch from the garden) will help avoid the need to trim claws.

In some countries (but not in the UK where it is considered inhumane) it is legal for veterinary surgeons to completely declaw cats, although some vets will not carry out this procedure as they do not think it ethical. Some owners prefer this to be done so that the cat cannot scratch them or their furniture.

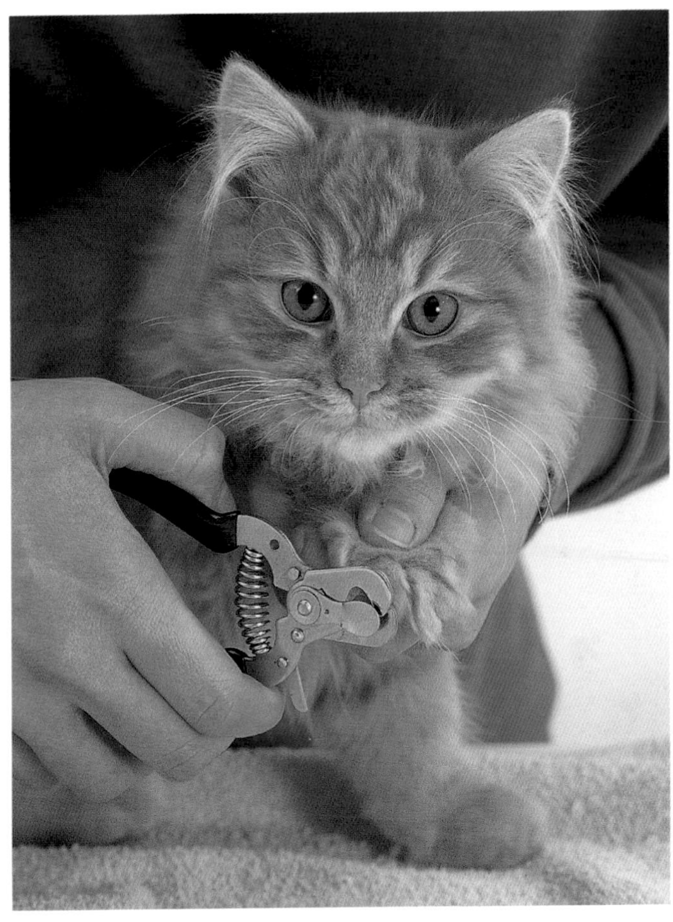

Guillotine-style claw-clippers designed for animal use are the best instrument for trimming claws.

Top tip

Claw clippers must be sharp, and the 'scissor' action must be springy. Always clean them after use with clipper oil and wipe them dry. Keep them in a dry place so they do not rust and become blunt, and resharpen them as necessary.

Grooming

Grooming is an integral part of cat ownership. As well as helping to keep your pet's coat in good condition, carefully and gently grooming him also helps you both to bond. Depending on the coat type of your cat, you will need the right tools for the job, comprising some or all of the items on the checklist.

Checklist

- ✓ blunt-ended comb
- ✓ fine-toothed ('flea') comb
- ✓ wide-toothed comb
- ✓ de-matter
- ✓ grooming mitten
- ✓ soft-bristled brush (for sparse-coated cats)
- ✓ bristle brush
- ✓ slicker brush
- ✓ toothbrush and cat toothpaste
- ✓ cotton wool
- ✓ guillotine-style claw-clippers
- ✓ fine round-ended scissors
- ✓ cat shampoo
- ✓ silk, velvet or chamois leather grooming pad
- ✓ grooming powder
- ✓ box for grooming equipment

Feline fact

Cats get stiffer and less flexible as they get older; seniors often need help to clean the back of their neck and the backs of their hind legs, as they find these areas hard to reach when grooming themselves.

A wide selection of grooming tools is available, for different coat lengths, thicknesses and conditions. Clockwise from top left: ***rubber grooming tool*** *used for gently and thoroughly grooming shorthair coats while massaging the skin and removing dead hair;* ***de-matting tool*** *used for slicing through knotted coats, but over-zealous use can result in a bald cat;* ***combs*** *(with differing tooth lengths depending on coat length) used for grooming short and long coats, particularly useful for longhair tummies, under chins and between the legs, taking care not to pull the skin;* ***slicker brush*** *comprising slender steel angled tines and good for all coat types, again being careful not to snag or drag the skin;* ***combined steel/bristle brush*** *which can be used on all coat types, the brush being particularly good for the head and tail.*

Why groom?

Cats spend much of their waking time grooming, and most are able to do a good job of keeping themselves clean without much help from us. However, longhaired, infirm, arthritic and injured cats do require their owners to groom them to keep their coats in tip-top order and so help them remain mentally and physically healthy.

Long, thick hair – especially the fluffy, soft variety found in Persians – will become tangled, and then form dense mats, if it is not brushed on a regular basis. Should matting occur, grooming the coat out would be far too uncomfortable for the cat, so the only alternative is to cut out the matted parts or, in very bad cases, have the coat clipped off by a vet. Longhairs can also suffer from litter clumping between their toes, so always check for this when grooming, and gently tease (or carefully cut) out any mats.

Regular grooming also reduces the amount of shed hair in the house – which is especially troublesome for owners who suffer allergies.

When grooming, part the fur so you can see down to the roots, and check for signs of ticks (as here) and fleas - either the actual flea or traces of their faeces. Grooming is also a good opportunity to check the cat all over for any unusual lumps and skin ailments.

Furballs

A furball (or hairball) is an accumulation of hair in the cat's stomach that occurs as a direct result of him grooming himself. A solid mass of hair forms which rubs against the lining of the stomach; this irritation prompts the cat to vomit the furball up. If the furball lodges further down the digestive tract, it may cause a blockage; if this occurs, the cat may show signs of a decreased appetite, constipation and general lethargy. Seek veterinary attention if you suspect a furball blockage. Grooming your cat regularly will help prevent problems of this nature.

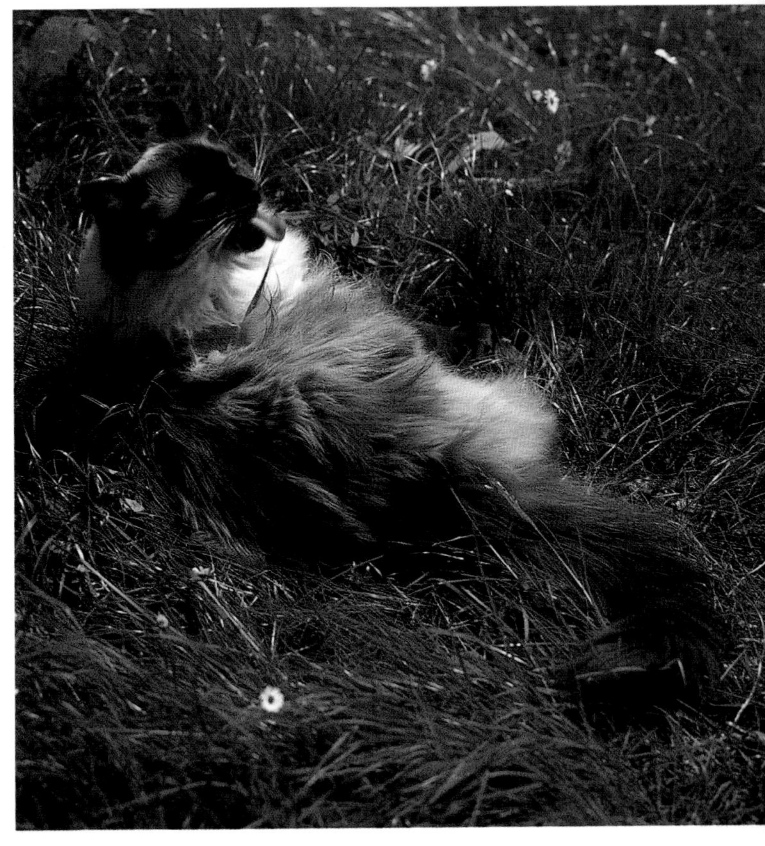

All cats produce furballs (or hairballs), but longhaired types tend to suffer more due to the quantity of hair they ingest while grooming themselves. The cat's tongue has a rough surface with a series of backward-facing spines that act like a comb, removing loose hairs, which the cat then swallows. Cats will often eat grass, which acts as an emetic, to help them vomit up furballs.

Step-by-step grooming guide for long coats

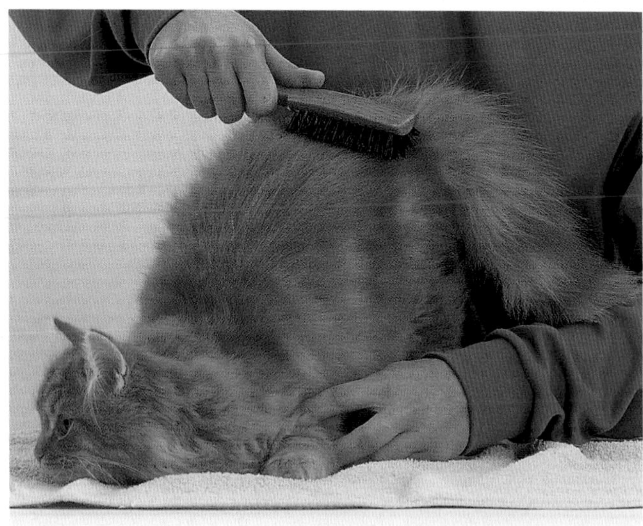

1 Do the back first: brush in the direction the hair is lying, working backwards from head to tail. Grooming powder can be used on especially soft coats that are prone to matting, as this will help separate the hairs, soak up excess natural coat oils and thus aid easier combing and brushing. Sprinkle the powder on and work it into the coat with your fingertips before brushing and combing it all out.

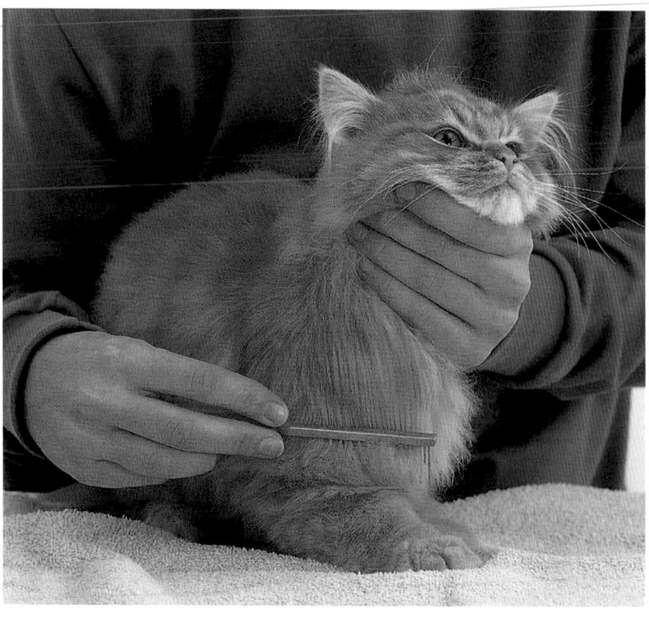

2 Comb out loose hair, without pulling on any knots, as this will be painful for the cat. Gently tease these out by holding the hair near the skin with one hand while the other combs. Don't tug at a knot.

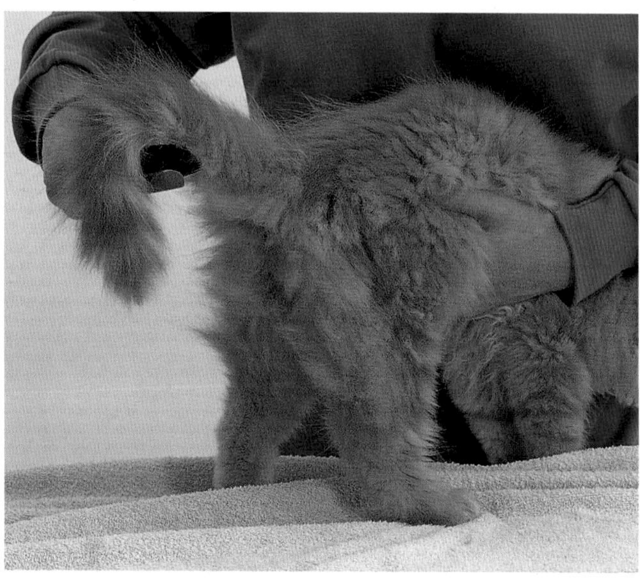

4 Use a soft brush on the tail, too, as this is very sensitive.

5 Wipe around the eyes and nose with cotton wool moistened with lukewarm water (squeezing excess out). Use a fresh piece for each eye and for the nose. Then very gently wipe under the tail with another piece of cotton wool. Use dry cotton wool to dry the areas wiped.

3 With a soft bristle brush, gently brush the tummy.

6 A toothbrush is ideal for grooming the facial area. Finish off grooming by stroking the cat all over with the grooming pad to leave a smooth, silky and shiny finish to the coat. If the claws need trimming, do this last (see page 109).

When to groom

Once a week for shorthaired cats should be sufficient, whereas longhairs ideally need daily attention. The more often you do it, the easier and quicker it is to keep the coat tangle-free, glossy and looking good. You need to pick your moment when to groom – waking the cat up to do it is not a good idea, and neither is grooming when he is fractious or unsettled for some reason. If your cat becomes fidgety and stressed by grooming because he was not accustomed to it from an early age, then do it little and often to gradually get him used to the procedure.

Never force the cat to be groomed; wait until he is in an amenable mood before trying again. Offering tiny morsels of his favourite food can help settle him and take his mind off what you are doing, as well as help him to associate grooming with something rewarding and pleasurable.

Having someone help by holding the cat can sometimes prove useful – they can talk to him and offer treats to distract him while you concentrate on the grooming.

Grooming short coats

Simply using your hand to groom will suffice for many shorthairs; this will loosen and stroke off dead hairs and tone muscles, while also being a pleasurable and soothing experience for both you and your cat.

Alternatively, use a moderately stiff brush to brush lightly but thoroughly from head to tail to remove any loose hair. Pay particular attention to the throat, armpits and inner thighs. Next, use a fine-toothed comb all over from head to tail to remove parasites, grit, scurf and loose hairs. Then use cotton wool moistened with lukewarm water to wipe around the eyes, nose and under the tail – use a clean piece for each. Finally, wipe over with the grooming pad to leave the coat soft and shiny.

Top tip

Always do a small skin patch test 24 hours before bathing with a wet or dry product to ensure your cat is not allergic to it.

When bathing your cat, take care not to get water or soap in his ears as all cats find this very distressing.

Bathing

Cats do not usually need bathing (in fact, most hate being wet at all), unless:

- you are preparing for a show.
- the coat has become very soiled or contaminated with chemicals or oil.
- the cat needs shampooing with a fungicidal or insecticidal wash for veterinary reasons (in which case you should wear protective plastic gloves). Always use a specially formulated cat shampoo and coat conditioner – never products intended for use on human hair, as these may prove harmful if absorbed through the cat's skin or accidentally ingested. You will probably need an assistant while bathing your pet, even if he has been accustomed to the procedure since kittenhood. It is easiest to bathe the cat in the kitchen sink.
- Quarter-fill the sink with lukewarm water (comfortable to the elbow-touch test) and place the cat in it.
- Ladle water over the body, until the fur is saturated.
- Use your hands to carefully wet the cat's face.
- Massage in the shampoo, but do not get any on the face or near the eyes.
- Refill the sink with clean lukewarm water (or use a spray attachment) and rinse all the shampoo out of the coat. You will probably have to replace the water several times to ensure no soap traces remain.
- If using a separate conditioner, massage this into the coat; leave for the recommended time, then repeat the rinsing process.
- Gently dry the cat as much as you can with a thick, warm, soft towel.
- Place the cat in a warm room to dry off thoroughly, and so that he does not become cold.
- Once dry, groom the coat into place.

Top tip

If the inside ear flap is dirty, use a piece of cotton or cotton wool moistened with water or baby oil to gently clean off wax or dirt. Never poke anything, such as a cotton bud, down into the ear, as you could damage this delicate organ.

Frequently asked question

Q My cat hates getting wet, but for shows I need to make sure his coat is spotlessly clean. Is there an alternative to wet bathing?

A Dry brush-in/brush-out shampoos are available, and also those that can simply be sprayed onto the coat and massaged in, and do not need rinsing out; both are well worth considering.

Brushing teeth

Regularly cleaning your cat's teeth will help prevent tooth decay, gum disease such as gingivitis, and bad breath. Toothbrushes specifically designed for kittens and cats are available from pet stores or veterinary surgeries, but a soft human toothbrush with a small head will suffice. You must not use human toothpaste – cats hate the taste and the froth it creates. You should also ensure that you take your cat to the vet for regular check-ups, when his teeth will be examined.

Start brushing your cat's teeth when he is a kitten, so he gets used to the treatment. Begin by simply dipping the brush in warm water, and placing it inside your kitten's cheek for a few seconds while gently holding his mouth closed. Reassure him with soothing words, and repeat with the other cheek. Do this every day, gradually extending the period the brush is held in your kitten's mouth, until he is no longer concerned about it. At this stage, begin to move the brush in a small circle, starting with the back teeth, as these are less sensitive than the front teeth. In a few weeks you should be able to brush both the front and back teeth without causing the kitten any concern. At this stage you can introduce a small amount of feline toothpaste. Rubber finger stalls may also be used instead of a toothbrush.

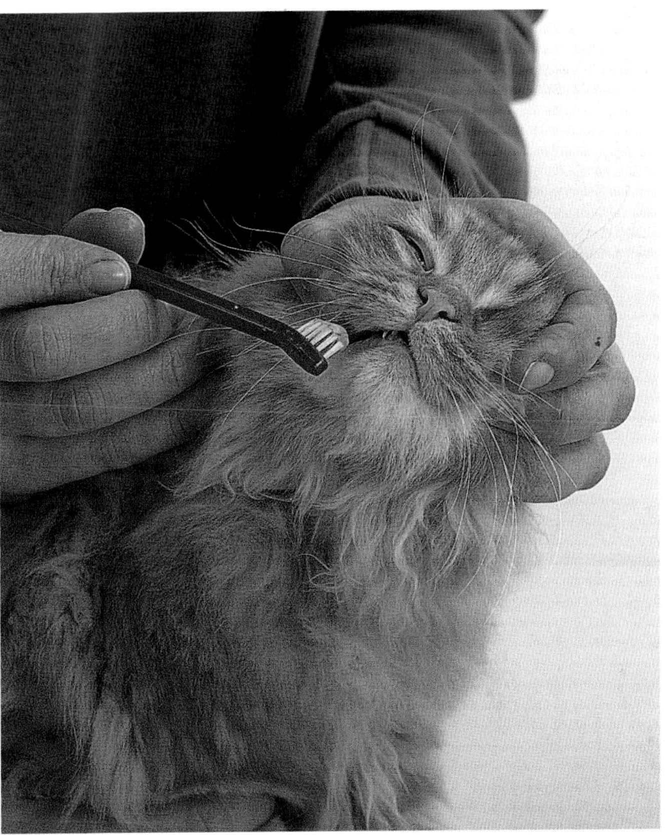

Brushing your cat's teeth with a child's soft toothbrush (or one designed for cats) and special toothpaste formulated for felines (never use one intended for humans) helps to prevent the tartar build-up on teeth that leads to gum disease and tooth decay. In order to be able to do this safely and effectively, ask your vet or a veterinary nurse to show you how to carry out this procedure.

Did you know ...?

Giving your cat a small strip of raw meat every day to chew on will help keep his gums and teeth in good order. Suitable meats include poultry, rabbit or beef that has been deboned.

Cats and travel

There are going to be occasions when you will need to be away from home – for holidays, visiting friends and family, going into hospital, business trips – and you will have to make arrangements for your cat to be looked after. There are several options to choose from (see the checklist) depending on the circumstances.

Checklist

✓ boarding cattery
✓ friends, family and neighbours
✓ petsitter
✓ taking the cat with you

Thinking ahead

Whichever option you choose, make the arrangements well in advance because:

• you will need to ensure your pet's vaccinations are up to date
• you may need to get a pet passport if taking your cat abroad
• good catteries get booked up quickly for peak times, as do petsitters, and you need to check them out first
• you need to be sure that caring for your cat is convenient for friends, family or neighbours while you are awa.
• if intending to take the cat with you, you need to check whether your accomodation is suitable for cats
• you need to get your pet used to travelling

Boarding catteries

Seek recommendations for local boarding catteries from vets and cat-owning friends, neighbours and relatives. Visit the establishment(s) first to check them out for yourself. Your cat will need to be vaccinated against relevant diseases before entering a cattery, so ensure his inoculations are up to

Feline fact

An older cat may present a problem at holiday times, as he may not settle well in a cattery. If this is the case, having someone come in daily to keep an eye on him and provide for his needs may be the best option in your absence if you are going to be away for more than a couple of days. This will avoid any major disruption to your cat's lifestyle, but it is not the same as having company at home, and may only work if your pet is used to letting himself in and out of the home through a cat flap. An indoor-only cat may suffer from loneliness and become depressed in this situation, so a petsitter may be a better choice.

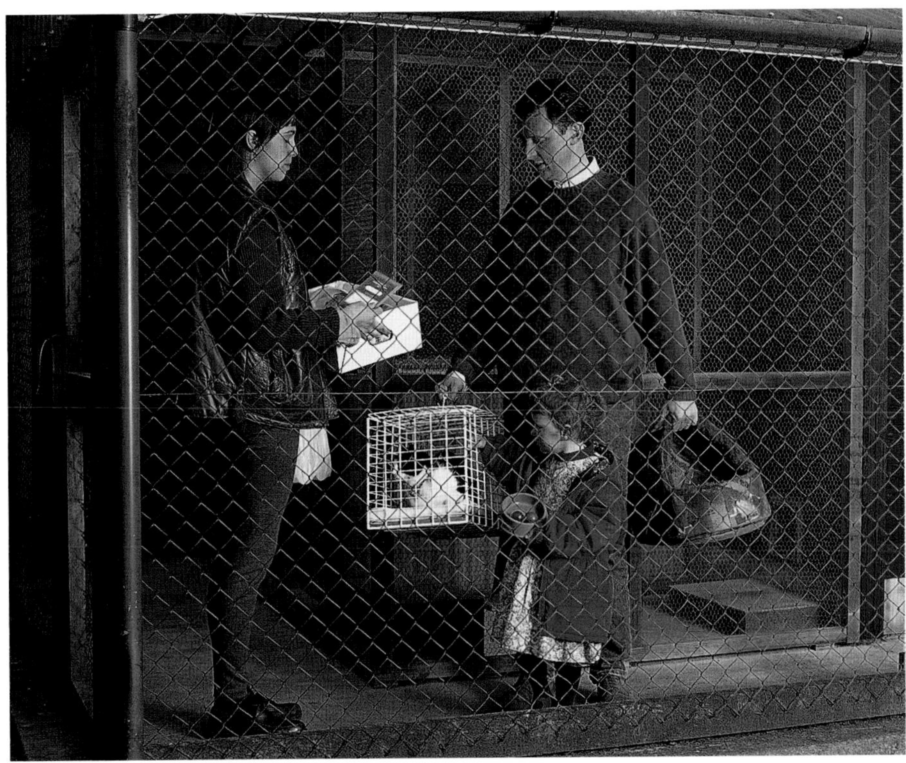

Taking the cat's bed, bedding and favourite toys with him to a cattery will help him settle and feel more at home.

Did you know ...?

If your cat suffers from a contagious disease, such as FeLV (see page 173), catteries will not accept him for fear of him passing the condition on to others. In such circumstances, you will have to make alternative arrangements for your cat when you are away. Similarly, if your cat is unwell on the day you present him at the cattery, the proprietor has the right to refuse to take him.

date well in advance. Take the vaccination certificate with you when you take your pet to the cattery, as they will want to check that it is current.

The best catteries are purpose-built, with each cat having his own small cabin and outdoor run. The cabin should be clean, dry and warm, with room for a bed, food and water bowls, and the cat's belongings; the adjoining run should be secure with room for the litter tray, exercise, a 'sunning/lookout' shelf, and a scratching post. Indoor catteries are not ideal as there is greater risk of infections spreading between cats due to inadequate airflow.

Petsitters

A good option, particularly if you have a number of pets, is to arrange for a petsitter to stay in your house while you are away for any length of time. Although this can be quite expensive, it does give you peace of mind knowing that both your pet and your house will be well looked after. Be sure to use a reputable agency – ideally one recommended by word of mouth – which chooses its staff carefully and offers insurance in case of any mishaps.

Petsitters are trained to look after all sorts of animals, with some specializing in and preferring particular species, so ask for someone who is cat-orientated. You can find petsitters advertised in cat magazines and on the internet.

Having a reliable person to come in at least twice a day to feed and water, clean out litter trays and provide affection can be an ideal solution for those cats who do not settle in catteries.

Top tips

If you are leaving your cat in the care of someone while you are away, give them the following details before you depart:

- feeding and litter-tray cleaning routine
- any specific dos and don'ts regarding your pet's care
- any medication information, if your cat is receiving any
- contact details for you in case of an emergency
- contact details of your vet (provide a map of how to get there if the person is not familiar with the area)
- your cat's insurance details

Cats should always be transported in a secure carrier. The more used they are to travelling, the less disturbing they will find it.

Taking the cat with you

If you want to take your cat away with you on a regular basis within your own country, then you need to get him used to travelling, whether by car or public transport. Train him to accept this from an early age, by taking him out for short journeys. Check with public-transport companies regarding pet travel, as some have specific rules and regulations about this.

To help him feel secure, put his blanket and favourite toy(s) in the carrier. Ensure the car is not too warm and that there is plenty of ventilation, otherwise the cat may become heat-distressed. Never let him out of the carrier, however, except in an emergency. Taking a fold-up pen with you can be a good idea, so that the cat is secure in your hotel room when you are not there.

Taking a cat abroad

Recent changes in legislation now allow for pet travel without the need for quarantine in many countries. Find out what the regulations are in your country, as the rules regarding pet travel do vary, and are constantly being updated and reviewed. To do so, contact the relevant government department (in the UK, it is the Department for the Environment, Food and Rural Affairs). The Pet Travel Scheme (PETS) now applies to pet cats and dogs that are resident in a PETS-qualifying country. Before you attempt to take your cat out of the country in which you are resident, and bring him back in again, you must find out:

- what, if any, restrictions apply
- what you need to do to comply with rules regarding pet identification, vaccination and parasite treatment
- how far in advance you need to do the above procedures

Frequently asked question

Q I would like to take my cat on weekend breaks away. Is this a good idea?

A Bear in mind that, being territorial creatures, some cats do not adapt very well to being removed from their home ground, and doing this can upset them greatly, which will lead to a miserable time away from home for all concerned. Outgoing, confident cats that are very owner/people-orientated tend to be better at coping with travel than more shy and retiring ones. If you understand your cat well, you will know whether taking him away with you would be a good idea or not. Some hotels and other types of accommodation welcome pets and have facilities to cater for them.

CARE OPTIONS	PROS	CONS
Cattery	• Least hassle to arrange • Safety and security • You know your cat will be looked after properly • Should he become ill or injured, he will receive appropriate and immediate treatment	• Expensive • Cat must be vaccinated • Disease-carrying and ill cats will not be admitted • Risk of contracting disease • Cat may pine
Visiting care at home	• No cost • Cat can remain in familiar surroundings • No need for vaccinations if you are against them	• Cat will not be supervised all the time • An only cat may get lonely • Can you rely on the carer to see to your cat at least once a day and care for him properly? • If the cat becomes ill or injured, he may not get immediate appropriate treatment
Staying with carer	• No cost • Cat will possibly have company all the time • No need to vaccinate	• Cat may escape and get lost • Cat may not settle well in unfamiliar territory and become depressed or develop behavioural problems
Petsitter	• Cat will have experienced company and care all the time • No need to vaccinate • Your house will also be looked after	• Expensive • You may not want a stranger in your home
Taking your cat with you	• You know your cat is receiving your proper and appropriate attention • Your cat will have company all of the time	• It can be difficult to find cat-friendly accommodation • Organizing PETS eligibility when going abroad (see page 120) can prove expensive and complicated • Your cat may escape and get lost • Your cat may not enjoy travelling • Your cat may not settle well • Your cat may contract a disease

HEALTH CARE

Like every other mammal, the cat has a body skeleton that protects his internal organs, enabling him to process food and reproduce. Powerful muscles are attached to the skeleton to allow motion. The cat mates with the opposite sex and the female bears live young which are suckled and reared by the mother until they are able to survive alone.

All cats, whatever their breed, share the same physiology (the way in which a living creature functions); they differ only in minor ways to produce a more compact or elongated conformation, with some displaying anomalies of fur, balance or bone structure caused by particular mutations or selective breeding.

Many medical problems can be avoided by ensuring that a cat has a good diet and good exercise, and by the owner being aware of early symptoms that all is not well with their pet.

From routine parasite control to vaccination, reproduction to neutering, this section tells you all you need to know about feline physiology and health.

The feline body

The feline body is a remarkable feat of natural engineering that has evolved into an animal possessing great beauty, grace and athletic prowess. To keep your cat in peak condition, it helps to know how your pet's body is constructed; how it works; how to recognize when something is wrong; what to do when your cat is ill or injured. Whatever the species, members of the Felidae family are characterized by the elements in the checklist.

Checklist

- ✓ a slender yet strong and supple body
- ✓ a short, round head in proportion to size
- ✓ erect ears that are broad at the base and taper upwards
- ✓ powerful legs, especially the hind legs
- ✓ dense fur
- ✓ whiskers
- ✓ great climbing and leaping agility
- ✓ five toes on the fore paws and four on the rear
- ✓ sharp, curved claws which retract (with the exception of the cheetah) on all toes
- ✓ 16 teeth in the upper jaw, 14 in the lower

Bones

A cat's body may be much smaller than a human's, but it contains more bones – some 230 to a human's 206. The skeleton of a cat is made up of a semi-rigid framework that supports other, softer structures.

The bones of the spine, limbs, shoulders and pelvis (working together with muscles and tendons), comprise a system of efficient levers to aid movement, while the skull, ribcage and pelvis protect the major organs they contain.

There are four distinct types of bone – long, short, irregular and flat bones – and each type has a particular function. They are joined together to make up the skeleton via tendons and ligaments.

Bones in the feline body

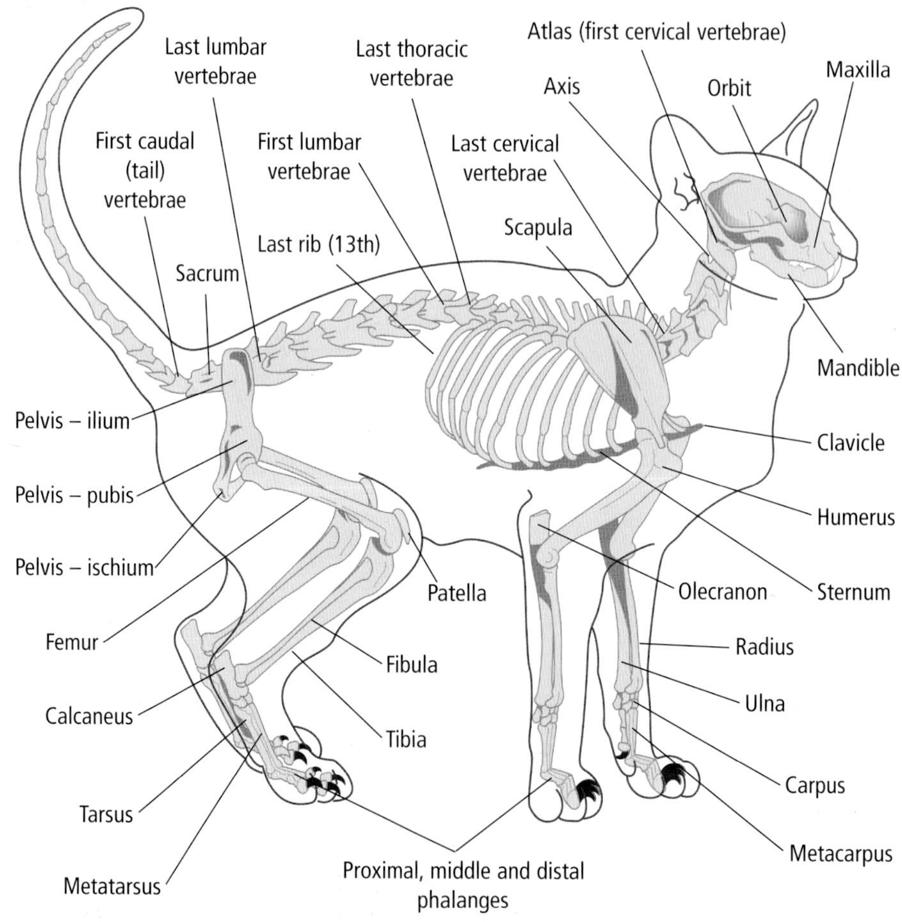

Long bones

These are cylindrical and have hollow shafts that contain the vital bone marrow in which blood cells are manufactured. They form the cat's limbs. Feline long bones are the humerus, radius, femur (thigh bone), tibia and fibula.

Short bones

These consist of a spongy core surrounded by compact bones. They are the bones in the feet and the patella (kneecap – where the femur joins the tibia).

Irregular bones

So called because of their irregular shapes, these bones are similar in structure to short bones. A long string of irregular bones make up the spine (vertebral column) and tail. The irregular projections of the bones in the spinal column serve as attachment points for the various muscles of the cat's back.

Flat bones

These are made of two layers of compact bone with a spongy layer sandwiched between them, and comprise the skull, pelvis and shoulder blades (scapulae). Flattened and elongated bones make up the cat's 13 pairs of ribs; these bones are not hollow but contain a substantial amount of marrow, which produces blood cells.

Ligaments and tendons

Ligaments are short bands of tough, fibrous connective tissue that connect bones or cartilage, or hold together a joint. They are also membranous folds that support organs and keep them in position.

Tendons are flexible but inelastic cords of strong fibrous tissue attaching muscles to bone.

Muscular system

Overlying the skeletal framework is a complex network of muscles that gives the cat his powerful and graceful movement, and is also responsible for his sinuous shape. There are three types of muscle in the feline body: cardiac, smooth (involuntary) and striped (voluntary).

Cardiac muscle

This specialized muscle forms the heart, and possesses unique powers of rhythmic contraction to pump blood around the body through a network of arteries and veins. A cat's heart works in the same way as a human heart – with four chambers and a double pump.

When jumping down, a cat stretches his body down as far as possible before pushing off, to reduce the distance covered and the shock of landing. Powerfully muscled hind legs allow the cat to leap up to five times his own height. Cats' finely tuned sense of balance enables them to land precisely where they want to.

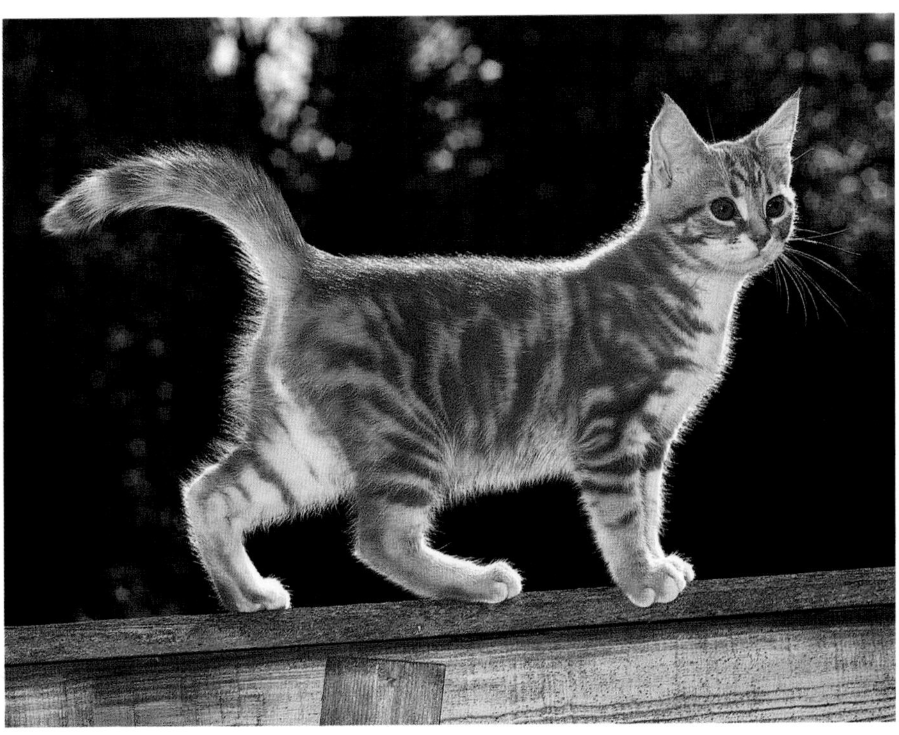

Powerful muscles at the root of the tail, combined with small muscles and tendons along the length of it, enable the cat to move his tail expressively, and also to use it as an important balancing aid.

Smooth (unstriated) muscles

These carry out muscular functions not under the cat's control, and include the muscles of the intestines and walls of blood vessels. They are also called involuntary muscles.

Striped (striated) muscles

These are muscle tissues in which the contractile fibres are arranged in parallel bundles (hence the term 'striped') and are attached to the limbs and other parts of the anatomy which are under the voluntary control of the cat – such as movement. They are also known as voluntary muscles.

Voluntary muscles are usually attached to bones that form a joint. **Extensor muscles** extend and straighten a limb, while **flexor muscles** flex and bend the joint. Muscles that move a limb away from the body are called **abductors**, and **adductors** move them back in again. There are more than 500 voluntary muscles within a cat's body, enabling him to be fluid in his movements.

Respiratory system

Respiration provides the cat's body with the oxygen that is vital for life. During respiration, the cat draws in air through his nasal passages via his nose and mouth. This air passes through the throat (pharynx) and down the windpipe (trachea), through the bronchi and into the lungs. In the lungs, gaseous exchange takes place: carbon dioxide from the blood filters into the air sacs as oxygen passes from the air to replenish the blood. The used air is then exhaled. Breathing is automatic: chest muscles contract and relax, acting like a pump on the ribs and diaphragm, driving air in and out of the lungs. The breathing rate varies in each individual and depends upon:

- age
- exercise
- emotion
- environmental temperature

The normal respiration rate of a healthy, resting, adult cat is 20–30 breaths per minute.

Frequently asked question

Q Why are cats' bodies so flexible?

A Compared with most animals, cats have a small collarbone and more supporting muscle. Their shoulders, therefore, are not rigid; this gives them great flexibility when grooming, or twisting and pouncing on toys and prey. Special vertebrae in the spine allow cats to twist and flex much more than they would be able to do with a more rigid backbone.

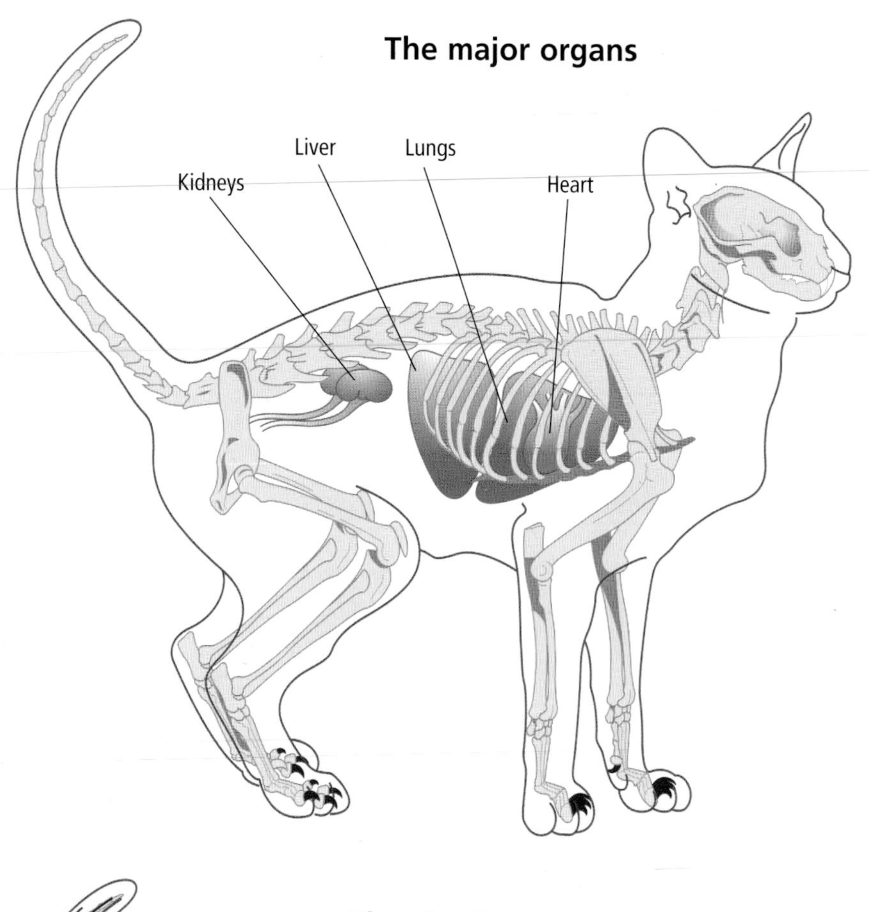

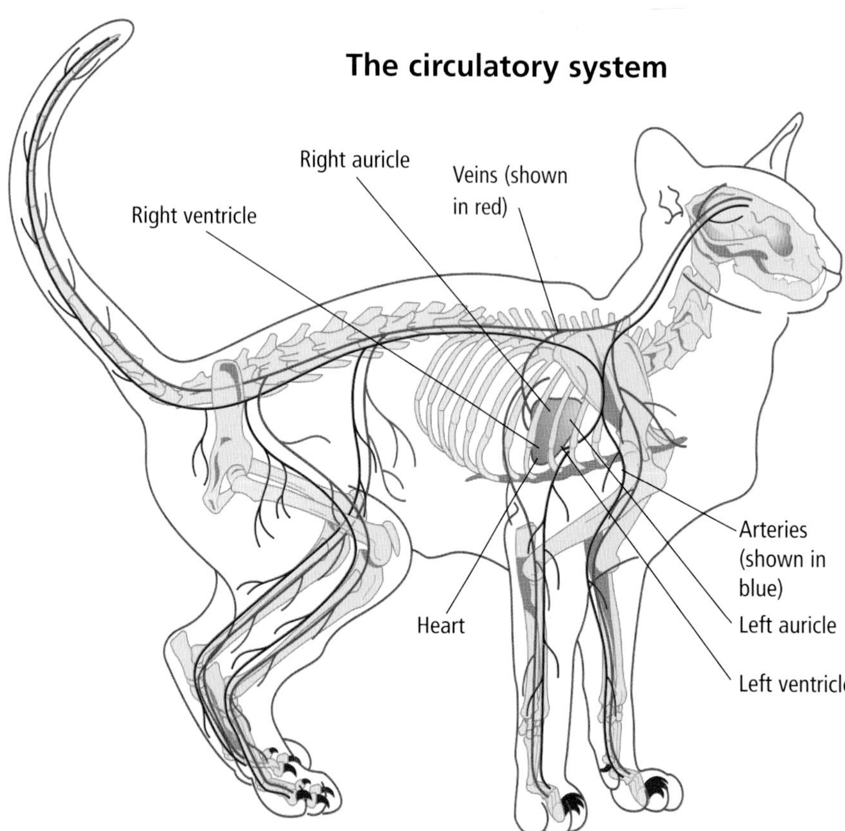

Circulatory system

Every body cell needs a supply of nourishment, and this is achieved via the blood, which delivers it and also removes waste products from the body. Blood is made up of red blood cells and white blood corpuscles that are contained in a fluid called plasma. Plasma contains platelets which contain a blood-clotting agent for use in the event of cuts and wounds.

Red blood cells transport oxygen, while white blood corpuscles collect and transport impurities and bacteria that have invaded the red cells.

Incredible journey

Blood is continually pumped around the body via the four-chambered heart, its journey beginning in the left auricle (upper chamber). Enriched with oxygen from the lungs, the blood from the left auricle travels into the left ventricle (lower chamber), and on into a great artery – the aorta – to run its course quickly through all the arteries and arterioles and into a fine network of capillaries throughout the body, distributing its store of oxygen and nutrients as it goes. As it releases these, the blood collects waste matter (bacteria, dead blood cells and carbon dioxide).

Leaving the capillaries, the blood enters tiny veins (venules) where it begins to slow down, laden with waste products, before passing into the great veins that transport it back to the lungs to dump its rubbish and be replenished with oxygen and nutrients. From here it enters the heart to repeat its journey.

Why cats are usually sleepy after meals

Extra nutrient-rich blood with its nutrients is required by different parts of the body at different times. After a heavy meal, for example, the cat's abdomen draws in extra blood to aid digestion, at the expense of the supply to the brain and other parts of the body. Hence the need of the cat (and indeed other animals) to rest or sleep after eating – the brain is less active and energy is being utilized in digestion rather than in other activities.

Pulse

Blood passing through the aorta causes its walls to expand, and a pressure wave (pulse) passes down the arteries. In a healthy adult cat at rest, the pulse rate is 160–240 beats per minute, depending on environmental temperature and the cat's emotional state at the time.

Digestive system

The cat's digestive system is adapted for a meat-eating hunter that may not always be successful in catching a meal, so may occasionally gorge at a large kill. His mouth construction means that a cat tears or bites at his food, then swallows it quickly, giving the salivary juices virtually no time for the preliminary breakdown of starches into blood sugars. Any starches present in the cat's diet are, therefore, of little nutritional value.

Feline gastric juices are more powerful than those of a human; they are, in fact, strong enough to soften bone. Cats can swallow large chunks of prey creatures (rodents and birds) and any parts such as feathers, hair and bones that are not quickly broken down in the stomach may be regurgitated.

In the stomach, protein is broken down into simple amino acids (basic constituents of proteins). These are then combined to form the building blocks necessary for replacement of cells throughout the cat's body. From the stomach, partly digested food passes through a valve called the pylorus to the small intestine. Further digestion changes take place, aided by secretions from the pancreas and liver. Fats are broken down and extracted, sugars are changed structurally (ready for storage) and minerals are absorbed.

From the small intestine, the now-fluid food contents pass into the large intestine, where they are acted upon by the specialized bacteria present there. Excess water is drawn off and utilized where appropriate, and the waste passes through the colon to be voided as faeces (solids) or as urine (liquid).

Feline fact

Cats can swallow and digest their food without chewing it.

Teeth

Feline teeth are designed to stab, slice and tear at raw, tough and 'chewy' food rather than chew it, and these actions help keep the teeth in good condition. Kittens shed their baby (milk) teeth as their permanent ones come through at around six months. When kittens are born, the teeth are just visible inside the gums, and soon erupt. At six weeks old, a kitten's teeth are strong and needle-sharp so, for obvious reasons, a mother cat will become reluctant to feed her babies, and a natural weaning process takes place, with the youngsters, ideally, having strips of raw meat to chew on.

Occasionally, 'double dentition' occurs, when a kitten does not shed

The skull and teeth

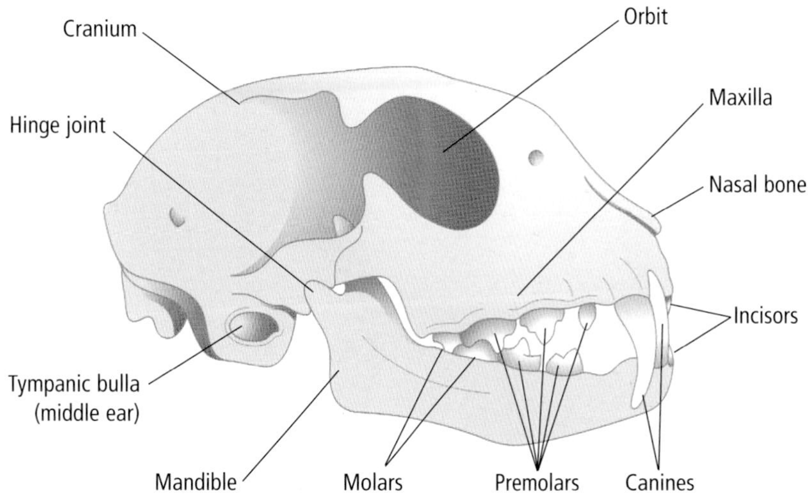

his milk teeth. It may be necessary in such cases for a vet to remove the problem milk teeth so that they do not interfere with secondary tooth growth and action, which could ultimately lead to digestive and other health problems.

Paws and claws

A cat's fore paws are made up of sets of three small bones, each of which forms a digit corresponding to the finger of the human hand. The tiny bones at the end of each digit are highly specialized and articulate so that the claws may be extended or contracted at will. The cat has no thumb, but a corresponding digit that comprises two bones which form the dew claw. In the hind feet the bones are longer and the first toe is absent altogether.

Claws are made up of keratin (the same material which forms hair), and grow continuously from the base, like human fingernails. There are five claws on the fore paws but only four on each hind paw; the fifth claw acts rather like our thumb, helping cats to grip when they climb and when holding prey.

Cats with extra digits (polydactyls)

Occasionally, a cat has more digits than is normal on either or both of the fore and hind paws. This anomaly sometimes occurs in cross-breeds, and is nothing to be concerned about (being no more than a gene mutation) because it does not usually affect a cat's health or movement. If, however, this condition occurs in pedigree cats, it has more serious implications for the breeder, though not for the cat. The cat will not conform to breed standards, and so will have little value. Pedigree cats who are afflicted should therefore not be bred from, so as not to perpetuate the condition.

Skin and fur

Feline skin is made up of two layers of tissue: the **dermis** (inner layer), and the **epidermis** (outer layer), which is constantly being replaced as it dies and sloughs away into tiny flakes of dandruff (dead skin). There are sweat glands on the skin, but these seem to exist mainly for excreting impurities from the body rather than for controlling body temperature. True sweat glands are to be found in the foot pads.

Sebaceous glands open into the hair follicles and produce a semi-liquid, oily substance, called sebum, to coat each new hair as it grows. Scent glands can be found on the

Did you know ...?

The hairless skin (known as leather) of the cat's nose and paws is extremely sensitive to the touch.

The skin and fur

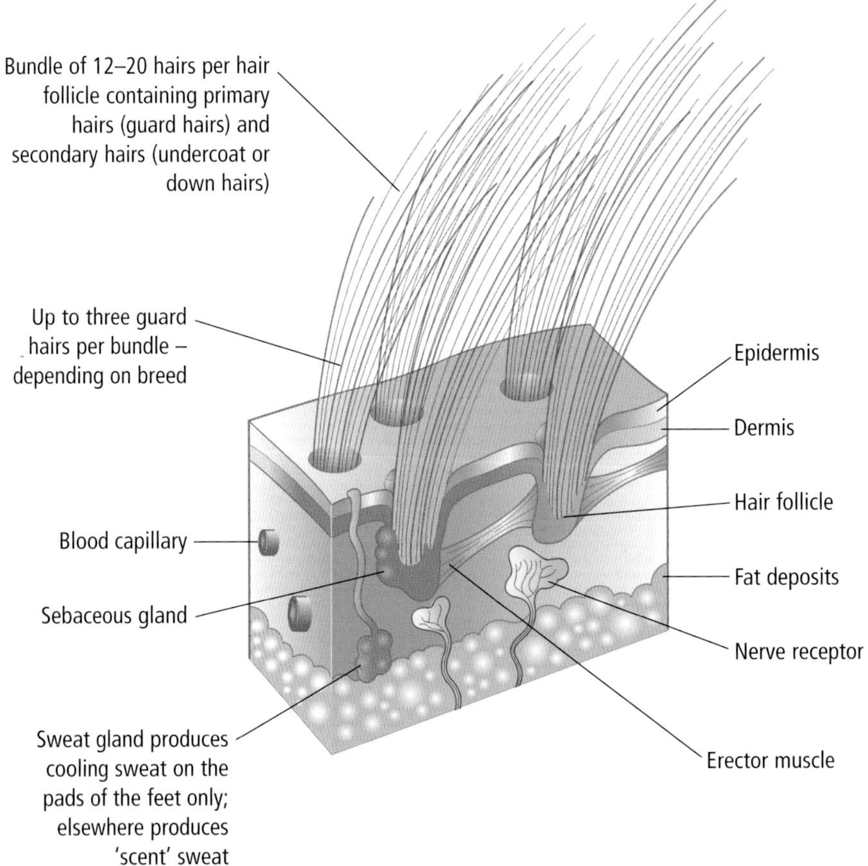

forehead just above the eyes (temporal glands), by the lips (perioral glands) and near the root of the tail.

Hair is derived from the outer layer of skin, and acts as insulatory cover. It is modified in certain areas to provide eyelashes, eyebrows and whiskers. There are three main types of hair.

- **Down hairs** or undercoat hairs are the shortest, thinnest and softest hairs; they lie close to the body and conserve body heat.
- **Awn hairs** form the middle coat and are slightly more bristly, with a swelling towards the tip before it tapers off. They are partly for insulation and partly for protection.
- **Guard hairs** are the thickest, longest and straightest; they form the top coat, which protects the fur below from the elements.

The ratio of down, awn and guard hairs varies greatly between the domestic breeds; in the wildcat, there are approximately 1,000 down hairs to 300 awn hairs and 20 guard hairs.

Whiskers on the side of the face determine whether a space is wide enough for the cat to get through; if the head and shoulders fit, the rest of the body will be able to follow.

Muscles attached to the large follicles enable the hairs to become erect and stand out at right angles to the skin; this occurs, for example, when the cat is alarmed or ill and has an abnormal temperature.

All hairs, especially the guard hairs, are sensitive to the touch, but even more sensitive are the **vibrissae** (whiskers, eyebrows, and similar hairs on the cheeks, chin and behind the forelegs), which are bigger and thicker. Whiskers are deeply embedded in the upper lip and are surrounded by a mass of tiny nerve endings which transmit information about any contact they make and changes in air pressure around them. The vibrissae also act as guides when it is too dark to see, enabling the cat to move without banging into objects.

Cats shed dead hair constantly (especially those that live in centrally heated environments), but those that spend a good deal of time outdoors will grow a thicker winter coat, and then shed this as the temperature warms up again in spring; it is not unusual for their coats to appear quite patchy during this time.

Top tip

In a fit, healthy animal, the skin is pliable; in a sick or dehydrated cat, it is stiff and unyielding. A sudden change from the normal pale pink colouring can indicate illness and needs veterinary investigation.

- **White** can indicate anaemia due to parasite infestation, dietary deficiency or shock.
- **Reddening** indicates inflammatory disease of the skin or underlying tissues.
- **Blue** indicates heart trouble, respiratory disease or poisoning.
- **Yellow** indicates jaundice (liver dysfunction).

Any change of colour in the cat's skin is usually first noticed on the ear flaps, nose, lips and gums.

Feline senses

The nervous and sensory systems of the cat are essential to his health and well-being. Perceptions and reactions to his environment are dependent on his senses; movement is controlled via the central nervous system (brain and spinal cord); and the endocrine system (hormone-producing glands) controls his behaviour patterns. The five faculties by which a cat's body perceives his surroundings are on the checklist.

Checklist

- ✓ sight
- ✓ smell
- ✓ hearing
- ✓ taste
- ✓ touch

The central nervous system

This controls and co-ordinates the cat's everyday activities. Information received by the sensory organs is constantly monitored by the system and dealt with according to its importance: it is acted upon immediately, discarded or stored away for future use, as appropriate. The brain has three clearly defined regions: the fore-brain, the mid-brain and the hind-brain.

When familiar cats meet, sniffing each other confirms visual recognition and gathers information about how the other cat is, where he has been and what he has been doing.

The brain and its functions

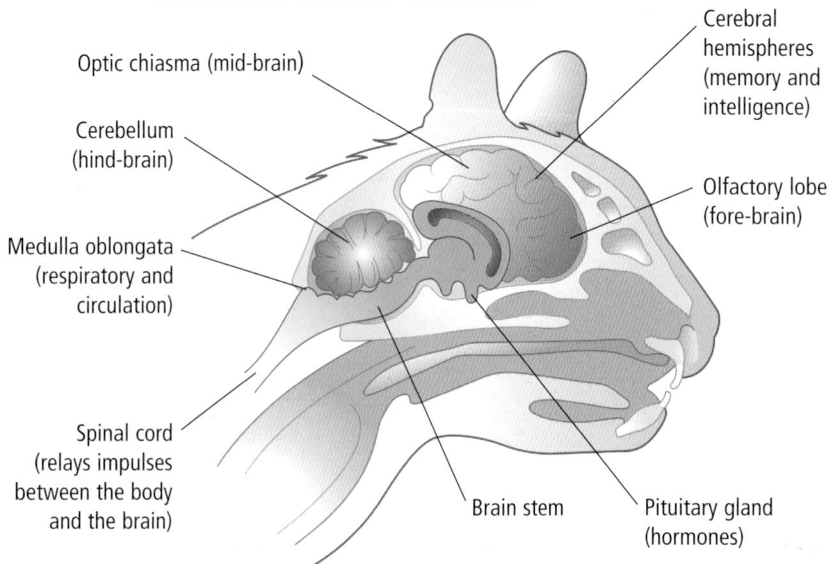

Feline fact

The pads of a cat's feet are very sensitive and incorporate many touch receptors. Some cats behave strangely just before an earthquake hits – perhaps they can detect vibrations of the earth through their sensitive foot pads.

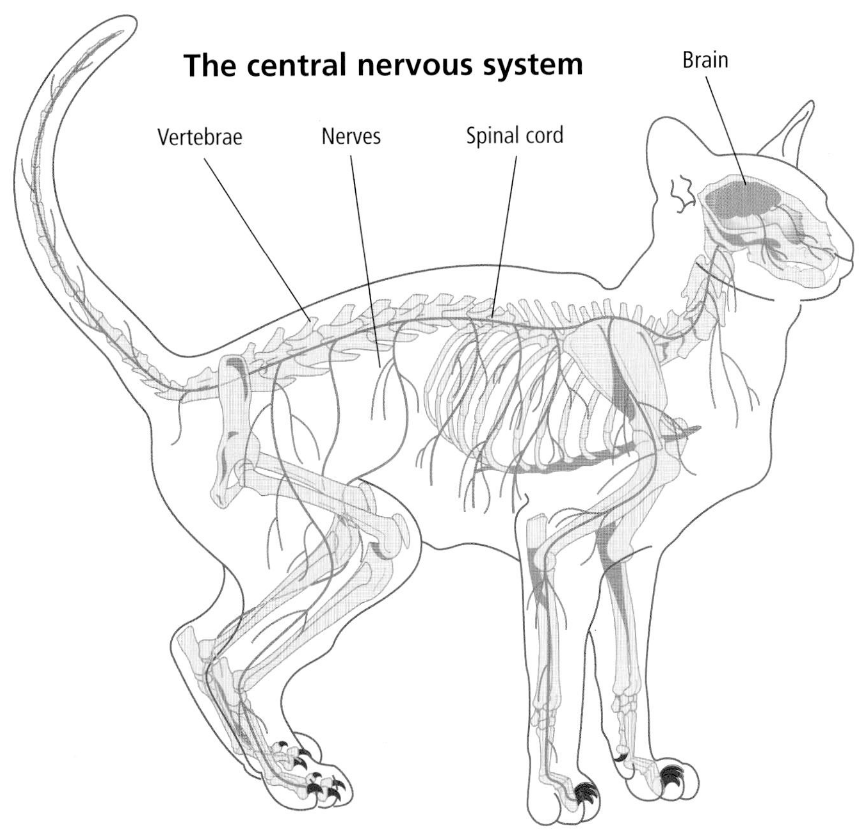

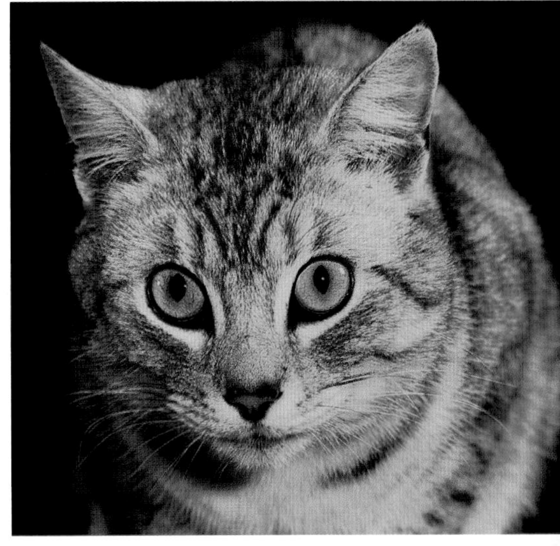

The pupil of the eye opens very wide to admit more light, which passes through the transparent cornea and lens to the retina at the back of the eye. Any light not absorbed by the retina bounces back to a layer of cells known as the tapetum lucidum, which reflects it back to the retinal cells, reinforcing the information transmitted to the brain by the nerves there. Any reflecting light still not absorbed creates the effect of the cat's eyes shining yellow, green or red at night.

Fore-brain

This area is concerned with the sense of smell via the olfactory lobe, memory and intelligence. It also contains the thalamus (which responds to impulses travelling from the spinal cord) and the hypothalmus (which controls the internal regulatory processes).

Mid-brain

This contains the optic lobes and deals with signals stimulated by light; therefore it is responsible for sight.

Hind-brain (core)

Here, the cerebellum controls balance and the enlarged end of the spinal cord forms the medulla, controlling the respiratory and circulatory systems. The pituitary gland (which produces hormones) is situated in this region, as is the limbic system that controls digestion. Unsurprisingly, this part of the brain is vital for the survival of the cat.

Sight

Cats need only one-sixth of the light humans need in order to distinguish the same detail of shape and movement. The eyes face forwards, allowing fields of vision to overlap and giving stereoscopic vision that is slightly wider than ours. This enables the cat to be accurate in judging distances for jumping, or springing and pouncing when hunting.

Being comparatively large, and set in deep skull sockets, feline eyes do

Frequently asked question

Q Why does my cat lie in baking-hot places, like in front of the fire, without appearing to feel discomfort?

A The ancestors of our domestic cats were originally desert-living animals. Consequently, they are comfortable lying in front of an open fire or close to a radiator, even on a surface that is heated up to a temperature too high for humans to stand.

The eye

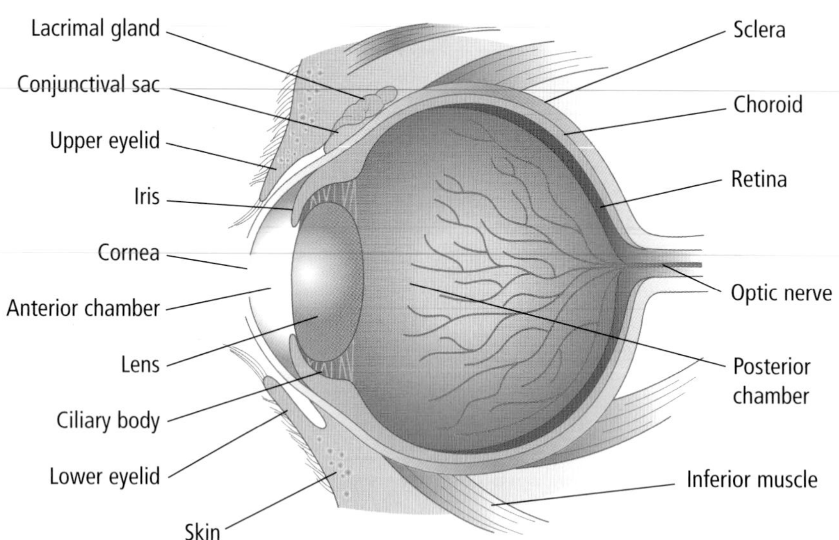

Feline fact

When the cat is out of condition, or ill, a tiny pad of fat beneath the eyeball contracts and causes it to retract slightly into the socket, which results in the haw extending partially across the eye. Being able to see the haw, therefore, is taken to be an indication of ill health.

not move freely, so the cat turns his head to bring objects into sharp focus. Cats are not colour-blind, but see the world in more subtle shades of colour than we do. Their eyes are protected from strong light by the iris contracting to form a slit-like pupil, limiting the amount of light reaching the delicate mechanisms at the back of the eye; when the iris contracts, the sharpness of vision is enhanced. In addition to the upper and lower eyelids, there is a third eyelid, which is called the nictitating membrane or haw. This is a thin sheet of pale tissue tucked away in the corner of the eye. Its function is to remove dust and dirt from the cornea by moving across the surface of the eyeball during any inward movement, and also to keep it moist and lubricated.

The positive response cats make towards fresh meat is more likely to be evoked by smell than by taste.

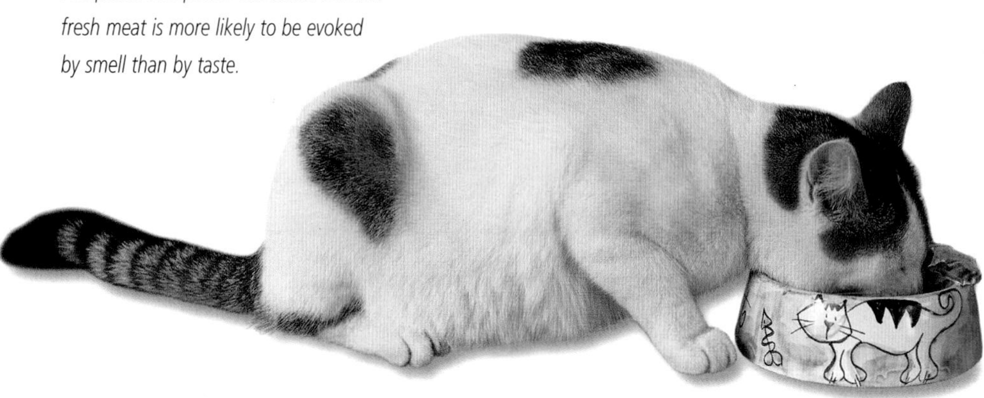

Did you know ...?

• Cats rarely eat carrion and find the smell of tainted or medicated food highly offensive. For this reason, they will rarely eat food that is not fresh or that has been treated with a deworming product.

• The area in the nose for detecting scent is ten times larger in cats than it is in humans. They also have a correspondingly larger part of the brain to help them decipher scent messages.

Smell

The feline sense of smell is about 30 times more developed than that of humans, and is essential to cats in relation to their sex life and hunting for food and water. A thick spongy membrane (olfactory mucosa) in the nose, with over twice the surface area of that of humans, contains 200 million scent-sensitive cells. When minute particles of odorous substances in the atmosphere are drawn in during normal breathing, they stimulate highly sensitive nerve endings of fine hairs within the nasal cavities.

In the roof of the mouth there is a special organ lined with receptor cells. Known as the Jacobson's organ, it is a tube, 1.2 cm (½ in) long, with its opening just behind the front teeth. Interesting odours are sucked into the mouth and directed to the Jacobson's organ to be investigated in more detail. The facial expression cats execute to do this (open mouth, lips drawn back and wrinkled nose) is called the Flehmen reaction.

Hearing

Feline hearing is exceptionally well developed, and cats can hear noises that are quite inaudible to the human ear. They can hear ultrasonic sounds that precede an activity, which is why they often react before we are even aware that anything is happening. The ear is made up of three sections: the outer, middle and inner ear.

The outer ear

The ear flap (pinna) acts as a funnel to direct sound waves down to the eardrum which is tautly stretched across the ear canal, separating it from the middle ear. The eardrum vibrates in response to sound waves.

Large ear flaps help a cat to focus sound and judge where it is coming from, thereby enabling him to pinpoint the position of prey even if he cannot see it.

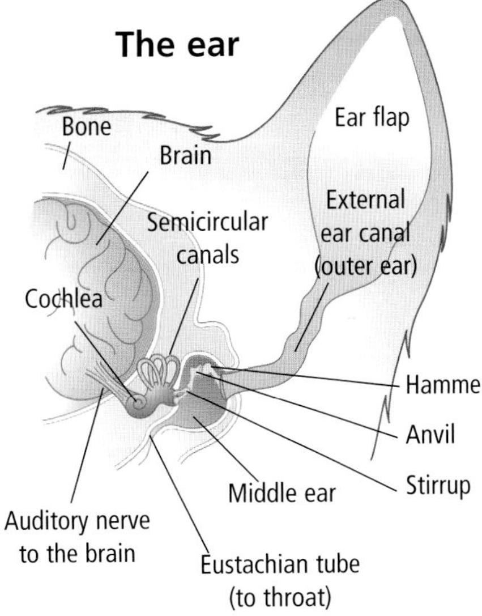

The middle ear

In here, three small bones – the hammer (malleus), anvil (incus) and stirrup (stapes) – transmit the sound relayed from the eardrum to the cochlea, which is contained within the inner ear.

The inner ear

The cochlea is a spiral cavity, containing the organ of Corti that converts the sound vibrations transmitted from the middle ear into nerve impulses. These are then passed along the acoustic nerve to the auditory cortex of the brain, where they are decoded and recognized by comparison with sounds stored in the memory bank.

Taste

It seems that the cat's tongue can differentiate between food items that taste salty, sour, bitter or sweet. Most cats appear to like salty things, but can vary considerably in their reaction to sweet foods. Taste alone does not seem to be important to most cats, but this is how tiny kittens, on first leaving the nest, test most new surfaces and objects – by licking them carefully and methodically, and with great concentration. Just how the information received in this way is analysed and stored is not known, and it occurs only during the most sensitive period of learning in the young cat.

Touch

Cats use their noses, paws and whiskers for examining objects by touch, after having first checked them out by smell. They rarely burn themselves with hot foods or liquids, as they use their noses as thermometers to test for temperature. Affectionate cats will often pat at their owner's faces or bodies to attract attention. Hunting cats touch prey with a paw to see if it is dead or alive. Mother cats often touch their kittens with their faces and paws. Cats also use their faces, whiskers and paws to touch each other.

Top tip

It is cruel to trim a cat's whiskers. Although the actual process of trimming them would not hurt, the cat would be left without vital sensors on his head to judge space either side of him, and how close he is to objects in the dark.

Routine health care

Knowing your cat, and his usual behaviour, will help you recognize when something is not quite right with him. If ailments are spotted quickly, then early treatment often helps to prevent more serious problems occurring; this usually results in less suffering for your pet and smaller veterinary bills for you. Monitoring your cat's mood and habits, and carrying out simple health checks on a regular basis, will enable you to assess his state of health. Things to look out for are shown in the checklist.

Checklist

- ✓ general condition, skin and fur
- ✓ appetite and thirst
- ✓ grooming
- ✓ mouth and teeth
- ✓ ears, eyes and nose
- ✓ weight
- ✓ faeces and urine
- ✓ ease of movement

Regular home checks

Keep an eye on all the following aspects of your cat's health, condition and demeanour.

General condition, skin and fur

The healthy cat is alert, interested in what is going on around him, curious, and looks well in himself. The skin should be clean, supple and pliable, while the fur should be soft and glossy, not dull and lank. Check for parasites, wounds, scurf, lumps and scabs (see also Top tip, page 129).

Appetite and thirst

Any change from normal eating and drinking patterns can indicate a digestive, urinary or mouth problem, and if this occurs it is essential to take your cat to a vet as soon as possible.

Grooming

A healthy cat constantly cleans and grooms his fur. A sick cat will neglect himself in this department and soon begin to look scruffy. Reasons for failure to wash include mouth soreness and joint stiffness (which could indicate arthritis), while female cats that stop cleaning their genital region could have a distasteful discharge.

Mouth and teeth

Cat breath should not be offensive: tooth decay is easy to diagnose because of the resulting unpleasant smell. The mouth area and tongue

Cats that are ill or in pain often withdraw into themselves and become quieter and depressed. If your pet has lost interest in life, seek veterinary advice. Checking your pet's vital signs (see page 99) on a regular basis can help alert you to early signs of problems.

If your vet knows your cat almost as well as you do, this familiarity often makes treating him more efficient and successful.

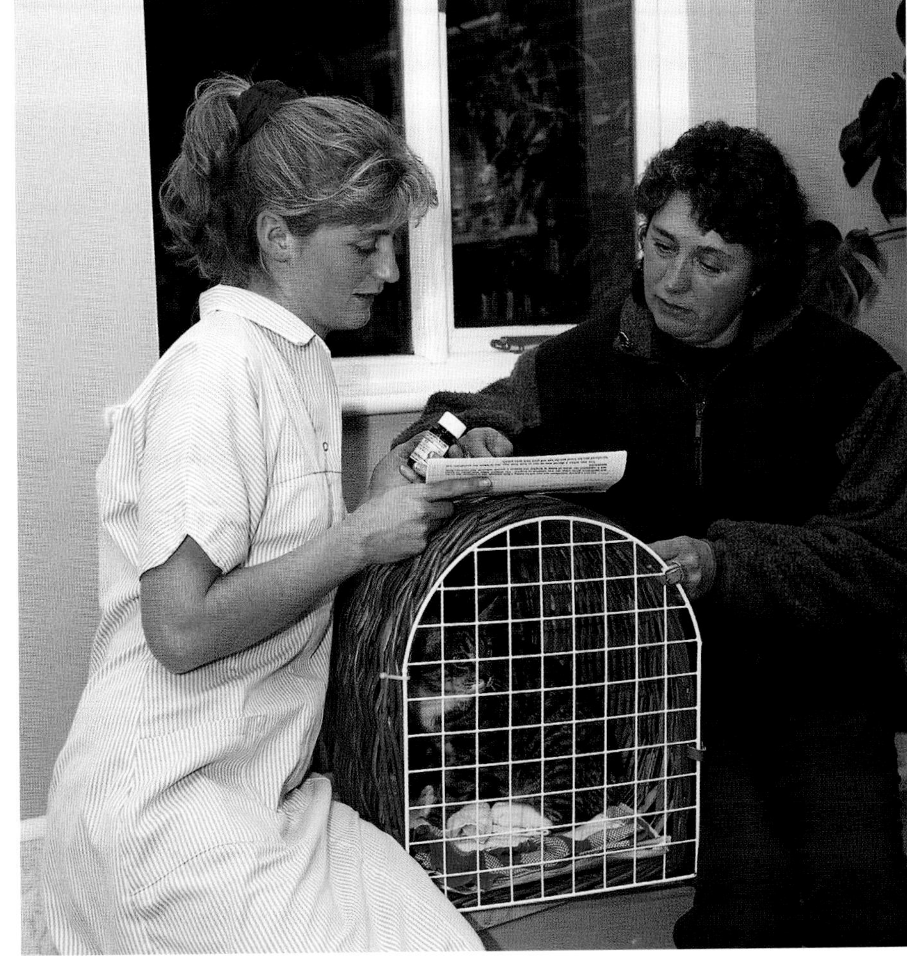

Top tip

If, for any reason, you feel that you would like a second veterinary opinion, it is within your right to ask for one, and your vet can arrange this; no one vet knows everything there is to know about his or her particular field of work. Your vet may even suggest consulting another expert in order to treat your cat most appropriately, especially if they do not have the specialized equipment or knowledge to deal with your cat's specific health problem.

should be pale pink in colour – white gums indicate anaemia, red bleeding gums are an indication of gingivitis (see page 166), and blue or grey gums suggest a circulatory problem. If your cat shows a reluctance or inability to eat, seek veterinary advice, as this could be due to a mouth abscess, a broken tooth or some other more serious ailment.

Eyes, ears and nose

The eyes should be clear, bright and free from discharge. Some breeds of cat with 'typey' facial features often suffer from eye discharge; this occurs as a result of the skull structure being deformed, meaning that tears cannot drain away as they would normally. Tearstains can be removed with cotton wool dipped in clean, boiled and cooled water. Any clouding of the surface of the eye requires veterinary attention. The pupils should be of the same size and the third eyelid (haw) retracted.

The inner ear surface should be clean, smooth and odour-free, and feel slightly greasy to the touch.

Frequently asked question

Q How often should I clean my cat's ears, and how should I do it?

A Cats do not usually need help in cleaning their ears. However, if the inside of his ear flaps (pinnas) are looking dirty, then you can gently clean them with cotton wool moistened with baby oil. Never poke cotton buds or anything else into the ear, or you may damage it. If you have any concerns about the cleanliness of your cat's ears, consult your vet.

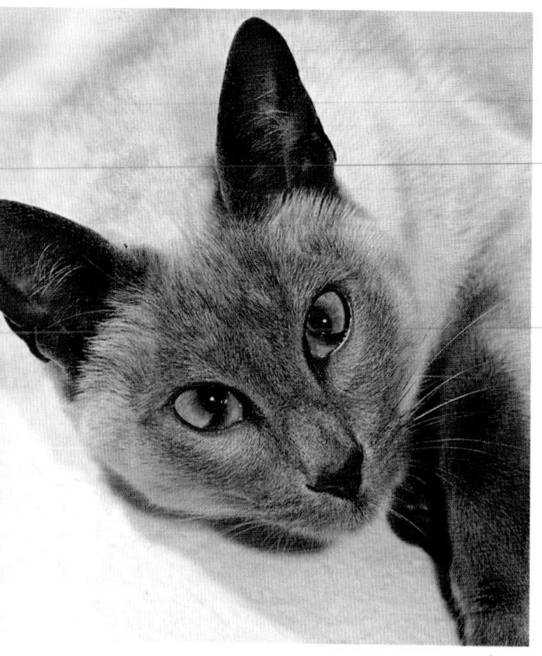

Raised haws (third eyelids) are an indication of ill health.

Did you know ...?

A cat that has been to the vet for any reason may come back smelling very different, and may be treated like a stranger by other cats in the household. Separating them and swapping their scents with a clean cloth can help reintegrate them, as can using a plug-in cat pheromone diffuser (see Smells familiar on page 88).

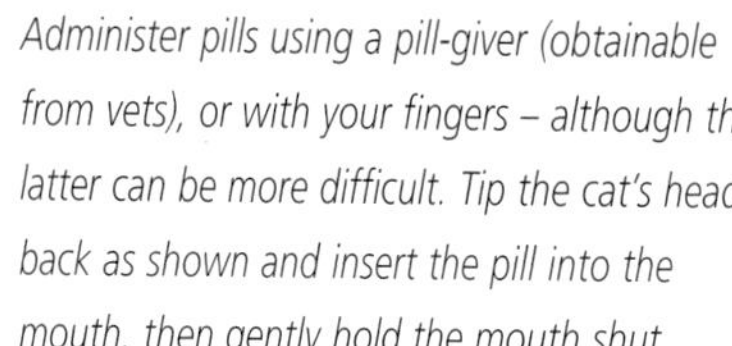

Administering medicine and pills

Only give medication as prescribed or advised by your vet, and administer it as directed. It helps to have someone to hold the cat while you give medicine or pills to him.

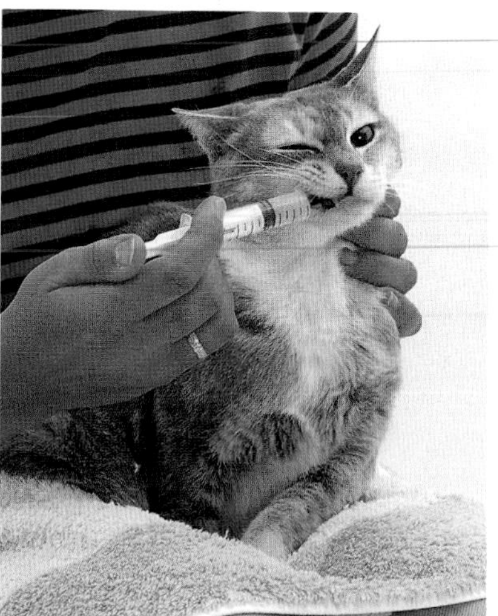

Giving medicine via a syringe (your vet can supply these) is the easiest way to administer it. Insert the nozzle in the corner of the mouth and squeeze a little at a time, stroking the cat's throat to encourage him to swallow.

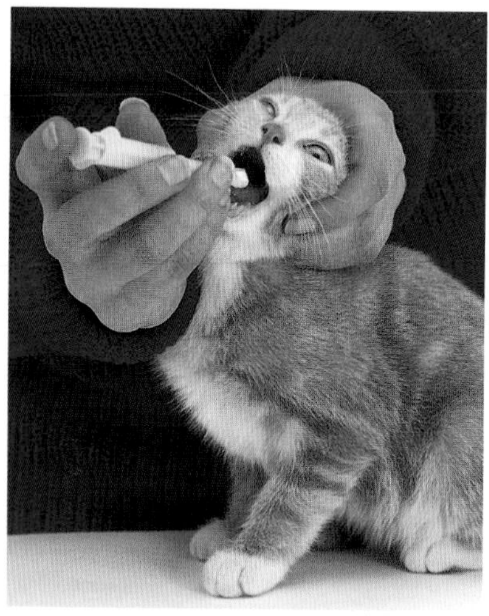

Administer pills using a pill-giver (obtainable from vets), or with your fingers – although the latter can be more difficult. Tip the cat's head back as shown and insert the pill into the mouth, then gently hold the mouth shut.

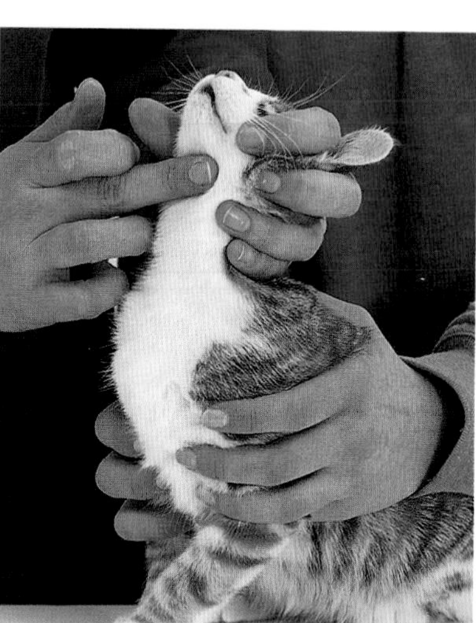

To encourage the cat to swallow the pill, gently stroke his throat.

Smelly or dirty ears need veterinary investigation, as this suggests there may be infection present.

The nose should be clean, slightly damp and free from discharge. Runny noses are often a sign of viral infection or allergy.

Weight

Cats, like humans, vary greatly in size and conformation. The average adult weight of a cat is around 4–5kg (9–11lb); a small cat may weigh only 2.5kg (5lb 8oz) and a large one as much as 5.5kg (12lb). Your vet will be able to tell you what your cat's ideal weight should be, and any deviation from this should be closely monitored. Obese cats have a shorter life expectancy than those of the correct weight, as carrying excess weight puts strain on the heart and

Applying topical treatments

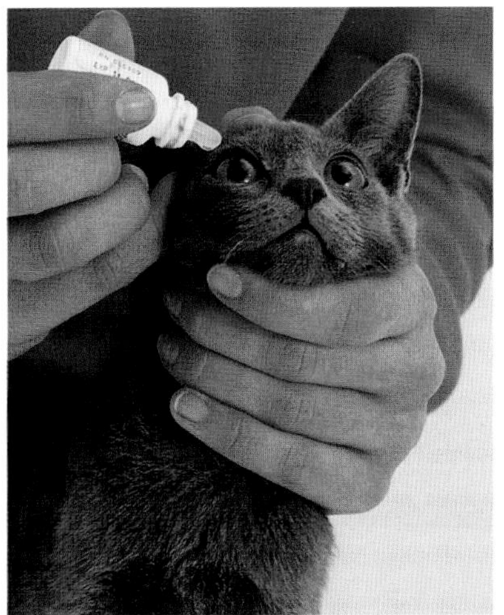

Only use treatments prescribed by your vet and apply them as directed.

When administering drops or ointment to the eye, hold the cat's head still and aim for the centre of the eye.

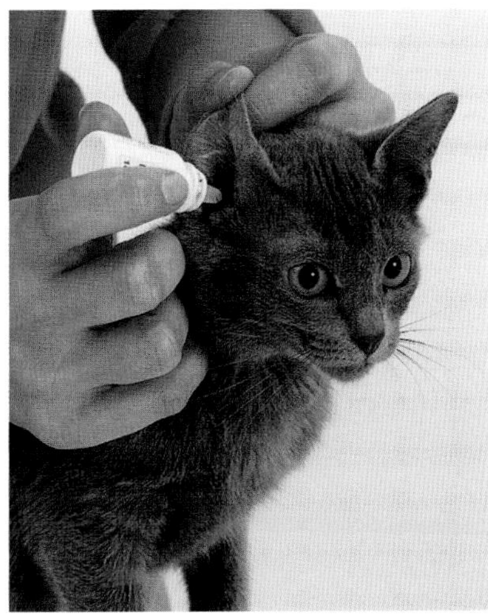

To apply ear drops, hold the head still, squeeze in the drops, and then gently massage the base of the ear to ensure the liquid is evenly distributed on the affected area.

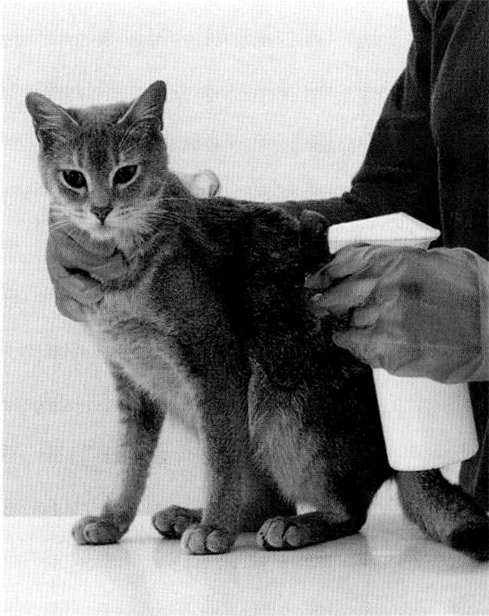

Wear rubber or plastic gloves to protect yourself when applying flea spray, massage it into the coat and wash your hands thoroughly afterwards.

limbs. Weight loss can indicate internal disease, or a parasite or pancreatic problem.

Faeces and urine

If your cat has difficulty in defecating or urinating, he needs very urgent veterinary attention. Stools should be firm, but not hard or loose, while urine should be pale yellow in colour and free from clouding and an offensive smell. Both should be free from traces of blood.

Ease of movement

Stiffness when moving around could indicate joint problems. Limping suggests a direct pain source such as a fractured limb, a wound, a thorn stuck in the foot pad, or an infected claw bed. A general reluctance to move around, combined with crying out when picked up, or even when touched, may be due to an internal injury or ailment.

Veterinary health checks

Choose a vet who specializes in feline health, and make the effort to cultivate a good relationship with

Symptoms of concern at a glance

- Blood in urine or faeces
- Breathing difficulty
- Coughing or sneezing
- Diarrhoea/constipation
- Difficulty in eating
- Difficulty in eliminating
- Dullness or fever
- Fur loss or failure to self-groom
- Haws showing
- Increased or decreased thirst
- Lameness
- Loss of appetite
- Marked change in behaviour
- Nasal discharge
- Pallor of lips and gums
- Scratching or licking
- Signs of acute pain
- Stiff or unsteady gait
- Swollen abdomen
- Ulceration of mouth
- Vomiting
- Weight loss or increase

him or her. An owner who takes their cat for regular health checks and routine vaccinations, and seeks advice on parasite control and dental care, is a valued customer for whom a vet will be prepared to give more time.

Take your pet for a check-up at least once a year (combine this with the annual vaccination booster), and every six months for old cats (aged 10 or more); this can often identify health problems before they become serious. Keeping a diary of your pet's behaviour and health and being able to explain any changes you have noticed, and when these first occurred, is very useful in helping your vet treat your cat appropriately and swiftly when the need arises.

Parasite control

Cats, especially those with access to outdoors, can suffer from a variety of external and internal parasites, including lice, fleas, fungal infections, ticks and worms – all of which cause ill health. There is a wide variety of preparations available to buy off the shelf at pet stores and supermarkets designed to treat these parasites, but they are not as effective as those that are available on prescription from your vet. So, while the former products may be cheaper and easier to obtain, they often prove to be false economy in the long run.

Never use more than one defleaing treatment at a time, otherwise your cat may overdose. You must also treat the indoor environment where your cat lives, or reinfestation will occur immediately. Vacuum-clean carpets and wherever your cat likes to sleep regularly, and wash your pet's bedding once a week or so to destroy flea eggs.

Intestinal worms (roundworm and tapeworm) are most efficiently controlled via all-in-one treatments prescribed and administered by your vet. A typical worming regime is to treat kittens aged four to sixteen weeks for roundworms every fortnight; from six months old, treat the cat every two to six months (depending on whether he is an outdoor or an indoor cat) for both roundworm and tapeworm. Consult your vet for advice about the most appropriate worming plan and treatment for your cat.

Vaccination

Cats, like any other animals, are susceptible to certain viral diseases, some of which can prove fatal. While they will not pass these on to humans (apart from rabies), they will transfer them to other cats, either in the air or through mating or other physical contact. It is advisable to have your cat vaccinated, where this is possible, in order to:

- help prevent your cat dying early from a feline viral disease
- help prevent feline viral diseases reaching epidemic proportions
- help eliminate feline viral diseases
- enable you to book your cat into a cattery when you go on vacation
- enable you to enter cat shows
- enable you to travel abroad with your cat if you so desire

Feline fact

There have been numerous cases where owners of both cats and dogs have tried to save money by treating their cats with defleaing preparations formulated for dogs – and ended up with dead cats. So never treat your cat with anything other than preparations formulated for felines.

When to vaccinate

Vaccinations are given via injection by a vet. Kittens can receive their first shots at about nine weeks of age, with a second dose given at 12 weeks. Full protection is not achieved until

Diseases your cat can be vaccinated against

- Feline leukaemia virus (FeLV), see page 173
- Cat flu (feline respiratory disease) – there are two forms of this disease: feline herpes virus (also known as feline rhinotracheitis virus) and feline calici virus (FCV), see page 164
- Feline infectious enteritis (FIE), also known as feline panleukopenia, see page 171
- Chlamydial disease, see page 169
- Rabies
- Feline infectious peritonitis (FIP) – the vaccination is currently available only in the USA, see page 173

Ideally, cats should be 100 per cent well before vaccinations are given, to reduce the risk of an adverse reaction to them.

seven to ten days after the second vaccination. Thereafter, cats should receive annual or two-yearly boosters (depending on the vet and whether tests are carried out to ascertain the level of immunity) to maintain their level of immunity, and also to satisfy boarding cattery, passport and show-entry requirements.

Vaccination risks

There are some risks associated with vaccination, but these are generally low and severe reactions are rare. The cat may have a small lump at the injection site, or may be quiet and off his food, for 24 hours after immunization, but should soon recover. If you are worried about your pet's behaviour or health after vaccination, contact your vet immediately for advice. On the whole, most vets recommend immunization to prevent certain feline diseases reaching epidemic proportions, especially in urban areas where there are large numbers of cats.

Did you know ...?

Some insurance companies will not pay out for treatment if a cat is not vaccinated – so check all of the policy clauses before parting with your premium. Shop around to find the best policy at the right price. Vets may be able to advise on the most efficient insurance companies to use, as they deal with them all the time.

Neutering

If you are going to breed from your cat, you will have a clear idea of whether you want to raise kittens or set up a stud. If not, and your cat is to be a pet only, then he or she should be neutered – whether male or female – in order to help prevent the situations in the checklist.

Checklist

- ✓ unwanted kittens
- ✓ potential behavioural problems, such as spraying in the house
- ✓ spread of disease
- ✓ straying
- ✓ the characteristic pungent male cat smell
- ✓ females continually calling for a mate
- ✓ health risks during pregnancy and birth

Why neutering is a good idea

A fully mature, unneutered male cat will spend a good deal of his time trying to pass on his genes. To do this well, he needs to defend a sizeable territory, compete with rivals and court females. Since all of these require large amounts of energy, tomcats often look thin and ragged, with numerous scars and abscesses from countless fights. Straying, too, can become a real problem with both male and female cats as they seek a mate (see page 86).

As well as the risk of unwanted kittens, there is also the real risk of cats, particularly feral cats, passing on diseases against which there is no vaccination and for which there is no cure, such as the feline immunodeficiency virus (FIV) – the feline equivalent to humans AIDS (although there is no danger of humans contracting this).

Neutering removes the great responsibility of having to find good, loving homes for kittens.

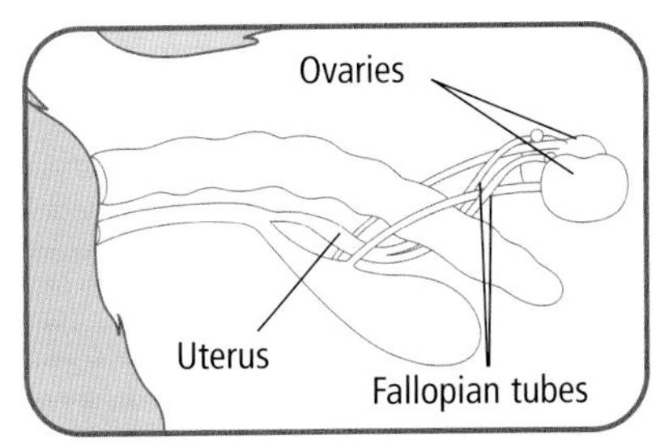

Queen

Spaying

Before spaying: the female reproductive tract comprises the ovaries, fallopian tubes and uterus (womb).

After spaying: the ovaries, fallopian tubes and uterus have been removed.

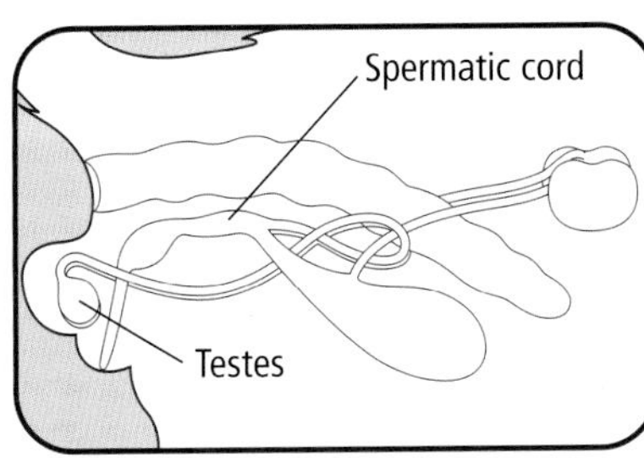

Tom cat

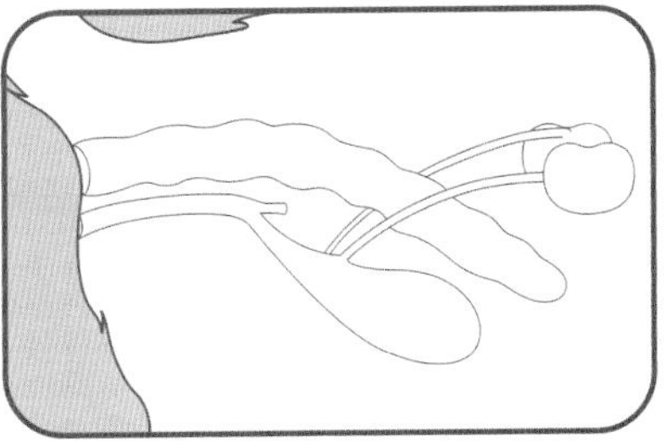
Spayed female

Castration

Before castration: the male reproductive tract comprises two testicles (testes) within a skin sac (scrotum), connected to the penis via the vas deferens (spermatic cord).

After castration: the testicles and part of the vas deferens have been removed.

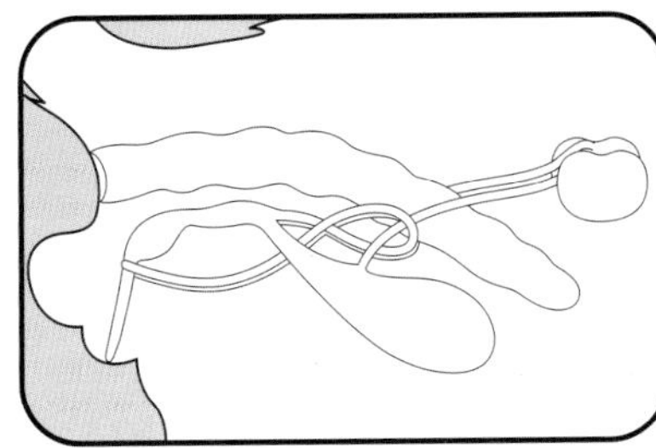
Neutered male

When to neuter

Neutering (known as spaying in females and castration in males) should be carried out when the cat reaches sexual maturity at around six months (the equivalent of adolescence in humans), and at any time afterwards. Individual vets have their own policy on spaying in-season females. This is due to the reproductive organs being enlarged with an increased supply of blood, so there can be greater risks involved in the surgery. The neutering of pedigree or show cats is often delayed to allow their full physical development.

What is involved?

Because the operation is more involved with female cats, the spaying procedure is more expensive than castration for males. Some animal charities have low-cost neutering schemes to help those owners on low income or receiving state benefits. Ask about this at your local animal veterinary clinic, or contact animal charities in your area.

Spaying females

The vet removes the ovaries, fallopian tubes and uterus under a general anaesthetic. They shave and clean the operation site to help prevent infection, then make a small incision on the mid-line (from the navel towards the hind legs), or in the flank, in order to remove the relevant organs. They close the wound with two or three stitches, which they will remove about a week later, unless they are using soluble suture material which gradually dissolves on its own.

Castrating males

The vet anaesthetizes the cat and removes his testes and part of the spermatic cord through an incision in the scrotum; this incision is so small that it does not even require stitches.

Did you know ...?

A female will keep coming into season (also called a 'heat') every 3 weeks during the breeding season (early spring through to late autumn) unless she becomes pregnant. When she is in season, she will make a distinctive and loud calling sound to alert toms in the vicinity that she is looking for a mate.

As they stray to find a mate, unneutered cats run a greater risk of contracting diseases from other felines as well as becoming involved in fights and road accidents.

Pre- and post-operative care

The cat must go without food and water for 12 hours before the operation, but most cats are up and about, eating, drinking and playing, within a few hours of their operation. Females who have had a mid-line incision may take slightly longer to recover – around 48 hours.

When you bring the cat home from the vet's, he or she will probably still be drowsy from the anaesthetic, so put them in a warm, quiet place to rest undisturbed – with water, a litter tray and a light meal of cooked white fish or chicken – until they feel ready to join in the family activities again. Your vet will advise whether you need to keep them inside or can allow them out. Gently discourage the cat from nibbling or excessively licking any stitches. If you have any worries at all following neutering, be sure to contact your vet for advice.

Feline fact

If you have a female in season, known as oestrus, visiting toms will loiter around her territory and you will have to put up with their spraying. There may be fights in the vicinity, as well as loud, persistent caterwauling during the night. Female cats sometimes also develop the habit of spraying, when their hormonal balance has been upset either by doses of contraceptive medication or by frequent periods of season.

Neuter behaviour

If neutered as kittens, the behaviour of male and female cats will be almost the same as it was before – at least from the practical point of view of an owner. Minor changes to expact are:

• their territories are much smaller than those of unneutered cats
• territorial fights may still occur, but will be much less of a problem
• both sexes tend to be more affectionate and amenable.
• they tend to spend more time at home
• although neuters may spray urine if they are emotionally disturbed by something, their spray smells nothing like the strong urine of a male cat, which is also sticky and difficult to clean from household furnishings

There is some truth in the observation that neutered cats become more inactive than unneutered ones as they age, although their life expectancy is greater. You may have to adjust a neutered cat's diet, as well as play with him every day and encourage him to exercise.

Top tip

Pedigree stud cats are kept confined to prevent them contracting infection from other cats and getting into fights. Although they have never experienced freedom, many of their natural desires will be frustrated and it is kinder to castrate them once their breeding days are over.

Contraception

It is possible to administer a hormone treatment to female cats to prevent unwanted pregnancies, but there are drawbacks to prolonged birth-control treatment. It could cause fertility problems if you wish to breed from the cat later; it could also result in side-effects that include increased appetite, weight gain, lethargy, behavioural problems and uterine disease.

It is also possible to use contraceptive drugs to prevent an unwanted pregnancy once mating has taken place (misalliance) – rather like the human 'morning-after' pill. This involves the vet giving an injection of hormones that override the queen's own hormones, making her body believe she has not become pregnant. This causes her to come into season (oestrus) again. Vets do not like to give this treatment, since it can have serious side-effects such as the development of pyometra (a life-threatening infection of the uterus).

Frequently asked question

Q I have heard that it is best for a female cat to have a litter before she is neutered. Is this true?

A This myth is based on human needs rather than scientific fact, as there is no evidence to suggest that it is necessary. If you want to raise a litter and are confident that you can then place the resulting kittens in good homes, spay the female soon after weaning to prevent any further pregnancies.

A cat born in early spring may come into season during the following autumn, whereas one born later in the year may not do so until the following spring. Some cats, depending on the breed, may come into season earlier than normal at five months, whereas others may not do so until they are as much as 12 months old.

REPRODUCTION

Once the female is ready, matings are repeated 10–20 times a day for up to six days. Only the fitter, stronger males can sustain this, which means that kittens in the same litter can sometimes have several fathers. This promiscuous behaviour not only ensures that the chances of conception are maximized, but also that the kittens have a variety of characters to increase the next generation's chances of successful procreation.

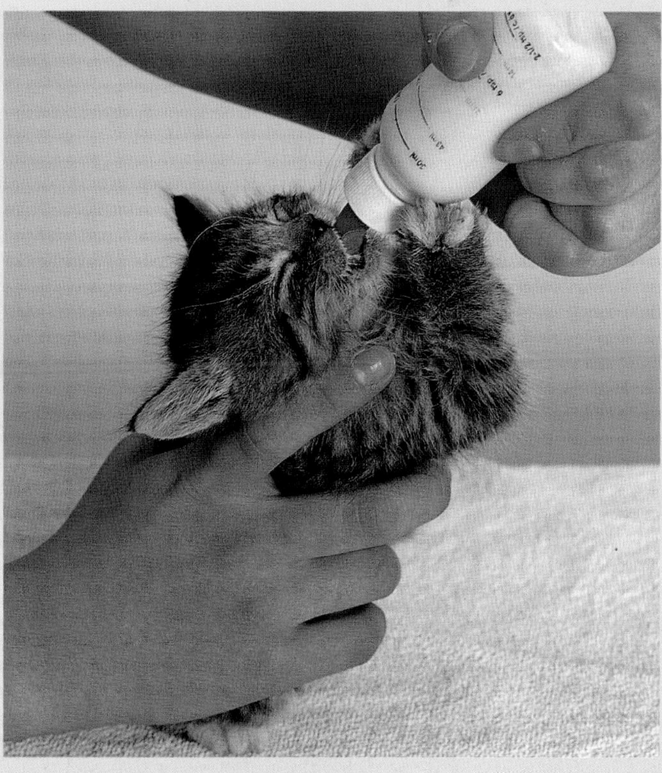

Mating and conception

As the female (queen) becomes ready to mate she rolls flirtatiously on the ground to attract males. Queens should be dewormed well before mating takes place.

Cat courtships can be prolonged affairs: despite wanting to mate, the female does not immediately accept the male's approach.

When she does accept him, the male firmly grips the back of the female's neck to hold her steady as he mounts her and mates.

After mating, as the male withdraws, barbs on the end of his penis (which stimulate the female to ovulate) cause pain inside the female, making her cry out, and she turns on him in self-defence. At this point, the male makes a hasty exit in case the female strikes out at him, his involvement in the reproduction process complete.

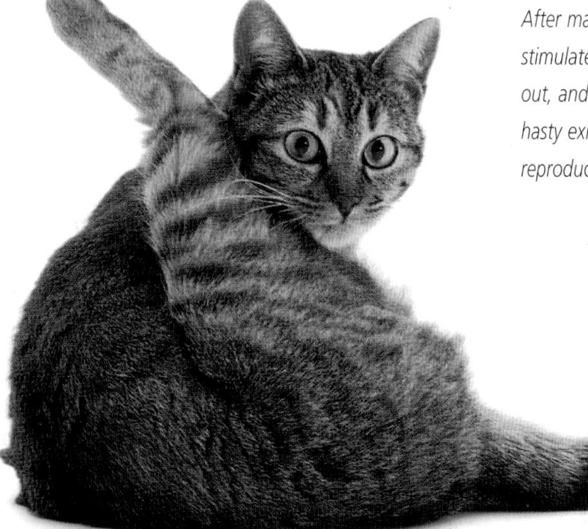

After copulation, the female rolls on the ground and then washes herself. Minutes later, she may be ready to mate again – this increases her chances of successfully becoming pregnant.

Pregnancy and birth

The gestation period in cats is nine weeks (approximately 65 days). Movement of the foetuses can be felt from the seventh week of pregnancy. As the birth nears, the female will begin to 'nest' and seek a private, preferably dark, safe place in which to give birth.

Once first-stage labour starts, the queen will pace around crying or growling softly, and look behind her in an agitated and puzzled manner. As second-stage labour begins, the queen goes into her nesting area or box, lies on her side and strains as uterine contractions move the kittens, one at a time, down the birth canal.

After delivering a kitten, the queen cleans away the birth membranes covering it, thus allowing and stimulating him to breathe. She passes the placenta, joined to the kitten by the umbilical cord, and eats it, severing the cord a short way from the kitten's body.

Once the kittens are born, the queen cleans herself, then settles down to suckle her babies, curling herself around them, and rests for about 12 hours.

Pregnancy, birth and kitten care

The urge to reproduce and pass genes on to the next generation is strong in unneutered felines, and a healthy female cat with access to males and a plentiful food supply can produce two or three litters of kittens a year. Species survival depends upon procreation, and pregnancy and birth are the most natural things in the world. Left to their own devices, cat courtship is a noisy affair, with several males attempting to mate with an in-season and responsive female, but usually one male is able to keep the others away and mate successfully.

Looking after the pregnant queen

Apart from increasing her diet (see page 42) with food specially formulated for expectant queens to cope with the demands being made on her body, treat the mother as normal during pregnancy. About halfway through the pregnancy, she will become more careful about jumping and passing through narrow openings, owing to her enlarged shape.

Take great care when picking her up and cuddling her as her pregnancy progresses – she may well not appreciate either, being uncomfortably full of kittens. If she becomes constipated, substitute one of her daily meals with oily food, such as pilchards or sardines, as this will aid the passing of motions.

Prepare a kittening nest, and place it in a quiet and undisturbed area of the house: a large sturdy cardboard box will do, with a hole cut into one side 15cm (6in) off the ground and wide enough for the cat to pass through easily. Line the base with newspaper for insulation and place a thick layer of paper towels on top to make a soft, absorbent

One day old
Newly born kittens cannot see and have very little control over their body movements.

Ten days old
A kitten's eyes usually open at about ten days.

Three weeks old
The kitten will start to experiment with solid food at this age.

Five weeks old
By now the kitten will be able to run and balance well.

Eight weeks old
The kitten will have learnt how to socialize with his siblings, and other pets in the household.

Did you know ...?

Some queens may suffer from mastitis due to a bacterial infection. Symptoms of this include hard, hot teats that produce bloodstained or abnormal-looking milk. The affected cat will be off-colour, may vomit and may have little or no appetite. Veterinary attention should be sought immediately so that the queen can be appropriately treated, and the vet can show you how to hand-strip her teats and hand-rear the kittens as necessary.

and disposable mattress for the birth. Show the queen where the nest is; bear in mind, however, that she may ultimately choose her own place – which could even be on or under your bed.

With longhaired queens, clip hair surrounding the birth canal (to aid hygiene and ease of delivery) and nipples (to facilitate ease of suckling). Gently sponge her anal area twice a day if she is carrying a large litter and is unable to clean this herself. Make sure she is free of fleas and mites in the 10 days preceding birth – consult your vet regarding suitable treatment.

Fourteen weeks old
The kitten's motor skills have imroved, his ability to balance is a its peak.

Five months old
Sexual maturity may be reached from this age, though it does vary from cat to cat.

Adult cat
Full size and maturity are reached at about one year of age.

Newborn kittens' eyes are sealed shut and begin to open at about 10 days old, although it may happen as early as the middle of the first week. A kitten cannot see with clarity or accuracy until he is about four weeks old; at 15 days old his ears are open and fully functional. Milk teeth begin to appear when the kittens are about 14 days old. Young kittens should be wormed, under veterinary advice, while still nursing, if necessary.

Labour and birth

Females give birth and raise their young following instinctive behaviour patterns that allow them to do so unaided, although they do get better at this with practice. In a natural colony of cats, however, other related females will help out, acting as midwives and surrogate nurses while the mother takes a break. This co-operation ensures greater protection and survival of the young.

Labour and birth normally proceed easily. Once second-stage labour begins (when the queen goes into the nesting box and lies down), a whole litter may be born in an hour or so, or they may be spread over 24 hours with long rests between kittens.

Birth problems

Occasionally things do go wrong. If the queen has been straining hard for two hours without results, call out a vet immediately to help her give birth. Sometimes, for various reasons, kittens do not survive. If the bereaved mother cat appears distressed, contact your vet for advice: the queen may require medication to suppress her milk and help prevent potential mastitis, or her loss may have a happy ending if the vet knows of orphaned kittens needing a foster mum. Other problems that can arise during pregnancy or following birth include:

Did you know ...?

False pregnancies can occur in cats. Also known as pseudo or phantom pregnancy, this condition is quite natural and may occur in a queen that has failed to conceive during a season. In some cases, the owner may not notice any difference in the female's mental or physical state; in other queens, the false pregnancy can result in a swollen abdomen and mammary glands that fill with milk. In the latter case, the cat may also spend time nest-building and crying, and be reluctant to exercise; she may even display the pushing actions of an actual birth. Such queens will form attachments to inanimate objects, such as toys, and some have 'invisible' kittens. In severe cases, veterinary advice and treatment where necessary should be sought.

Until the kittens are old enough to relieve themselves outside of the nest, the mother licks them after each feed to stimulate them to eliminate, swallowing the body waste to keep the nest hygienic.

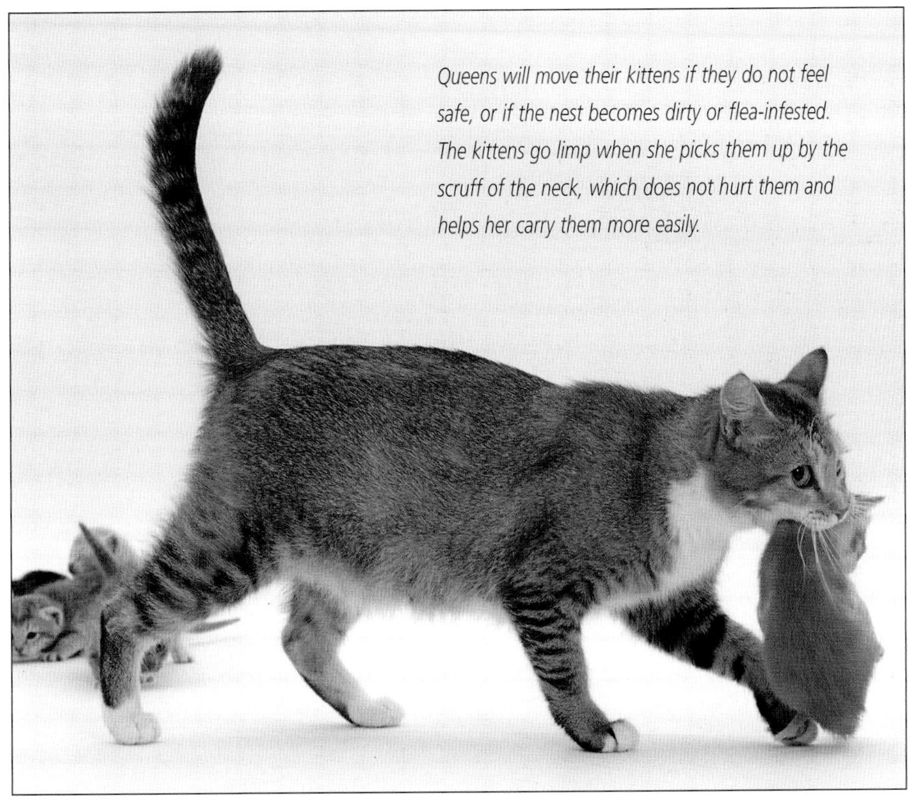
Queens will move their kittens if they do not feel safe, or if the nest becomes dirty or flea-infested. The kittens go limp when she picks them up by the scruff of the neck, which does not hurt them and helps her carry them more easily.

Feline fact

Once mating has taken place, the male cat plays no further role, except to defend the territory where his females raise their young from other marauding males that may kill the kittens so that they can perpetuate their own genes.

- **miscarriage**, due to illness or because the foetuses are not healthy
- **uterine infection** after birth, indicated by fever, vomiting, lack of appetite, dark coloured vaginal discharge
- **prolapsed uterus**, indicated by a swollen red mass appearing out of the vulva

Consult your vet immediately if any of these occur.

Mother and baby care

Kittens are totally dependent on their mother and her milk for the first three weeks. After this, they begin to experiment with eating the solid food that their mother brings back in the form of prey for them to eat, or which their human carer provides. The mother will eat and drink more than normal to maintain a plentiful milk supply. Four good meals daily should be enough for her, depending on the number of

Frequently asked question

Q A friend's cat died of eclampsia and she had to raise the kittens herself. What is this condition, and what should I do if my pregnant queen gets it?

A Also known as milk fever or lactation tetany, eclampsia is the paralysis of milk production in the mother's teats after kittening. It is usually due to a calcium deficiency in the diet, and can occur up to 21 days after kittening. Occasionally, it can occur just prior to kittening. Seek veterinary attention immediately.

Symptoms of eclampsia include salivation, anxiety, aversion to light, lack of co-ordination, high temperature and convulsions. If the condition is not quickly treated with calcium and glucose injections, the queen will die.

Orphaned kittens

In the rare instances when unweaned kittens are abandoned or orphaned, it is necessary to hand-rear them. This is a hugely time-consuming and tiring business, although usually ultimately rewarding if the helpless babies grow into healthy and independent young cats. If the kittens are left without a mother for whatever reason, consult your vet immediately – he or she may know of a potential feline foster mother, be able to put you in touch with an experienced breeder for tips, or offer advice themselves on how to hand-rear the kittens.

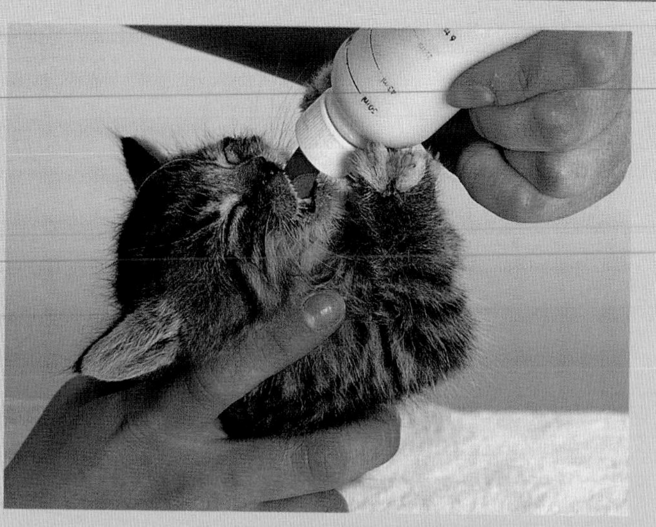

When you are hand-rearing, kittens need feeding every two hours for the first week.

kittens. The meals should comprise small and fresh food, preferably one formulated for lactating queens, to make sure she receives the nutrients she needs to maintain her own body as well as her offspring.

Keeping kittens clean is a vital role for mothers, whose kittens may otherwise die of disease. The mother continues to wash them all over until the babies learn how to do this themselves.

Early learning

Begin to handle the kittens from two weeks old, to start the vital feline-human socialization process. At this age, the mother cat will not be too anxious about familiar humans touching her babies. By the age of three weeks, kittens can stand quite well and toddle around on short, unsteady legs. At this stage, they can roll over and right themselves, and play with their siblings with paw pats and bites. By the fourth week, the kittens can move around confidently and can often run and balance well by the end of the fifth week. However, it will be another five to six weeks before they can run, jump and leap with accuracy, balance and co-ordination.

Weaning

At four weeks, the kittens start to explore outside the nest, and experiment more with solid food (see pages 40–45 for feeding guidance). Supply them with food specially formulated for kittens to make sure they receive the nutrients their rapidly growing bodies need.

As they eat increasing amounts of solids, their excreta changes and their mother stops cleaning up after them – so now it is time to provide them with their own litter tray. If they do not learn to use it from their mother, place them on it after every meal; leaving a small amount of excreta in the tray from their last elimination will help them recognize where to go at first.

Queens naturally wean their kittens themselves as their milk gradually dries up five to six weeks after the birth. At this age, the kittens should be fully weaned on to solid kitten food, although they may still return to mum for the occasional comfort suckle if she allows it. By eight weeks, the kittens are usually fully independent of their mother as regards food and hygiene requirements, and are ready for rehoming. For information about kitten care from eight weeks onwards, see pages 102–109.

Top tip

Although when playing with them and teaching them to fight, the mother can sometimes appear to be quite rough with her babies, even making them squeal, she is not really hurting them, so this is nothing to be alarmed about.

A large cat pen, complete with litter tray in which to put the kittens for brief periods when weaning begins, will provide the mother cat with periods of much-needed rest; it will also encourage the kittens to use the tray.

Did you know ...?

If the kittens are unwanted, and you cannot place them with a new owner or a charity, then veterinary euthanasia is the legal and most humane method of disposing of them. Consult your vet or local animal charity.

The mother encourages her kittens to play from an early age – as soon as they start to toddle around. Through play, the kittens practise social, fighting and hunting skills to equip them for adult life.

FIRST AID AND ILLNESS

Despite your best attention, things can always go wrong, and it is wise to be ready for any eventuality concerning the health of your cat. Try to minimize the possibility of accidents occurring around your home, and be vigilant about keeping an eye out for any signs of ill health that may need addressing.

First aid

A knowledge of first aid can prove useful, and in some instances essential. Accidents tend to happen when we least expect them to, so it is sensible to be prepared. Emergency situations need immediate action; if you know what to do you may be able to limit the injuries sustained by your pet, and perhaps even save his life. When administering first aid, the points of action to take are shown on the checklist.

Checklist

- ✓ always remember your own safety is paramount
- ✓ assess the situation
- ✓ protect yourself and others from injury
- ✓ examine the cat
- ✓ diagnose injuries
- ✓ treat injuries or pain as appropriate
- ✓ keep the cat warm, calm and quiet
- ✓ protect the cat from further injury
- ✓ contact a vet for professional advice and treatment

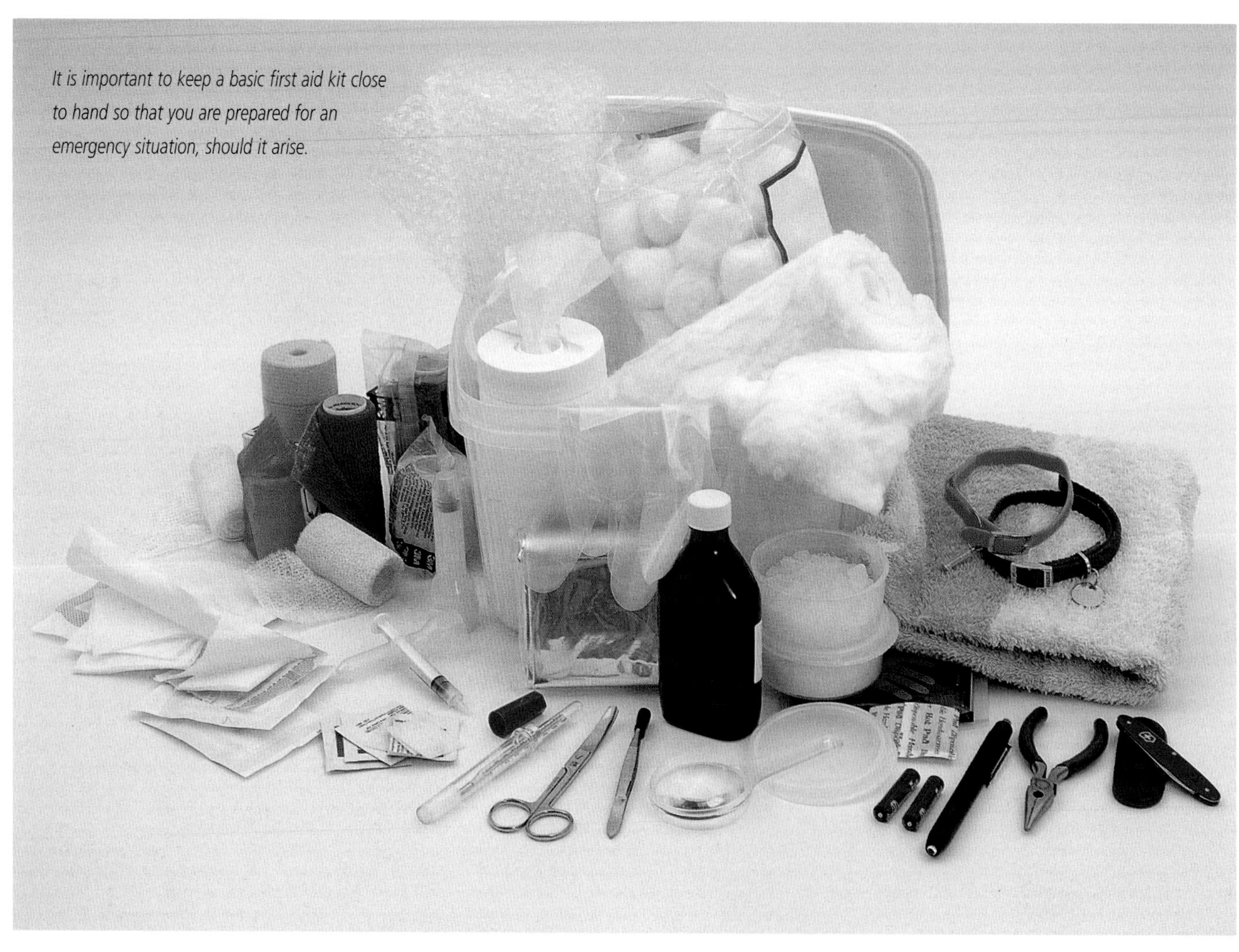

It is important to keep a basic first aid kit close to hand so that you are prepared for an emergency situation, should it arise.

First aid training

Having a basic training in the subject will give you the confidence to deal with an emergency situation calmly and efficiently until an expert practitioner can take over from you. Some vet clinics run courses in basic first aid, and it is well worth enlisting on one of these. Practising first-aid procedures on a healthy cat when you not under pressure is the best way to learn what to do in a real situation.

You can buy an Elizabethan collar from your vet or pet store, or make your own from a small plastic bucket by slitting it down one side and cutting a hole in the centre to comfortably fit around your cat's neck; alternatively, use a piece of strong cardboard.

First-aid kit

It is useful to have a home first-aid kit with which to treat minor injuries, to minimize adverse effects on the cat. Basic first-aid items can be bought from your vet, local pharmacy or good pet stores. A first-aid kit should contain the following:

- **absorbent paper kitchen roll** to wipe up any liquid mess
- **antihistamine** to ease insect stings and bites
- **antiseptic lotion** for cleaning wounds – particularly animal bites
- **antiseptic wound powder** for treating wounds and promoting healing
- **bandages** to keep dressings in place
- **cat claw-clippers** choose the guillotine variety
- **conforming ('sticky') bandage** – useful for holding dressings in place
- **cotton buds** – dampen these and use to remove grass seeds or other foreign objects from the eyes and to clean wounds and apply ointments
- **cotton wool** to bathe eyes, clean wounds and use as a dressing – dampen first to prevent strands breaking off and sticking to a wound
- **curved, round-ended scissors** to clip fur and trim dressings to size
- **elizabethan collar** to prevent a cat from interfering with dressings or sutures
- **glucose powder** – mix one tablespoon of glucose with one teaspoon of salt in 1 litre (1¾ pints) of warm water to make a rehydrating fluid for cats
- **heavy-duty protective gloves** for restraining a cat
- **lubricant jelly** to lubricate the thermometer before insertion
- **non-stick dressings** – useful for cuts
- **pencil torch and batteries** to inspect the mouth and ears
- **rectal thermometer** to ascertain body temperature. You may prefer to use an aural thermometer, which is more expensive but can be much easier to use
- **round-ended tweezers** to remove insect stings
- **small stainless steel or plastic bowls** to contain saline or antiseptic solutions when bathing wounds
- **space blanket or large sheet of plastic 'bubble wrap'** to maintain body temperature in cases of shock and hypothermia
- **squares of clean cotton material** (old linen or cotton bed sheets are

Did you know ...?

To clip fur around wounds, use a pair of scissors with curved blades and rounded ends. Dip the blades in clean, preferably boiled and cooled, water, and then carefully clip the fur around the wound; the fur will stick to the wet blades, preventing it from falling into the wound. Dip the scissors in the water again to swill off the clippings.

ideal) to place over wounds or stem blood flow

- **sterile eye wash** – contact-lens saline solution can be used
- **sticky surgical plaster tape** to hold dressings in place
- **surgical gloves** for when treating wounds
- **surgical spirit** to remove ticks
- **syringe plunger** to administer liquid medicine
- **table salt** to make saline solution (two teaspoons of salt dissolved in one litre of warm water) with which to clean wounds and counter infection
- **thermometer** (see page 157, rectal thermometer)
- **towel** to wrap the cat in when administering medication, and also to restrain it in event of accident

First-aid basics – ABC

The basics of first aid for a cat are as simple as ABC – airway, breathing and circulation. The first priority is to make sure that the cat's airway is clear, so that he is able to breathe, and that he is breathing. Next check that his blood is circulating properly (his heart is beating). You can then deal with any other symptoms as appropriate.

Airway and breathing

If the cat is unconscious in a collapsed state, check that he is breathing. If there is little or no breathing and the tongue is blue-black, open the mouth and remove anything that is blocking the airway. Gently lift the chin to extend the cat's neck to open the airway. If he still does not breathe, administer **artificial respiration**:

1 Hold the cat's mouth shut and cover his nose with your mouth.
2 Gently breathe up the cat's nose – 30 breaths every minute (taking your mouth from his nose between breaths to allow him to exhale).
3 Keep this up until the cat begins to breathe on his own, veterinary help arrives or you believe the cat to be beyond help.

Circulation

Next, check for a heartbeat. Do this by putting your ear on the cat's chest on the left-hand side, just behind his elbow, and you will be able to hear it. Also check for a pulse – place a couple of fingers in the same place as you put your ear, or on the inside of the cat's thigh in the groin area (see page 99). If there is no heartbeat, begin **chest compression**:

1 Place one hand either side of the cat's chest, just behind his elbows.
2 Squeeze the chest in a smooth action, giving two compressions every second (always use the flat of the hand – never the fingers). Do not use too much force, as it is easy to break

Top tip

One way of checking whether a cat is breathing is to place a small mirror close to his mouth and nose – if it mists and demists, then he is breathing.

Cover an unconscious cat with a blanket, towel or even a sweater to keep him warm while awaiting veterinary attention.

A sick cat is seldom co-operative. He feels vulnerable and defensive, so beware of his claws and teeth when handling him or doing something he does not feel happy with. Always wrap him in a towel for your own protection.

Top tip

A seriously injured or dangerously ill cat is better nursed at an animal hospital than at home, where full facilities and veterinary skills are not available.

the ribs.

3 Give two breaths to the cat for every four compressions. Keep this up until the cat's heart begins to beat, you cannot do any more, or a vet takes over. Keep checking for a heartbeat or pulse throughout your attempts at heart massage.

Moving an injured cat

Approach the injured cat carefully, looking for any signs of injury, and also assessing any danger to both yourself and the cat. Speak softly and reassuringly to him to help soothe him and keep him calm.

If the cat is in the road, move him to the side if it is safe to do so. Try not to aggravate any injuries when picking him up; the best way to do this is to slide a board under him as a makeshift stretcher, or slide both hands under him, keeping him in a horizontal position. A common injury sustained in road accidents is a ruptured diaphragm, so it is very important to keep the cat horizontal to stop his internal organs moving.

Emergency situations

Advice on what to do in a number of first-aid situations is given below.

Road accidents

As well as checking for obvious signs of injury, inspect the back of the neck for lumps and swellings that may indicate broken bones or trauma swellings. Seek veterinary attention as soon as possible, informing the vet of any signs or symptoms of injury you have spotted. Even if the cat appears to have suffered no external injury, a thorough veterinary check-up is essential in case there is unseen internal haemorrhaging which could be life-threatening if not detected and treated as soon as possible.

Burns and scalds

Cool the burnt area with iced water (if you can stand the cat in a bath or sink, pour this on for about 10 minutes) to reduce the pain and the severity of the burn. Cover the burn lightly with a cool, damp, clean cloth (handkerchief or tea towel), wrap the cat in a space blanket (or equivalent), place him in a warm carrier and take him to the vet without delay.

Chemical burns

Put rubber gloves on and wash the affected area under cold running water – either by standing the cat in the bath or sink and running water over the burn, or using a hosepipe in the garden. Prevent the cat from licking the area and follow the instructions as for burns and scalds.

Sunburn

Treat as for burns and scalds.

Poisoning

If you suspect your cat has ingested a poisonous substance (profuse salivating is the most obvious sign; extreme sleepiness is another and is commonly associated with rat poison), contact your vet immediately, giving the name of any poisons you suspect. This will allow the practice to obtain any relevant information from the poison

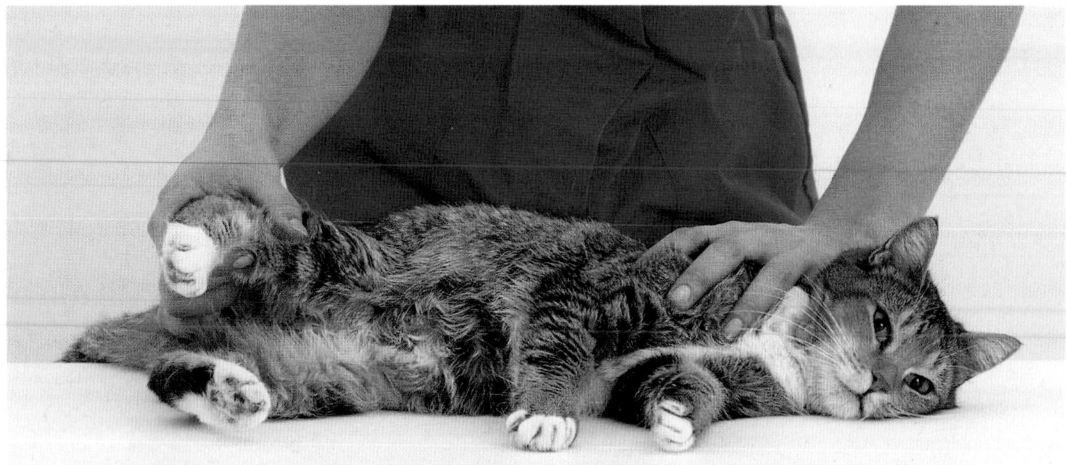

A cat with broken bones will not be easy to handle and may well bite and scratch any one who tries to approach or move him.

manufacturer while you transport your cat to the surgery. If you are instructed by the vet to make your cat vomit, in order to rid his digestive system of as much of the poison as possible, place one or two small washing soda (sodium carbonate) crystals, if you have them, at the back of the cat's throat. Alternatively, use mustard or salt mixed with a little water. Get the cat to the veterinary clinic without delay. Keep all hazardous substances securely locked up, especially when there are curious kittens in the house.

Broken bones

Signs of fractured bones – apart from them protruding from the skin – include extreme pain on moving a limb, swelling, tenderness, loss of control of and/or deformity of the limb, unnatural movement of the limb, or the sound of the two ends of the bone grinding against each other (called crepitus). Keep the cat as quiet and warm as possible and take him to a vet immediately.

Electrocution

Once the power supply has been turned off, check that the cat is breathing – if not, begin artificial respiration (see page 158). If it is not possible to switch off the power supply, do not approach the cat. Electrocution will almost inevitably cause burns, which will need treating as detailed on page 161. A big danger in treating cats that have been electrocuted is the threat to the first-aider. It is easy to rush in to help the stricken animal without considering any risk to yourself – so think before you act.

Insect stings and bites

A cat will frantically claw at the area of his body where he has been stung. If the cat has been stung in the throat, seek immediate veterinary attention, as swelling may block the airway and kill the cat. For stings elsewhere on the body, clip the fur from around the affected area so you can see what the problem is, and wash it with saline solution. Bees leave their sting in the victim, but wasps do not. If you can see the sting, and judge it is removable with tweezers, then do so carefully, and wipe the area with cotton wool dampened with surgical spirit.

To neutralize the effect of a wasp sting, wipe the area with vinegar or lemon juice; use bicarbonate of soda dissolved in a little water for bee stings. Then dry the area thoroughly, but gently, and apply a wet compress to help reduce the irritation and swelling. For other insect bites, clean and dry the area, then apply antihistamine spray or ointment to reduce itching and irritation.

Animal bites

Cats are at risk from bites by other cats, and by rats. If you suspect your cat has been bitten by another cat, clip the fur away from around the bite and clean the wound thoroughly with saline solution, followed by diluted antiseptic lotion. Dry the area, then apply a liberal dusting of antiseptic wound powder. Repeat twice daily – it is important the wound is kept clean, or it may fester, become infected and result in an abscess. Cat bites almost always end up infected if they are not treated adequately.

Rat bites are especially dangerous, as these rodents carry many harmful diseases. Treat immediately as for cat bites, then take your pet to a vet who may administer an antibiotic injection and prescribe an antibiotic dusting powder for the wound.

In areas where venomous snakes are encountered, it is not unusual for cats to attack them and be bitten in the process.

Snake bites

It is extremely important to keep the injured cat as calm as possible and prevent him running around, or even making any movements, as this will speed up the circulation of the venom around his body. Try to remain as calm as possible and seek immediate veterinary attention.

Drowning

Pull the cat out of the water, and hold him upside down (if possible) to drain the water from his lungs. Then lay him flat and rub his body fairly vigorously to promote respiration. If he is not breathing, commence artificial respiration (see page 158) and summon veterinary help as soon as possible.

Foreign bodies

In most cases, it is best to leave the removal of foreign bodies lodged in an area of the cat's body to a vet – contact your veterinary clinic for advice. If the cat is pawing at the affected area, gently restrain him to prevent further damage occurring until your vet takes over and deals with the problem. You can sometimes flush grass seeds out of the eye using a syringe filled with saline solution, and extract thorns from paws fairly easily – but check that the end has not broken off and been left in the wound. If this happens, seek veterinary treatment, or it may fester.

Choking

Choking warrants immediate action: taking the cat to a vet will waste time and may result in death from asphyxiation. Securely wrap the cat in thick material and open his mouth to see if there is anything stuck in his throat. The main worry is that, in trying to remove a foreign object, you will push it further down the throat and make matters worse. If you have a helper, ask them to hold his mouth open while you remove the blockage.

If whatever is blocking the airway is wedged in place, do not try to pull it, or you may cause more damage. Instead, with the cat on the floor in front of you but facing away from you, sit down, take the cat's hind legs and lift them to your knees, and hold the legs between your knees. Place one hand on either side of the chest and squeeze using jerky movements, to try to make the cat 'cough'. Squeeze about four or five times and the cat should cough out the object. Let your cat rest, then take him for a

Frequently asked question

Q How loose or tight should bandages be?

A If you have not done a veterinary first-aid course, bandaging is best left to vets and veterinary nurses, since incorrect application can do more harm than good by restricting blood circulation. Ask your vet clinic to show you what different bandages are used for, and how to apply them correctly.

veterinary check-up. If the object does not come out, take the cat to the vet immediately.

Lameness

Check for foreign objects lodged in a limb or paw, and also for broken bones. Seek veterinary attention as soon as possible.

Fits and convulsions

Limit how far the cat can move – put him in a large, well-padded cardboard box. Seek veterinary attention urgently. Seizures are extremely serious and potentially life-threatening.

Shock

Shock following an accident, injury or terrifying experience causes an acute fall in blood pressure, and is life-threatening. Signs of shock include: cool skin, pale lips and gums (due to a lack of blood circulation), faint, rapid pulse and staring but unseeing eyes. Keep the cat quiet and warm by wrapping him in a space blanket (or equivalent), and promote blood circulation by gently but firmly massaging his body, taking care not to aggravate any injuries in doing so. Seek veterinary attention as soon as possible.

Bleeding wounds

Most cuts and lacerations heal on their own fairly quickly; treatment consists simply of keeping them clean with cotton wool dampened with saline solution. Initial bleeding, which may be profuse, helps clean the wound of debris, thus lessening the possibility of infection. Seek veterinary attention immediately, however, if:

Clean any wounds carefully with saline solution and cotton wool.

- the wound is spouting bright red (arterial) blood in jets.
- there is a constant flow of dark red (venous) blood that refuses to cease.
- the wound is deep or serious enough to cause concern, as sutures may be required.
- gunshot wounds are suspected.
- the skin has been punctured – these wounds appear tiny on the surface, but can be quite deep and are thus particularly prone to becoming infected. Never attempt to remove a foreign object from such a wound as this may aggravate the injury and/or allow large amounts of bleeding to occur (while it is in place, the object acts as a plug and may be preventing massive blood loss).
- cuts affect toes or a limb, as tendon damage may have occurred.

In the case of minor wounds, you can stem the blood flow by means of gentle direct pressure using a dampened clean pad of cotton material, before cleaning them. Where arterial or venous bleeding is present, apply indirect pressure (not on the wound itself) to the appropriate artery or vein if you can feel it under the skin on the heart side of the wound; otherwise press a cotton pad over the wound to help stem the flow of blood. Elevating the injury, if possible, will enable gravity to help reduce the blood flow.

Internal injuries

These can be detected by abnormal swelling of the abdomen; bleeding from the mouth, nose, ears, eyes, sex organs (not to be confused with a queen's natural oestrus) or anus; bloodstained urine and/or faeces; shock; or signs of bruising on the skin. Seek veterinary attention immediately.

DON'T MAKE IT WORSE!

SITUATION	WHAT NOT TO DO
Wounds	DON'T apply direct pressure to a wound with an object impaled in it, or with bone protruding from it, or attempt to remove any objects from wounds, since this may aggravate massive blood loss; leave this to a vet.
Severe bleeding	DON'T apply a tourniquet, since it can cut off the blood flow completely, causing severe – often life-threatening – danger to the cat.
Chest compression	DON'T attempt chest compression if a chest injury is suspected.
Choking	DON'T attempt to remove an object wedged in the mouth or throat, other than by the coughing method described on page 161. If this fails, leave it to a vet.
Burns	DON'T apply too much cold water at once to the affected area, since too sudden a drop in temperature may cause more disastrous problems. See page 161.
Electrocution	DON'T touch the cat without first switching off the power supply to prevent you from also being electrocuted.
Chemical burns	DON'T attempt to treat the cat without first putting on gloves and protective clothing, to prevent the chemicals burning you.
Fits and convulsions	DON'T attempt to hold down a fitting cat.
Fractures	DON'T try to splint a broken bone – leave this to a vet.
Poisoning	DON'T make the cat vomit unless the vet gives specific guidelines to do so.
Fights	DON'T try to break up a cat fight using your hands – use a long broom-handle or stick to separate the cats.
Eye injuries	DON'T apply a bandage or compress to an eye if you suspect there may be a foreign body in it.
Ingested string	DON'T try to pull foreign bodies from the mouth or anus if you meet with resistance in doing so – seek veterinary attention instead.

Common ailments

Cats suffer from a variety of illnesses, many of which can be treated successfully. You must seek veterinary advice and treatment quickly, and faithfully follow instructions given regarding medication and care. It will help the vet treat your cat more effectively if you can provide as many details as possible about your pet. This is where knowing your cat well can be, quite literally in some cases, a lifesaver. Details to provide your vet with are shown on the checklist.

Checklist

- ✓ your pet's symptoms
- ✓ when they started
- ✓ how long they have been present
- ✓ how your cat's usual behaviour is affected

Feline influenza (feline respiratory disease/cat flu)

Flu in cats is not uncommon and, in houses where more than one cat lives, and particularly in catteries, can soon spread to other cats. Generally, the mortality rate in cats infected by cat flu is low.

Symptoms

These vary, but may include loss of appetite, fever, sneezing, depression, inflamed or reddened eyes, yellow or thick green discharge from the nose, occasional coughing and ulcers on the tongue.

Causes

The two main causes are viral. One is known as feline calici virus (FCV). The other is known as feline herpes virus (FHV) or feline viral rhinotracheitus (FVR). It is transferred from the affected cat through aerosol droplets from sneezes. Unfortunately, some cats are carriers, and although they do not show any signs of the condition they can still pass cat flu to another cat.

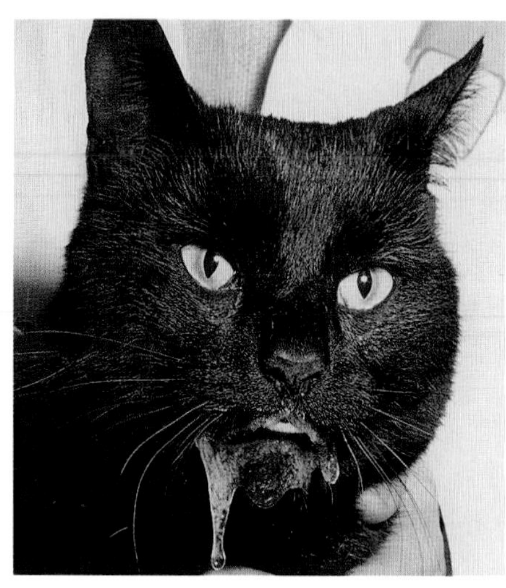

Salivation is a common symptom of cat flu.

What to do

Isolate an affected cat as soon symptoms are noticed and contact the vet within 24 hours. The incubation period is two to ten days, but even after successful treatment many cats are still carriers of the virus. In such cases, it is best if the affected cat is never allowed to come into contact with another cat. Vaccinations – both injected under the skin and sprayed up the cat's nose – can provide some protection.

Treatment

There are two parts to treatment. The first is to nurse the cat to get him eating and drinking again, and the second is to administer drugs to alleviate his suffering. The vet may prescribe antibiotics and mucolytics (which help clear the mucus from the respiratory system).

Halitosis (bad breath)

This is one of the most common mouth problems suffered by cats; most show symptoms before they are three years old.

Symptoms

Foul-smelling breath, tender gums, loss of appetite and excessive drooling. Plaque and calculus (a build-up of minerals) on a cat's teeth can lead to heart and kidney disease if left untreated. Yellow-brown stains on the teeth where they meet the gums are a classic symptom.

Causes

Usually gingivitis (inflammation of the gums), or food becoming trapped

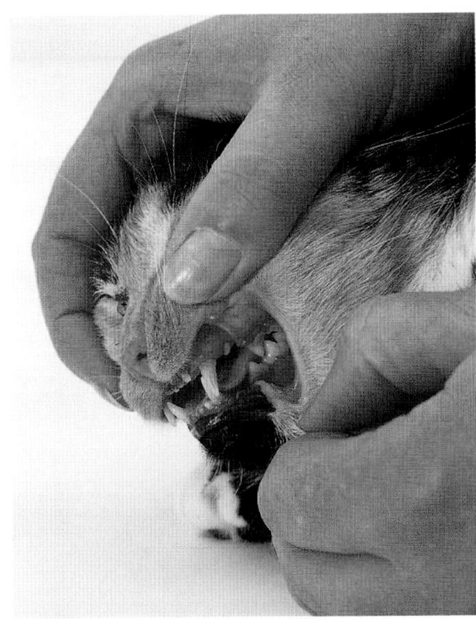

Rotten teeth and diseased gums are causes of bad breath or halitosis.

between the teeth, which attracts bacteria that will decay them. It is also a symptom of renal failure.

What to do

Keep the cat's teeth in good condition. Regularly cleaning them can act as a prevention measure, and also as a way of inspecting the cat's teeth, and finding minor problems while they can still be dealt with. Take your cat for a regular check-up which includes a mouth examination.

Treatment

If your cat suffers from gingivitis, it may be helpful to use an antiseptic spray in his mouth. Ask the vet for advice on this. Feeding mainly soft, tinned food may adversely affect the teeth, so provide some crunchy food (kibble or biscuit-type feed) at every mealtime, as this will help clean teeth. Feline 'dental toys', if the cat will play with them, may also help to keep his teeth clean.

Vomiting

This is a symptom of another condition and not an illness in itself.

Symptoms

A forceful expulsion of the contents of the cat's stomach and/or small intestine through the mouth.

Causes

These include:

- sudden change in diet
- motion sickness
- heatstroke
- conditions that affect the chemical composition of the blood, such as diabetes mellitus, renal failure, liver disease or a bacterial infection
- a foreign body in the stomach
- gastric dilation/torsion
- stomach cancer
- parasitic worms
- fear and stress
- trauma to the head
- infections
- ingestion of emetic substances, such as grass
- furballs

What to do

If your cat suddenly and repeatedly vomits, you should withhold food and water, and contact the vet. Keep the cat where you can see him, covering the floor with newspaper, or something similar, to keep your home clean. Note the times of vomiting, and also the consistency, colour and quantity of the vomit. By doing this, you will help the vet to find the cause and therefore treat the problem effectively. Occasional vomiting is normal, and no action need be taken in such cases. In cases of recurring vomiting, or where large amounts of vomit are produced, or there is blood in the vomit, seek veterinary advice.

Vomiting may be caused by furballs, but regular grooming will reduce the risk of these developing.

Vomiting that you consider to be a result of your cat's scavenging, and which is therefore spasmodic and not severe, is best treated by starving the cat for 24 hours. During this time, it is vital that the cat is offered regular small amounts of water to drink, to help prevent dehydration.

After this time, reintroduce food with small, light meals, such as scrambled eggs or boiled chicken, gradually building up to his former feeding regime. If the vomiting continues, or starts again when food is reintroduced, seek veterinary advice as soon as possible.

You can help prevent some of the causes of vomiting by treating your cat on a regular basis for internal parasites (worms), discouraging him from scavenging, not making sudden changes to his diet, not feeding him prior to travelling, and not overfeeding him.

Treatment

In severe cases, it is not unusual for the affected cat to be placed on an intravenous drip to keep him hydrated. Where a foreign body is wedged somewhere in the digestive system, surgery will be needed to remove it.

Diarrhoea

Like vomiting, diarrhoea is a symptom of an underlying condition and is not an illness in itself.

Symptoms

Pungent, liquid-like faeces; these may be passed frequently, necessitating many trips to the litter tray, or appear as 'accidents' around the home. If your cat is suffering from colitis (an inflammation of the colon), his faeces will contain quite a lot of mucus and bright red blood. Another symptom of colitis is tenesmus, where the cat strains to defecate; this latter symptom is often mistaken for a symptom of constipation. Diarrhoea often leads to dehydration, so your cat may appear slightly disorientated.

Causes

Diarrhoea may simply be a symptom of overeating or stress. Intestinal worms are a common cause of diarrhoea, as are foreign bodies in the digestive system and fungal infections.

What to do

Prevent the cat from eating anything, but ensure that he is given adequate amounts of drinking water. If the diarrhoea is acute, provide the cat with a rehydrating fluid (see First-aid kit on page 157) and contact the vet. Keep your cat where you can see him, covering the floor with newspapers, or something similar, to keep your home clean. Note the times of his motions, and also the consistency, colour and quantity of the diarrhoea. By doing this, you will help the vet to find the cause of the sudden diarrhoea, and to treat the problem effectively.

Treatment

The treatment for diarrhoea depends upon the underlying cause. If it is due to internal parasites, then anthelmintics (wormers) will be used to rid the cat of the infestation, while antibiotics will be used for infections. Diarrhoea can cause the cat to dehydrate, and can lead to irreparable body damage (particularly of the kidneys) and even death. In all cases of severe diarrhoea (where overeating is not the cause), if it persists, or if there is blood in the motions, consult your vet immediately so the cat can be treated at once.

Enteritis

This is inflammation of the intestines, causing diarrhoea.

Symptoms

Diarrhoea, and signs of blood in the loose motions, may indicate this condition.

Causes

Enteritis is very common among young cats and can be caused by different things, but often it is the bacterium *Escherichia coli* (referred to as E. coli) that is the culprit. Another major cause of enteritis is

Diarrhoea and the risk to humans

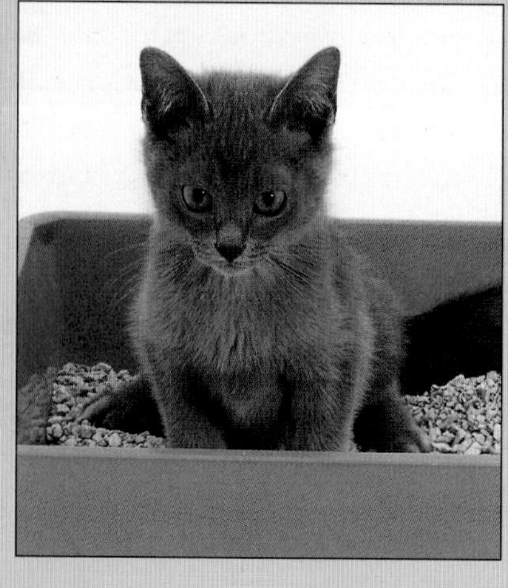

Diarrhoea in your cat may be caused by a zoonotic disease – one that can be transmitted to humans. Such diseases include campylobacter and salmonella, both caused by harmful bacteria. To reduce the chance of any of these diseases being passed on to you and your family, always wash your hands after handling your cat – and particularly before eating. Isolate the affected cat and keep him on water and electrolytes for 24 hours, dosing with kaolin solution (available from vets, doctors and pharmacies), about every two hours. After the fast, food intake should gradually be built up again; cooked chicken, rabbit and fish are excellent foods for a recovering cat.

campylobacter bacteria; in humans, 'food poisoning' of this type is known as dysentery.

What to do

Observe your cat's actions, and the amount, colour, consistency, and smell of his motions. In particular, look for any signs of blood in the faeces.

Treatment

Immediate treatment with a broad-spectrum antibiotic, together with regular doses of kaolin, may cure the condition. Sometimes more than one antibiotic is needed, or more than one course. Enteritis can be life-threatening, and treatment must start as soon as possible.

Constipation

Constipation comprises a failure by the cat to pass faeces (or passing fewer motions, and less frequently than usual). It is a symptom, not a disease, which may have many underlying causes, and is fairly common in elderly cats.

Symptoms

A cat producing extremely dry faeces, or straining to defecate, is probably constipated. Every cat and his lifestyle is different, but cats should be expected to defecate one to four times daily.

Causes

Any debilitating disease can cause constipation, as can a foreign body blocking the cat's digestive system (usually this occurs in the intestines). Constipation can also be a symptom of prostate problems in male cats.

Provide an incontinent cat with litter trays throughout the house, to reduce the risk of 'accidents'.

What to do

Providing your cat with a diet high in fibre and giving a good overall balanced diet will help prevent many cases of constipation.

Treatment

Where an internal blockage is the cause, the cat will need surgery. In cases linked with diet, laxatives and a change of diet may be all that is needed. Constipation is potentially very dangerous, so always consult your vet when it occurs.

Urinary incontinence

This is the inability to control urination.

Symptoms

The cat will have 'accidents', particularly when resting. He will not have urinated deliberately, but because of his condition the urine will dribble out involuntarily when he is lying down.

Causes

There are many possible causes of urinary incontinence, which may include faulty urethral valves, congenital defects of the cat's urinary system, urolithiasis (crystals or 'stones' of insoluble calcium in the urinary system), cancer or prostate problems (in male cats). Urinary incontinence is seen particularly in older queens.

What to do

When taking your cat for veterinary examination, provide a fresh sample of your pet's urine for testing; this will reveal if any diseases are causing the problem. It is unfair to punish or reproach a cat for incontinence. The cat's bed is likely to become soiled, so bedding must be changed and cleaned at regular and frequent intervals, preferably daily.

Treatment

Surgery may be needed to treat faulty urethral valves, congenital defects of the cat' urinary system, urolithiasis, cancer or prostate problems (in male cats), while drug therapy may be used to improve the effectiveness of the urethra in sealing the flow of urine. Urinary incontinence is not life-threatening in itself but, because some of the possible underlying causes may be serious, it is better to seek veterinary advice sooner rather than later.

Arthritis

This causes inflammation of the joints. There are two forms of arthritis that may affect cats – osteoarthritis and traumatic arthritis.

Symptoms

Swollen joints, difficulty in walking, and lameness.

Causes

Osteoarthritis may be a condition in itself or a result of other conditions. It is a progressive and painful disease that will seriously affect the quality of life of the affected cat. It may affect one or more joints, and the seriousness of the condition will depend on which joints are affected, and the general health of the cat. Osteoarthritis is not nearly as common in cats as it is in dogs. Overweight cats are more prone to osteoarthritis. Traumatic arthritis is caused as a direct result of an injury to the joint; for example, it may be the result of a road traffic accident or a sprain while exercising.

What to do

Your vet will advise you on what action you should take, as this will depend on the underlying causes and treatment being given.

Treatment

The treatment for arthritis may include anti-inflammatory drugs and painkillers, and in some cases surgery may be needed. All cases of osteoarthritis should be treated seriously. Don't wait until your cat cannot walk before consulting the vet. A physical examination and observation of the cat's movement, along with X-rays and analysis of joint fluid, will give the vet an indication of how serious an arthritic problem is.

Poor exercise tolerance

Sometimes a normally active cat will develop problems that make exercise difficult for him.

Symptoms

Pain and discomfort during what should be normal exercise.

Causes

This is often a direct result of inflammation of the joints (arthritis). Where a muscle is diseased (for example with a bacterial infection), it is referred to as myopathy; where a muscle is inflamed, it is referred to as myositis.

What to do

Be very careful with regard to administering painkillers, unless under veterinary instruction. Painkillers can easily lull a cat into a false sense of security, causing him to use injured joints which will result in more damage.

Treatment

In cases of mild myopathy, for example where your cat develops a slight limp for 24–36 hours, simply resting him will probably relieve the problem (sometimes it will be necessary to confine him to a limited space, such as a pen). If the limp persists beyond this time, veterinary advice and treatment should be sought. When a joint is damaged, the injury is referred to as a sprain, and may involve damage to cartilage and/or ligaments. While not dangerous in itself, the condition is painful. If not treated adequately, a sprain may lead to osteoarthritis. Damage from osteoarthritis is usually permanent.

Blindness

This may mean limited vision, or total lack of vision.

Symptoms

Your cat may bump into furniture and objects for no apparent reason. It is also quite common for an elderly cat to have more problems with his eyesight in bright light and in darkness, and he may be reluctant to venture out at such times.

Causes

There is a variety of causes – from injury to hereditary diseases and

Cloudy or opaque eyes indicate a sight problem; many cats adjust remarkably well to being blind in one or both eyes.

conditions. As cats age, it is quite common for a bluish colour to appear in the eyes as the lens of the eye deteriorates.

What to do

Any cat showing symptoms of failing eyesight should be taken to a vet without delay.

Treatment

This depends upon the cause, but many cases of total blindness are untreatable.

Feline chlamydial infection

Chlamydia consists of infection with *Chlamydia psittaci*, a bacterium that causes conjunctivitis.

Symptoms

Conjunctivitis (reddened eye) and a thick, ocular discharge. Sneezing and a nasal discharge are also common.

Causes

Cats become infected by *Chlamydia psittaci* which is spread by other infected cats in their bodily discharges.

What to do

Seek urgent veterinary treatment for any eye infection.

Treatment

The vet will prescribe antibiotics, and the whole course must be completed. If feline chlamydial infection is not treated quickly and adequately by a vet, it can infect the gastrointestinal (digestive) and genital systems of the cat, and may cause reproductive problems in queens.

Feline chlamydial infection, common in kittens of one to nine months, causes conjunctivitis.

Ear mites

These are insect parasites very common in cats.

Symptoms

Persistent ear-scratching. A build-up of wax in the ears, dotted with black specks, is an indication that a cat may have ear mites; the black specks are probably spots of dried blood. The mites can move down the ear canal and infect the middle ear; such an infection will cause the affected animal to lose his sense of balance. The cat may be unable to hold his head straight or, in more serious cases, may constantly fall over.

Causes

Ear mites (*Otodectes cynotis*), which are common in cats and also in wild rodents.

If left untreated, the irritation caused by ear mites will cause the cat to scratch, sometimes until his ears actually bleed.

What to do

Seek veterinary advice in all cases of ear mites, or if your cat suffers balance loss. All animals that have been in contact with the infected cat must also be treated, as ear mites can infect other animals that may not show any symptoms for some time.

Treatment

In mild cases, the vet will prescribe ear drops. If the cat's ears are irritated, they may also prescribe anti-inflammatory drugs. Mites are easily treated if caught early enough. The ear mites are usually white or colourless and are not visible to the naked eye – a magnifying glass lens or otoscope is required (although otoscopes may not be able to detect them as the mites hide under pieces of wax). A special instrument called an otoscope is used to inspect the inside of a cat's ears.

Ear canker (otitis)

An inflammation of the skin lining the ear, otitis is one of the most

common conditions in cats, and may occur in one or both ears.

Symptoms

These may include regular ear-scratching and head-shaking, a discharge or smell from the ear and reddening of the inner ear flap and/or the ear hole. The cat may well hiss at anyone who ventures to touch him around the ear.

Causes

Normally, the amount of wax produced in a cat's ear is exactly the same amount that is lost naturally. Much of the wax is lost through evaporation of the water from the wax. Problems occur when the ears do not get proper ventilation and the wax builds up. This excess wax causes irritation, and the ear is stimulated to produce even more wax. This leads to ideal conditions for normally harmless fungi and bacteria to grow and prosper. Ear mites, foreign bodies in the ear and skin problems can also cause otitis.

What to do

Take any cat showing any of the symptoms of irritated ears to the vet as soon as possible – immediately if you suspect a foreign body is lodged in the ear. *Never* attempt to remove a blockage yourself, as you may damage the cat's ear permanently. Don't put any liquid, ointment or other medication inside the cat's ears unless on the direction of your vet, and don't attempt to put any solid object inside the cat's ear, including cotton buds, which may also damage the ear.

Discharge from the ear should not be interfered with until your vet has had a chance to see it, as this may provide some clues about the ear problem.

Treatment

Treatment may include syringing of the ear, or the application of a topical medicine, such as ear drops or ointment. Whatever medications are prescribed, it is important that you administer them exactly as instructed, and always finish the course of treatment. In serious cases of recurring otitis, surgery may be necessary to improve ear ventilation. Even though otitis is not a serious condition, if not properly treated it can become chronic, causing severe problems and possibly damage to parts of the ear and the cat's hearing.

Ear flap wounds

These are scratches or tears to the ear flaps (pinnas).

Symptoms

Any ear wound, no matter how minor, is likely to bleed a great deal. Even if the actual wound does not cause the cat any real pain, the irritation of blood running down the ear is likely to cause him to scratch at his ear and shake his head.

Causes

Ear flaps are often bitten and scratched during fighting, and some felines, particularly farm cats, may injure their ear flaps in their usual day-to-day life.

What to do

With someone restraining the cat, the wounds should be cleaned using saline solution. Once cleaned, it will be possible to see the extent of the damage; if this is significant, seek veterinary treatment as the wounds may need suturing.

Treatment

After cleaning with saline solution, cover minor wounds with antiseptic ointment, cream or powder. If the wounds look inflamed within a few days of the injury, consult the vet, as antibiotic treatment may be required.

If ear-flap wounds are not treated, they may become infected and far more serious.

Due to the long-term nature of the intensive treatment required for renal failure, veterinary costs will be high.

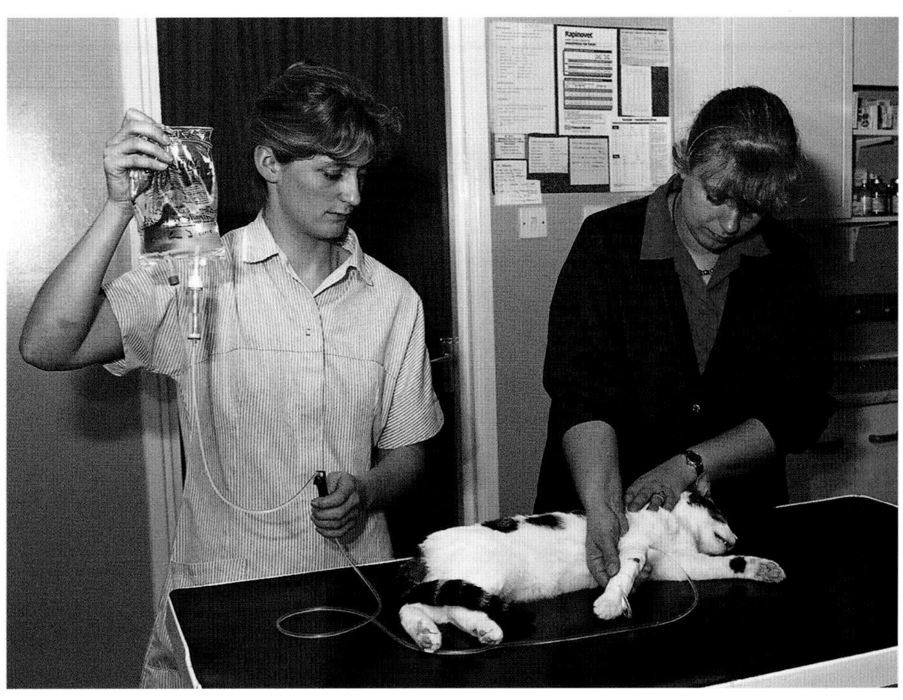

Kidney (renal) failure

Kidney failure is probably the most common problem seen in elderly cats. It is also a symptom of polycystic kidney disease (PKD), a hereditary condition which is often found in Persian cats.

Symptoms

These include a seemingly insatiable thirst, the passing of large amounts of urine either in one go or at very frequent intervals, vomiting, diarrhoea, loss of appetite, weight loss, halitosis and anaemia.

Causes

For various reasons, including infections and physical damage, the nephrons (parts of the kidneys that remove waste products from the blood) may fail to do their job properly, and this leads to chronic renal failure. This is an extremely serious and usually irreversible condition with a very poor chance of recovery. The condition rarely occurs in cats under 5 years of age.

What to do

Renal failure is life-threatening. Don't hesitate to contact the vet if you suspect this condition in your cat.

Treatment

Treatment of an affected cat may include a period of intensive care, during which the cat will have fluids administered via an intravenous drip, and a special diet, coupled with a restful lifestyle and a prescribed course of medication. A cat suffering from renal failure will die, and you may choose to have him put to sleep.

Feline infectious enteritis (FIE)

Also called feline panleukopenia, this widespread, life-threatening viral disease attacks the white blood cells and the cat's gut.

Symptoms

These include loss of appetite, persistent vomiting and/or diarrhoea.

Causes

The virus is passed from one infected cat to others by direct or indirect contact.

What to do

This disease is highly infectious, so isolate any infected cats. To guard against it, make sure your cat is vaccinated and receives regular boosters.

Treatment

There is no real treatment for FIE, but special care and intensive nursing may alleviate the symptoms. Seek immediate veterinary treatment for any cat showing symptoms of this disease. A severe infection may kill a young cat or kitten very quickly.

Diabetes mellitus (sugar diabetes)

In this hormonal condition, the cat is unable to control his blood-sugar levels.

Symptoms

Increased appetite, particularly if coupled with other symptoms such as an increase in the amount of urine passed, lethargy, weight loss and maybe cataracts. Very often, symptoms of diabetes mellitus are seen in queens just after they have started oestrus. Many of the conditions associated with diabetes mellitus are also common symptoms of other, less serious, diseases or other factors. For example, an increased thirst may simply be due to your cat being fed on a dry diet.

Causes

A lack of insulin (produced by the pancreas) or an increase in blood-sugar levels (hyperglycaemia). It is most common in cats over 8 years of age. Due to the increased levels of progesterone (a hormone) in the blood during phantom or pseudo pregnancies, unspayed queens are said to be more than three times more susceptible to diabetes mellitus, and obese cats of either sex are also at increased risk.

What to do

Take any cat showing symptoms of diabetes for examination by a vet as soon as possible.

Treatment

Treatment for this condition is likely to be long-term, as your cat may need regular insulin injections and other treatment, so the costs in terms of both time and money will be fairly high. Typically, you will need to collect and test a sample of urine from your cat every morning to check the glucose levels, calculate the amount of insulin needed and administer it by injection, and feed your cat an extremely regulated (high-fibre) diet at specific times. Your vet will advise you on all of these matters. In queens, spaying will keep the cat's condition stable.

Voracious hunger can sometimes be an indication of diabetes mellitus.

Diabetes insipidus

This renders the body incapable of regulating the use of water.

Symptoms

These include polydipsia (excessive thirst) and polyuria (production of large amounts of urine).

Causes

Diabetes insipidus is caused by lack of the anti-diuretic hormone ADH (produced in the cat's pituitary glands), or the failure of kidneys to respond to this hormone. Normally, the production of ADH is increased when there is little water intake, and decreased when the cat drinks large quantities of water, thus controlling the body's water balance.

What to do

Any sign of abnormal water intake should be investigated by a vet as soon as possible.

Treatment

Depending on which form of diabetes inspidus is present, treatment may involve the administration of ADH to the affected cat; this is administered through nasal drops.

Abnormal water intake

This is an increased or decreased need to drink water.

Symptoms

The cat either drinks more or less water than is normal for him. Other symptoms include an increased or decreased need to urinate.

Causes

It can be a symptom of cystitis, tapeworm infestation, diabetes insipidus or diabetes mellitus.

Increased thirst can also be due to a cat being fed on a dry diet.

What to do

Keep an eye on urine deposits in the litter tray; if you know what is generally normal for your pet, then a change will be detected early. Cystitis is indicated by discomfort and straining to urinate, while tapeworm infestation is signalled by the visible presence of worms in faeces, and also tiny white segments of them sticking to fur around the anus.

Treatment

Take your cat for a veterinary examination: treatment will depend on the cause of the condition. If tapeworms are to blame, deworming will be in order, while cystitis is treatable with antibiotics.

Feline leukaemia virus (FeLV)

This viral infection affects the cat's immuno-response system.

Symptoms

Lethargy, high temperature, lack of appetite and enlarged lymph nodes in the neck area, in the 'armpits' and in the groin area.

Causes

A virus which is contained in blood, semen and saliva; it is spread through mating and bite wounds.

What to do

There can be a delay of as much as three years between the cat becoming infected and showing signs of the condition, so there is no real urgency to seek veterinary treatment unless the cat exhibits severe symptoms that cause him pain or discomfort.

Treatment

There is no cure for FeLV. Many cats infected with the disease will make a reasonable recovery naturally, but will then become carriers, spreading the condition to all other cats with which they come into contact. If you have more than one cat in your home, the vet may recommend that the infected cat is euthanized in order to limit the risk of the infection spreading to other cats. If you have just one cat, you must not allow him to go outside, where he may come into contact with, and therefore infect, other cats in your neighbourhood. Some owners prefer not to risk their cat infecting others, so choose to have him euthanized. There is a vaccine available for this condition, and owners are advised to have their cat vaccinated on a regular basis.

Feline infectious peritonitis (FIP)

Caused by a virus that affects cat under about three years of age, this infection is known to spread rapidly among cats, and so is particularly dangerous in households where there is more than one cat.

Bites sustained in fights are a common means by which FeLV is transferred from one cat to another.

Symptoms

These include loss of appetite, a swollen abdomen, loss of weight, breathing problems and a fever.

Causes

A virus (feline coronavirus) which is passed from one infected cat to another by direct or indirect contact.

What to do

Isolate infected cats and seek urgent veterinary advice.

Treatment

There is no treatment for FIP and most cats die as a direct result of this infection. It may be advisable to have your cat put to sleep; your vet will help you to make this decision.

Feline immunodeficiency virus (FIV)

Also known as feline T-lymphotropic lentivirus (FTLV) and feline AIDS, this viral infection affects the RNA (ribonucleic acid) that is involved in the manufacture of proteins within the cat's cells. It prevents the body's immuno-defence system from fighting off infections.

Symptoms

This virus allows many infections to become established in the affected cat but has no symptoms as such.

Causes

The virus multiplies in the white cells in the cat's blood and is often transmitted through cat bites.

What to do

You must take any cat suspected of suffering an FIV infection to the vet. Infected cats will suffer chronic long-term illnesses, weight loss and other debilitating conditions as a result of the infections caused by the lack of immuno-response.

Treatment

There is currently no treatment available for a cat infected with FIV and euthanasia is usually recommended.

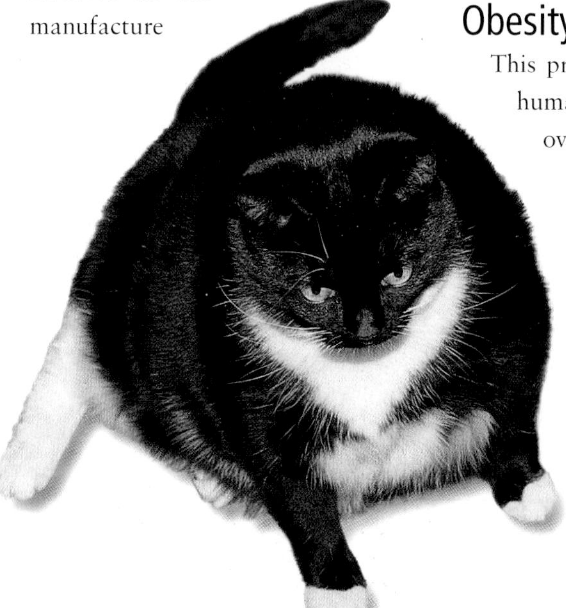

Old cats are prone to obesity if they are not very active.

Obesity

This problem is not confined to the human population – many owners overfeed and under-exercise their pets, sometimes with the best of intentions.

Symptoms

The cat is overweight, even grossly fat, signified by rolls of fat under the skin. This can cause breathlessness and a reluctance to exercise. It can predispose the cat to joint problems and other illnesses associated with obesity, such as heart and major organ failure.

Causes

Old age, when the cat does not exercise as much as he may once have done, overeating, or being fed an unsuitable diet.

What to do

Consult your vet regarding a suitable diet plan.

Treatment

Encourage your cat to exercise more by playing, and hide his food ration around the house so he has to hunt for it, thereby expending energy. Follow your vet's diet plan strictly; if the cat is old, a specially formulated low-calorie diet for elderly felines will probably be recommended.

Heatstroke

This is a fever caused by the failure of the body's temperature-regulating mechanism when exposed to excessively high temperatures.

Symptoms

Agitation and extreme distress. First, the cat will stretch out and pant heavily, then drool and stagger as if drunk. Finally, if untreated, it will collapse, pass into a coma and die.

Causes

Usually due to being in a car – either on a long journey or left inside one. Inside a car, there is poor ventilation and the temperature rises to a

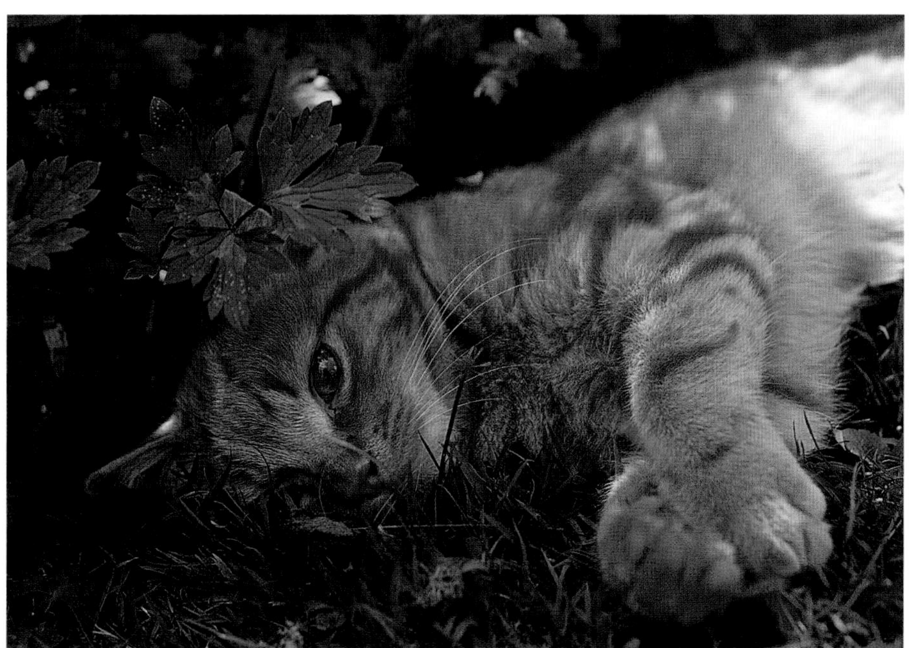

Cats will naturally seek shelter from the sun, or move to a cooler area of the house, when they feel they are getting too hot.

dangerous level quickly, even in the cooler sunshine of spring or autumn.

What to do

You must act fast. In mildly affected cats, simply moving them to a cool place and ensuring a steady passage of cool air will usually be sufficient.

Treatment

In bad cases, cool the cat down with cold water from a hosepipe (using a fine misting spray) or by gently pouring bowlfuls of cold water over it. In very bad cases, cover the cat with wet towels, including the head (but keeping the nose and mouth clear) and keep dousing him with cold water. Seek veterinary assistance urgently. In all cases of heatstroke, it is vital to keep the head cool, as the brain may literally be cooked, and brain death can occur.

Flea dermatitis

Irritation and soreness of the skin occurs around flea bites.

Symptoms

Red, raw areas and scabs caused by the cat scratching himself obsessively; these may be found all over the cat's body, or just in localized areas such as near the base of the tail and behind the ears. Some cats are more sensitive than others to flea bites and can be driven almost to distraction with the resultant itching.

Causes

A reaction to the saliva of the fleas when they bite the cat in order to feed on his blood.

What to do

Consult your vet.

Treatment

The cat may require a course of treatment to alleviate irritation, along with treatment to kill the fleas and prevent reinfestation.

Ringworm

This is a fungal infection of the skin.

Symptoms

Scratching, and circular areas of hair loss, with the visible skin becoming scaly and raised around the edge of the lesion.

Causes

Fungi, including *Microsporum canis*, *Microsporum gypseum* and *Trichophyton mentagrophytes*. Spores of these fungi may be wind-borne or found in the soil.

What to do

Some of the fungi responsible for ringworm are zoonotic (contractable by humans), so take care that you and your family are not infected. Only your vet can prescribe effective treatment, so seek urgent advice.

Treatment

Washing the cat in fungicidal wash prescribed by a vet will help kill the fungi. Topical applications of fungicidal treatment may also be recommended.

Telltale signs of ringworm infection include a circular area of hair loss and scaly, flaking skin.

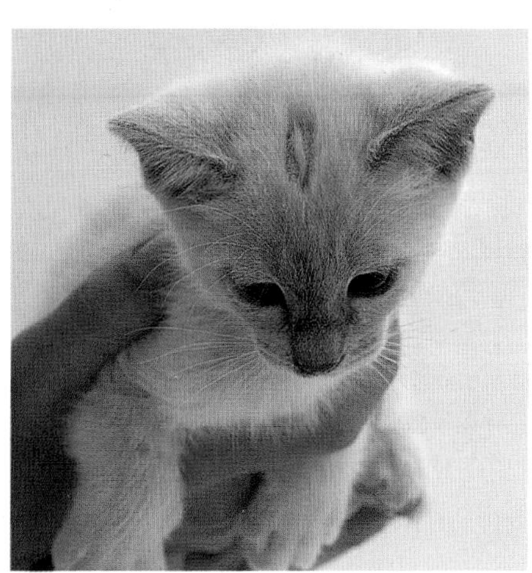

Complementary therapies

More and more vets are now adopting a natural approach when treating sick animals, cats included. Natural medicine denotes the use of complementary (natural and traditional) therapies and remedies, as opposed to conventional medicine (synthetic drugs and remedies). A more holistic view is taken of ailments whereby the whole animal is considered, rather than simply the condition(s) that he is exhibiting. Diagnosis takes into account everything on the checklist.

Checklist

- ✓ overall physical health
- ✓ mental health
- ✓ environment
- ✓ exercise
- ✓ daily routine
- ✓ companionship
- ✓ nutrition (food and water)
- ✓ hygiene

What is involved?

When the vet or practitioner has ascertained what is ailing your cat, and why, he or she will decide upon the appropriate action or treatment. In some cases, treatment may simply involve making improvements to your cat's living environment or exercise levels, or changing his diet to one that better suits his digestive system. In other instances, it may well be that a course of treatment – acupuncture for example – may have the desired effect in curing whatever is ailing the animal. Sometimes the provision of extra companionship, either human or in the form of another animal, can have the desired effect of alleviating anxiety-induced health problems.

Do these therapies work?

Many people and vets believe and advocate that they do, and can recount innumerable case histories showing how natural medicine triumphed where conventional treatment failed. There appears to be little scientific research to substantiate such claims where some therapies are concerned (such as spiritual healing and feng shui), but these remedies have been used for a long time, even thousands of years – and something that does not work is unlikely to be persevered with. With most forms of complementary therapy, as long as they are applied with expertise and knowledge, the worst that can happen is that they have no effect.

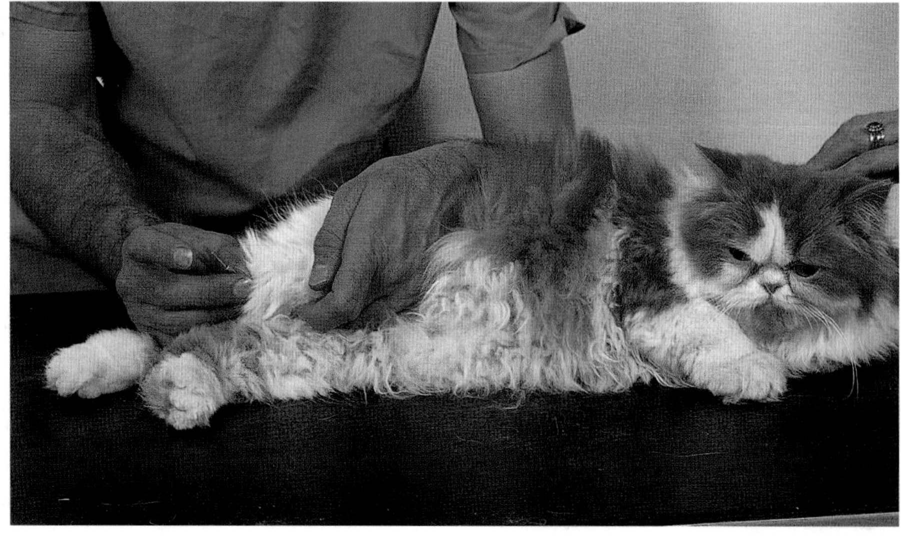

Acupuncture has been used for thousands of years to treat a variety of ailments – animal and human.

Top tip

Complementary therapies should not be considered the last resort by pet owners but as viable forms of treatment that are well worth trying. The range of ailments and conditions that can benefit from natural therapies is vast. A tiny selection of these includes poisoning, diabetes mellitus, osteoarthritis, gingivitis, constipation, cancer, nervousness, aggression, skin diseases, internal and external parasites and anal gland disorders. Ask your vet's advice for practitioners in your area.

When to try them

Complementary therapies are so called because most of them are complementary to each other, and many of them can be used alongside, or in conjunction with, conventional medicine. Better results or speedier recoveries can sometimes be obtained by using a combination of two or more therapies to treat a health problem, depending on what the problem is.

Correctly administered, complementary therapies have been known to bring about seemingly miraculous results.

Finding a practitioner

An increasing number of vets are using natural healing treatments, so it shouldn't be too difficult to find an experienced and trustworthy practitioner. Even if your own vet does not personally practise traditional medicine in the particular field you are interested in, he or she may be able to refer you to a reputable person who does. The internet is another valuable resource for finding a practitioner.

Frequently asked question

Q My vet is quite old-fashioned and won't entertain the idea of any form of 'alternative' treatment, but now I would like my cat to be treated naturally wherever possible. What should I do?

A If your vet will not refer you to a complementary practitioner, it may be advisable to take your business to a veterinary clinic that will. You are quite within your rights to do so – after all it is your cat's health that is important, not the feelings of your vet. Ring around veterinary practices in your area – or further afield if you have no other choice – to find one that suits you and your cat's needs. Bear in mind, though, that the further you have to travel the less convenient it may be in an emergency.

THERAPY	WHAT IT INVOLVES
Acupressure	Non-invasive pressure is applied to acupoints on the body via the practitioner's fingers or thumbs to induce the same reactions in the patient as acupunture.
Acupuncture	Fine copper or steel special needles are inserted in the skin at specific points (acupoints) on the body to relieve illness and also mental and/or physical stress. This treatment has been shown to alleviate pain, heal damage, promote bodily chemicals that produce a sense of well-being, improve the appetite and raise energy levels.
Aromatherapy	Essential plant oils – diluted, undiluted or contained in a bland base oil as appropriate – are used to treat ailments. They are applied either by allowing the cat to choose and smell certain oils as its body dictates, or by applying them topically (to the surface of the body) where appropriate. They can be used for a whole host of complaints, from fleas to emotional problems.
Biochemical tissue salts	A form of homoeopathy (see opposite) using 12 energized mineral salts.
Chiropractic	Manipulative method of treating disorders and displacements of joints, especially those in the spine. It can prove useful in cases of back pain, lameness and joint injuries.
Colour therapy	Colours have an effect on physical and mental well-being, so can be used to treat a variety of ailments.
Crystals and gems	Through energy waves, each type of crystal can help heal mental and physical ailments. Once the symptoms of the ailment have been determined, the practitioner chooses appropriate stones for the cat to wear, have around his body while resting and/or have in his bed.
Dowsing	Although not a healing treatment in itself, it works as a method of ailment diagnosis by means of a divining rod or pendulum held over the patient.
Electro-crystal therapy	This enhances the effects of crystals through an energy field created by a small electric charge. Special equipment is used to administer this painless treatment.
Feng shui	This ancient Chinese art involves arranging your cat's home environment to optimize his mental and physical well-being. Acupuncture was derived from this practice.
Flower remedies	These are essences derived from specific flower petals which are floated in water to transfer their healing properties into the liquid, to which a tiny amount of alcohol (usually brandy) has been added to preserve them. Essences are available for all sorts of behavioural problems, including anxiety, aggression, timidity and shock. They appear also to alleviate physical ailments, if these are linked to mental or emotional problems.
Herbalism	Plant-based natural medicines for both external and internal use. For example, the willow tree is a source of salicylic acid (aspirin), while digitalis (heart medicine) is derived from foxglove. An infusion of mallow can be used to bathe swollen areas to reduce swelling, while comfrey can be taken internally to help repair bone fractures.

THERAPY	WHAT IT INVOLVES
Homoeopathy	Remedies derived from animal, mineral and vegetable substances through a special process called 'potentization' that releases their therapeutic properties. It works on the principle of 'like cures like': if a substance causes adverse symptoms in an animal, a minute 'energized' dose of it can also cure those same symptoms. Remedies include those from seemingly strange sources such as lead, poisonous snake venom, arsenic, egg yolk and animal tissue, among many others.
Iridology	Ailments are diagnosed by examining the iris of the eye; minute changes in its colour and shape can inform the practitioner about the patient's health status, the location and type of disease present in the body, and whether the cat will have a tendency towards disease in the future.
Kinesiology	Testing muscles that relate to an organ system through an energy field (the cat) to determine imbalances.
Magnotherapy	The use of magnets to promote healing, through increasing blood supply to the afflicted area.
Osteopathy	Manipulative adjustment of muscles and joints to relieve misalignment that is causing pain.
Physiotherapy	This involves body manipulation, massage, exercise, specialized machines (such as ultrasound) and the application of warmth or cold as appropriate to help treat disease, injury or deformity.
Radionics	This distance healing works by the practitioner assessing a 'witness' (a lock of hair, for example) from the cat to determine what ails him, then directing healing energy vibrations at him through a specialized radionics instrument known as the 'black box'.
Reflexology	Diseases of body organs are treated by applying pressure to particular joints.
Spiritual (faith) healing	The 'laying-on of hands' on the animal or his affected area: healing powers are directed at the patient through the healer. This form of healing has proven effective with 'incurable' diseases such as cancer, though is not guaranteed to work – it depends on the individual cat.
Touch massage	Gentle, repetitive massaging movements, which are said to generate specific brainwave patterns in the recipient that help promote mental and physical healing.

TWILIGHT YEARS

The company of an ageing cat in good health is delightful and soothing, and just as rewarding as playing with a kitten. To care for an older cat, you may need to make a few changes in his everyday regime, and make a few allowances for his age, but it will be well worth the effort.

Caring for the older (senior) cat

A cat can be considered old when he starts to take things easy and spends more time than usual sleeping. The old cat's reactions are sharp, his movements are subtle, and he may even deign to chase string and pat feathers, as long as he is not made to feel foolish. Just because he sits around a lot and is undemanding and quiet, an elderly cat should not be ignored. To remain happy and in the best possible health, he needs everything on the checklist.

Checklist

- ✓ lots of love and affection
- ✓ particular attention to claws and teeth
- ✓ extra care with diet
- ✓ help with grooming
- ✓ twice-yearly veterinary check-ups
- ✓ patience and understanding if 'accidents' occur
- ✓ unchanging daily routine
- ✓ minimal upheaval in his life
- ✓ plenty of sleep

Lifestyle

Just like elderly people, old cats are resistant to and can be upset by major changes in their routine and lifestyle. If changes do have to happen, try to incorporate them gradually to allow your cat time to get used to them. Everything should be done to keep the elderly cat feeling as good as possible. (For holiday care, see pages 116–119.)

Disturbed behaviour patterns may be the result of chronic illness in the old cat. For example, a previously clean cat may have 'accidents', making puddles on chairs and carpets. Should this happen, it may be best to keep the cat in areas of the house where such accidents don't matter – but that does not mean he should be shut away or limited in his access to his family, as this would be unfair and cruel.

Very old cats doze most of their days away, and prefer to be where they are most comfortable, feel safe and can relax and sleep deeply.

It would also be unfair and cruel to chastise or ban the cat from the house for something that is beyond his control. Carpets can be replaced, but loving companions cannot.

Older cats are more prone to constipation, so keep a watch for this and seek veterinary attention if it occurs.

Companionship

Some people consider getting a kitten when their established cat gets old. This can be a good or bad decision, depending on the temperament and nature of the aged cat. If he likes the kitten, then he may gain a new lease of life. If, however, he does not, then he may resent the newcomer and become depressed and withdrawn, stop eating and, ultimately, become very ill. If the old cat is the only one in the household and has always been a loner, then it would be kinder not to get another cat or kitten.

If your elderly cat displays an increased need for your company, always give him plenty of attention and reassurance – even consider moving his bed into your bedroom at night if necessary. Leaving a radio on low while you are out can help provide 'company'.

Diet

Foods specially formulated for elderly cats are available, and these contain all the nutrients the ageing body needs to remain in the best possible condition, and help delay or alleviate the onset of conditions such as senility. As older cats can often suffer from urinary-tract problems, a totally dry diet may not be the best choice; it may be wise to consult your vet regarding the best type of food for your cat. See also Feeding your cat, pages 36–43.

Bad teeth and inflamed gums are not uncommon in old cats; at this stage, your cat will find soft moist or semi-moist food easier to eat. Make sure there is always a plentiful supply of fresh, clean water.

A cat tends to slow down as he ages, and may tend towards obesity if you don't monitor his diet closely.

Frequently asked question

Q How old are cats in human terms?

A By the time a kitten is 12 months old he is thought to be the equivalent of a 15-year-old human, and is considered physically mature, depending on his breed and type; 14 months equates to 18 years; 2 years is equivalent to 24 years. From then on, to calculate his approximate age in human years, add 4 years for every year that your cat lives. For example, a 10-year-old cat would be 56 in human years and a 16-year-old would be 80.

LEFT *Because their bodies do not regulate temperature as efficiently as their younger counterparts, older cats seek out warm places to rest – on top of a boiler being a favourite spot. They also prefer to stay indoors when it is cold or wet outside.*

BELOW *Keep an eye on senior cats when they are allowed outside, particularly senile, blind or deaf pets – these are at risk from getting lost and potential hazards such as predators and traffic.*

Feline facts

- Unless you know his birth date, it is extremely difficult to age a mature, fit and active cat aged between three and 13 accurately, because there are no specific signs of ageing to look for and cats age much more gracefully than their canine counterparts.
- On average, cats now live to around 14 years of age, thanks to improved geriatric feline veterinary care and nutrition. Many cats live until their late teens in reasonable health, although at this age they can look a little unkempt.

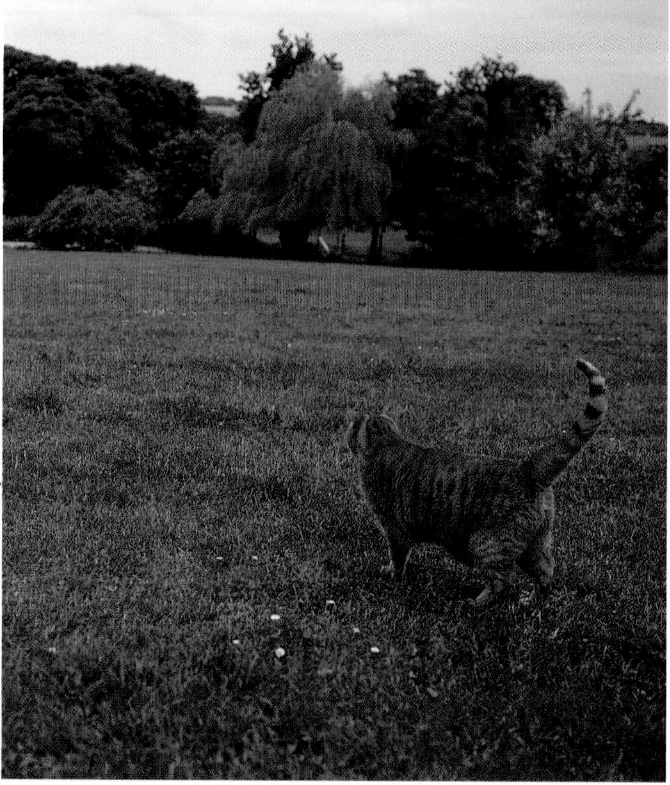

An older cat may not be able to defend his food as well as he once could, so if you have other cats and/or dogs ensure they are not allowed to steal his meals, or intimidate him while he is eating and scare him off.

Being less active as he grows older, it is easy for the cat to pile on weight, which can put undue strain on his heart and joints; keep a careful watch on this. Equally, he could lose weight rapidly and starve if he is not eating for some reason. Weighing your cat once a week can help you monitor his weight – and this is quite simple to do. First, weigh yourself on your bathroom scales, and then weigh yourself again while holding the cat; deduct the first weight from the second to ascertain your pet's weight. It may be easier for a helper to read the weights while you stand still on the scales.

Common ailments

As a cat ages, his body tissue starts to degenerate. This is inevitable and cannot be prevented, although with care from both owner and vet the effects can be eased. Old cats are prone to a number of particular ailments:

- claw wounds, owing to a decreasing ability to retract them efficiently
- coat and skin complaints, owing to inefficient self-grooming
- cold-related problems, owing to decreased body temperature regulation
- constipation, owing to decreased digestive efficiency
- deafness
- heart disease
- high blood pressure (hypertension)
- incontinence
- increased predisposition to furballs
- injury, owing to decrease in agility
- joint stiffness and arthritis
- kidney disease
- liver failure
- loss of appetite
- obesity-related problems
- senility
- sight problems
- tooth and gum problems

Seek veterinary advice for all of these ailments – the more quickly they are dealt with the more likely it is that the treatment will be successful, and your cat's comfortable life prolonged.

Excessive drinking can indicate a urinary-system problem that may need immediate veterinary treatment.

Time to say goodbye

Eventually the older cat sleeps more and more, and is increasingly reluctant to exercise. He may drink lots of fluids, but take little food. While he is able to function normally, if only in this modified way, he is probably quite contented. If his bladder and bowels begin to fail and he is unable to eat, you must seek veterinary advice, for the only humane thing to do in these circumstances is to have the old cat put to sleep, allowing him to die painlessly and with dignity. It is the last kind thing you can do for a much-loved companion and friend. (See pages 186–189 for information on bereavement and euthanasia.)

Top tip

The key to good health care for your old cat lies in vigilance. Twice-yearly check-ups by a vet will alert them to early signs of problems; some vets run clinics for older cats, recognizing the need to spend a little extra time on these much-cherished companions. Extra attention should be given to grooming the old cat as he may find self-grooming difficult if he is stiff or suffers from arthritis – especially in hard-to-reach places, such as the back, rear of the neck and under the tail. Claws may need trimming regularly if the cat is not keeping them worn down through outdoor exercise or stropping.

Bereavement

When a companion animal dies, or his death is imminent, this often has a huge impact on those humans who loved and cared for him. Losing a much-loved pet is just the same for many owners as coping with the death of a family member or close friend. Individual people deal with this trauma in different ways, but all or some of the stages of grief that are often encountered, are shown on the checklist.

Checklist

- ✓ anticipation of loss
- ✓ shock
- ✓ denial
- ✓ anger
- ✓ depression
- ✓ acceptance

Why pet cats die

There are two reasons for a cat dying:

1 sudden death through accident or illness.
2 euthanasia (being 'put to sleep' or 'put down') following an accident, or because of old age or illness, when a cure is not possible and the cat's quality of life is or will be poor.

In the case of the former, you will not be prepared for your pet's death and it will no doubt come as a huge shock. In the case of the latter, you can prepare for the inevitable, although it does not make it any easier to bear. Many owners blame themselves for their pet's death, and agonize

Feline fact

Sometimes, understandably, owners cannot bear to lose their pet and delay having him put down when really this should be done. However, a caring owner will put their pet's needs first, not their own – whatever the cost to themselves. However hard it may be to face up to the loss, having him euthanized is the kindest thing you can do for a cat that is suffering, to save him from further distress.

If you know your cat well, you'll know when the time has come to let him go with dignity and minimal discomfort.

over whether the death could have been prevented if they had done things differently. This is a normal reaction, but sadly it cannot change what has happened. The important thing, for your sake, is to focus on the many happy times you enjoyed with your cherished pet and to hold and treasure those memories.

Euthanasia

Other than sudden death, having a cat 'put down' is the most humane way for him to die. A prolonged natural death can be traumatic for both pet and owner, as well as painful for the cat. While the process may be upsetting to read about, it can help to understand how euthanasia is achieved.

Talk it over with your vet first, and decide whether having it done at home or at the vet clinic would be more suitable and practical. Also discuss the options of what to do with your pet's body. Once this has been mutually agreed, arrange a date, preferably sooner rather than later, so as not to prolong your pet's suffering, as well as your own, unnecessarily.

At the veterinary clinic

Arrange a time when the vet clinic is likely to be quiet, or you can enter and leave through a private entrance so that you do not have to face a crowded waiting room. Have a supportive person drive you there and back; you may well be upset, and therefore in no fit state to undertake this yourself. Take a blanket in which to wrap your pet to bring him home again, if this is what you want to do.

Make the journey there as smooth, stress-free and quiet as possible. If you will be able to bear up in your pet's last moments, then be with him. If you feel you will go to pieces, then ask your vet and the vet nurse to deal with it; if you are terribly distressed, it may make your pet equally so, and his passing may not be as peaceful as it should be.

At home

This is more expensive, but may be the preferred option if you are unable to get to the clinic, your cat is too ill to move, he finds travel upsetting, or you would prefer euthanasia to be carried out in familiar and comfortable surroundings. Request that a veterinary nurse attends, as well as the vet. The former can help out as required or where necessary, and help to keep you and the cat calm, thereby making the process as stress-free as possible.

Did you know ...?

Being animal-lovers themselves, many vets find euthanizing pets as painful as the owners do (especially if the pet is well known to them), although it does not stop them being professional about it. Just because a vet may appear to be detached about the process does not mean that he or she does not care; they do, it is just that they have to remain strong for the animals' – and often the owners' – sake. Many vets are now more aware of the fact that owners suffer great emotional pain when they lose a pet, and are better equipped to cope with this than they may have been years ago; and because of this they offer a much more sympathetic and caring service.

On the day, keep your cat's routine beforehand as normal, but give him lots of extra attention and cuddles if he will allow you to – he may not understand why you are being extra-affectionate, but may appreciate it nonetheless. It will make you feel better, as well as make the most of those last precious moments.

The process

Properly carried out, the process is quick and relatively painless. The vet may administer a sedative injection if the cat is very distressed, or is difficult to handle or restrain. They usually shave a fore leg to identify where the relevant vein is situated. They then inject a concentrated solution of phenobarbitone (an anaesthetic overdose) into that vein. For thin cats, the vet may need to inject directly into a kidney. The cat almost immediately goes to sleep. Breathing swiftly ceases, and the heart stops beating.

In some cases, the circulatory system is not working efficiently, and therefore the necessary vein on the fore leg is not easy to find in order to administer the lethal injection. When this occurs, the vet may need to inject directly into the heart or kidneys. Owners can find this distressing and be unable to cope efficiently in holding their pet and keeping him calm, so this is where the experienced handling and sympathetic soothing afforded by a veterinary nurse can prove beneficial to all concerned.

Afterwards

If you wish, the vet will dispose of the body, arranging to have it buried or cremated on your instructions. Alternatively, you can take your cat home, if this is allowable, to bury him in a favoured area of the garden. Graves should be at least 1m (3ft 3in) deep and well away from water courses (your local environment agency should able to advise you). Pet cemeteries and crematoriums will advise you on the costs, and what is involved.

Frequently asked question

Q I am getting on in years, and am worried about what will happen to my cat if I die before he does. How can I make sure my feline friend will be well cared for when I am gone?

A This is a very real worry for caring senior owners who may not be in the best of health, or know they are quite likely to die before their pet does. If no relatives are willing to give the cat a good permanent home, then some animal charities will take on this responsibility and find the cat a home of which his old owner would have approved. To ensure that this happens in the event of death, the owner (or his/her representative) should contact a charity that makes such provisions to find out what they need to do beforehand, so that when the time comes the cat can be transferred to the charity or new home with the minimum of fuss and stress.

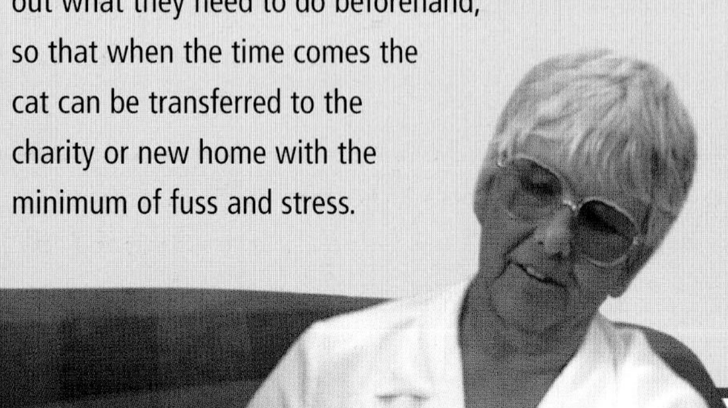

For an elderly person, or one with limited time available, a more mature cat that is already house-trained and more independent, may be easier to accommodate.

Grief

Only the owner can understand how they feel after losing a pet that meant the whole world to them, and it is important to realize that grieving is an essential part of the healing process after bereavement. There is no set time limit as to how long owners should grieve; some are able to accept and recover from the loss more easily than others, who may not get over it for months, even years – and this is perfectly normal. However long it takes, do not be afraid to grieve when you feel the need to; bottling up grief inside you is bound to affect your own mental and physical health.

Help when you need it most

Sometimes you may feel as though you are over the loss, but then grief hits you again at unexpected moments – such as when something triggers memories of your pet – and feelings of extreme sadness engulf you all over again. Again, this is normal. However, do not be afraid to lean on supportive family and friends when you feel the need, and do make use of the many excellent pet-bereavement counselling services that are available through phone, letter and email – many animal charities provide such a service, as do some pet-insurance companies.

If overwhelming sorrow persists longer than you feel able to cope with, then go and see an understanding doctor (but not necessarily your own if you do not feel comfortable doing so, or you find he or she is not sympathetic and helpful); it may be that you need additional counselling, or even prescribed medication, to help ease debilitating grief and allow you to function with some normality again. Just talking to a sympathetic and understanding trained bereavement counsellor can help you come to terms with your loss.

Physically marking your cat's passing with a grave and monument of some kind, whether a headstone, tree, shrub or plant, to mark where he lies and who he was, can prove therapeutic. You have somewhere tangible to go to mourn your pet, and then something to remember him by with gladness when the raw grief subsides.

Everyone, even other pets, need time to grieve before new pets are introduced to the household.

Children and pet loss

Depending on their age, children react differently to the death of a pet. For many it will be the first time they experience this inevitable part of life. This being the case, it will help enormously for a parent to talk things through with a bereavement counsellor as to how to approach and explain pet death. The child may also find such supportive third-party help invaluable.

Never underestimate a child's grief or reaction to the death of a pet, as it can affect them in many different ways that can have long-lasting and detrimental effects on their behaviour, health, learning ability and socialization. One thing you should *not* do is say that the pet was 'put to sleep', as this can create false hope; the child may think that one day their pet friend will wake up and come back again.

Whether a child should be allowed to see the body of the pet depends on the age and psyche of the child. A qualified counsellor will be able to advise on the best course of action to take.

Top tip

After the death of a cat, do not get another one just on the basis that you think it will be beneficial to surviving pet(s) (although in some cases this has proved a success), as they may resent an intruder. If you do get another cat, wait until you feel emotionally and physically ready to cope with a new addition to the household (see pages 76–79 and 82–83).

Pet grief

It is not just the owner who grieves over the loss of a pet; so can other animals in the household. Some people prefer to let the other animals see the body of their friend so they recognize he has died and can say 'goodbye'. The best thing to do is to carry on with the remaining pets' routine as normal, and to let them work out a new hierarchy among themselves. Perhaps the last thing you need right now are the potential problems that introducing a new pet into the equation may well bring.

Time for a successor

Only you will know when the time is right to get another cat. When it is, remember that there are plenty of homeless felines, young and old, waiting in rescue centres to fill the gap in the life of a special someone who can offer them the life they deserve – a good, caring home and lots of love.

INDEX

G

H

I

J

K

L

M

N

O

P

R

S

ACKNOWLEDGEMENTS

Executive Editor Trevor Davies
Executive Art Editor Leigh Jones
Editor Katy Denny
Designer Jo Tapper
Picture Librarian Jennifer Veall
Senior Picture Researcher Christine Junemann
Senior Production Controller Jo Sim
Index compiled by Indexing Specialists

Photographic Acknowledgements in Source Order

Ardea 73 bottom/**Jean-Paul Ferrero** 10
Bruce Coleman Collection/Heral Lange 121 bottom left, 129/**Kim Taylor** 124
Corbis UK Ltd/Lynda Richardson 7 bottom left, 67 bottom
Frank Lane Picture Agency/David Dalton 18 top/**Philip Perry** 66 bottom/**Walther Rohdich** 142
Getty Images/Kathi Lamm 59 top right, 71/**Maria Spann** 57/**Arthur Tilley** 80
Octopus Publishing Group Limited 6 bottom right, 12 bottom right, 18 bottom, 41, 43 left, 114/**Jane Burton** 1, 2-3, 9, 12 top right, 20 top, 21 top right, 21 bottom right, 21 bottom centre, 24, 30 left, 30 right, 30 centre, 32 top, 34 top left, 34 top right, 34 bottom left, 35 top, 35 bottom, 36 top, 36 bottom, 38, 40 top, 40 centre, 40 bottom, 42 left, 42 right, 42 centre, 44, 48 top, 50 bottom right, 52 bottom, 53, 54, 56, 60 centre, 63 top left, 66 top, 69 bottom, 77, 78 top, 78 bottom, 81 left, 91 bottom right, 91 bottom left, 93 top left, 93 top right, 98, 101, 102, 103 top left, 103 top right, 103 bottom right, 103 bottom left, 104, 107 top left, 107 top right, 107 bottom right, 107 bottom left, 108, 109, 112 top left, 112 top right, 112 bottom right, 112 bottom left, 113, 113 bottom, 115, 136 top right, 136 bottom right, 136 bottom left, 137 left, 137 centre, 139, 140, 143, 145 top left, 145 bottom left, 149 right, 149 centre 150 top, 151 top, 153 top, 153 bottom, 156/**Stephen Conroy** 43 right/**Nick Goodall** 117 top left/**Steve Gorton** 5 top left, 5 centre left, 8, 11, 13 top right, 13 bottom right, 20 bottom, 22, 26, 27, 47, 48 bottom, 49, 50 top left, 52 top, 55, 58 top right, 58 bottom left, 59 top left, 59 bottom right, 59 bottom left, 60 bottom, 61 top left, 61 centre left, 61 top right, 62 top left, 62 top right, 64, 65, 67 top right, 68 top left, 68 bottom right, 69 top, 70, 73 top, 74, 75, 76, 79, 81 right, 82, 83, 85 Top, 85 bottom, 86 top, 87 top left, 87 bottom right, 87 bottom left, 88, 89 top left, 89 bottom right, 90 bottom right, 93 bottom left, 94, 100, 106, 111 bottom, 117 bottom right, 120 top right, 120 bottom right, 120 bottom left, 130, 132, 133, 172, 173 bottom, 181 top right, 181 bottom right, 181 bottom left, 183 top, 184 top, 184 bottom, 188/**Rosie Hyde/Stonehenge Veterinary Hospital** 135, 171/**Peter Loughran** 16 top right, 37, 39, 71 top, 145 top right, 150 bottom right, 175 top/**Ray Moller** 15 top, 16 bottom left, 17 bottom right, 19 top left, 60 centre right, 61 centre right, 61 bottom right, 63 centre/**Dick Polak** 159/**George Taylor** 118
Marc Henrie 7 bottom right, 25, 46, 51, 134, 155 bottom right, 169 Top, 170, 174, 176, 181 top left, 182
RSPCA Photolibrary/Angela Hampton 154 bottom right, 165 right, 168
Dr A H Sparkes 164
Warren Photographic/Jane Burton 4, 5 Top, 5 top centre, 5 bottom right, 5 bottom left, 5 bottom centre, 6 top right, 6 bottom left, 7 top left, 7 top right, 12 bottom left, 13 top left, 13 bottom left, 14, 15 centre, 15 Bottom, 16 centre, 16 bottom right, 17 bottom left, 19 Bottom, 23, 28, 29, 32 Bottom, 33, 60, 60 Top, 60 top left, 62 centre, 62 bottom left, 63 bottom right, 84, 90 top left, 90 top right, 90 bottom left, 92, 96, 97, 99, 99 top right, 105, 110, 111 Top, 116, 121 top left, 121 top right, 121 bottom right, 123, 125, 131, 136 top left, 137, 144 Top, 144 bottom right, 144 bottom left, 145 bottom right, 146 top left, 146 centre left, 146 top right, 146 centre right, 146 Bottom, 147 top left, 147 centre left, 147 top right, 147 Bottom, 148, 148 left, 148 right, 148 centre left, 148 centre, 149 left, 151 Bottom, 152, 154 Top, 154 bottom left, 155 top left, 155 top right, 155 bottom left, 157, 158, 160, 161, 162, 165 left, 166, 167, 169, 175 Bottom, 177, 179, 180 Top, 180 bottom right, 180 bottom left, 183 Bottom, 185, 186, 189